Philoponus

Against Aristotle, on the Eternity of the World

Philoponus

Against Aristotle, on the Eternity of the World

Translated by
Christian Wildberg

Cornell University Press
Ithaca, New York

First published 1987 Cornell University Press.

Library of Congress Cataloging-in-Publication Data

Philoponus, John, 6th cent.
Against Aristotle, on the eternity of the world.

(The Ancient commentators on Aristotle)
Translation of extant fragments of: De aeternitate mundi contra Aristotelem.
Bibliography: p.
Includes indexes.
1. Aristotle. 2. Eternal return—History.
I. Wildberg, Christian. II. Title. III. Title: On the eternity of the world. IV. Series.
B485.P48 1987 113 86–47973
ISBN 0–8014–2052–0

Phototypeset by Input Typesetting Ltd., London
Printed in Great Britain by Redwood Burn Limited, Trowbridge.

Contents

General Introduction

Richard Sorabji

The 15,000 pages of the Ancient Greek Commentaries on Aristotle are the largest corpus of Ancient Greek philosophy that has not been translated into English or other modern European languages. The standard edition (*Commentaria in Aristotelem Graeca*, or *CAG*) was produced by Hermann Diels as general editor under the auspices of the Prussian Academy in Berlin. Arrangements have now been made to translate at least a large proportion of this corpus, along with some other Greek and Latin commentaries not included in the Berlin edition, and some closely related non-commentary works by the commentators.

The works are not just commentaries on Aristotle, although they are invaluable in that capacity too. One of the ways of doing philosophy between A.D. 200 and 600, when the most important items were produced, was by writing commentaries. The works therefore represent the thought of the Peripatetic and Neoplatonist schools, as well as expounding Aristotle. Furthermore, they embed fragments from all periods of Ancient Greek philosophical thought: this is how many of the Presocratic fragments were assembled, for example. Thus they provide a panorama of every period of Ancient Greek philosophy.

The philosophy of the period from A.D. 200 to 600 has not yet been intensively explored by philosophers in English-speaking countries, yet it is full of interest for physics, metaphysics, logic, psychology, ethics and religion. The contrast with the study of the Presocratics is striking. Initially the incomplete Presocratic fragments might well have seemed less promising, but their interest is now widely known, thanks to the philological and philosophical effort that has been concentrated upon them. The incomparably vaster corpus which preserved so many of those fragments offers at least as much interest, but is still relatively little known.

The commentaries represent a missing link in the history of philosophy: the Latin-speaking Middle Ages obtained their knowledge of Aristotle at least partly through the medium of the commentaries. Without an appreciation of this, mediaeval interpretations of Aristotle will not be understood. Again, the ancient commentaries are the unsuspected source of ideas which have been thought, wrongly, to originate in the later mediaeval period. It has been supposed, for example, that Bonaventure in the thirteenth century invented the ingenious arguments based on the concept of infinity which attempt to prove the Christian view that the universe had a beginning. In fact, Bonaventure is merely repeating arguments devised by the commentator Philoponus 700 years earlier and preserved in the meantime by the Arabs. Bonaventure even uses Philoponus' original examples. Again, the introduction of impetus theory into dynamics, which has been called a scientific revolution, has been held to be an independent invention of the Latin West, even if it was earlier discovered by the Arabs or their predecessors. But recent work has traced a plausible route by which it could have passed from Philoponus, via the Arabs, to the West.

The new availability of the commentaries in the sixteenth century, thanks to printing and to fresh Latin translations, helped to fuel the Renaissance break from Aristotelian science. For the commentators record not only Aristotle's theories, but also rival ones, while Philoponus as a Christian devises rival theories of his own and accordingly is mentioned in Galileo's early works more frequently than Plato.[1]

It is not only for their philosophy that the works are of interest. Historians will find information about the history of schools, their methods of teaching and writing and the practices of an oral tradition.[2] Linguists will find the indexes and translations an aid

1. See Fritz Zimmermann, 'Philoponus' impetus theory in the Arabic tradition'; Charles Schmitt, 'Philoponus' commentary on Aristotle's *Physics* in the sixteenth century', and Richard Sorabji, 'John Philoponus', in Richard Sorabji (ed.), *Philoponus and the Rejection of Aristotelian Science* (London and Ithaca, N.Y. 1987).

2. See e.g. Karl Praechter, 'Die griechischen Aristoteleskommentare', *Byzantinische Zeitschrift* 18 (1909), 516–38; M. Plezia *de Commentariis Isagogicis* (Cracow 1947); M. Richard, '*Apo Phônês*', *Byzantion* 20 (1950), 191–222; É. Evrard, *L'École d'Olympiodore et la composition du commentaire à la physique de Jean Philopon*, Diss. (Liège 1957); L. G. Westerink, *Anonymous Prolegomena to Platonic Philosophy*

for studying the development of word meanings, almost wholly uncharted in Liddell and Scott's *Lexicon*, and for checking shifts in grammatical usage.

Given the wide range of interests to which the volumes will appeal, the aim is to produce readable translations, and to avoid so far as possible presupposing any knowledge of Greek. Footnotes will explain points of meaning, give cross-references to other works, and suggest alternative interpretations of the text where the translator does not have a clear preference. The introduction to each volume will include an explanation why that work was chosen for translation: none will be chosen simply because it is there. Two of the Greek texts are currently being re-edited – those of Simplicius *in Physica* and *in de Caelo* – and new readings will be exploited by translators as they become available. Each volume will also contain a list of proposed emendations to the standard text. Indexes will be of more uniform extent as between volumes than is the case with the Berlin edition, and there will be three of them: an English-Greek glossary, a Greek-English index, and a subject index.

The commentaries fall into three main groups. The first group is by authors in the Aristotelian tradition up to the fourth century A.D. This includes the earliest extant commentary, that by Aspasius in the first half of the second century A.D. on the *Nicomachean Ethics*. The anonymous commentary on Books 2, 3, 4 and 5 of the *Nicomachean Ethics*, in *CAG* vol. 20, may be partly or wholly by Adrastus, a generation later.[3] The commentaries by Alexander of Aphrodisias (appointed to his chair between A.D. 198 and 209) represent the fullest flowering of the Aristotelian tradition. To his successors Alexander was The Commentator *par excellence*. To give but one example (not from a commentary) of his skill at defending and elaborating Aristotle's views, one might refer to his defence of Aristotle's claim that space is finite against the objection that an

(Amsterdam 1962) (new revised edition, translated into French, Collection Budé, forthcoming); A.-J. Festugière, 'Modes de composition des commentaires de Proclus', *Museum Helveticum* 20 (1963), 77–100, repr. in his *Études* (1971), 551–74; P. Hadot, 'Les divisions des parties de la philosophie dans l'antiquité', *Museum Helveticum* 36 (1979), 201–23; I. Hadot, 'La division néoplatonicienne des écrits d'Aristote', in J. Wiesner (ed.), *Aristoteles' Werk und Wirkung* (Paul Moraux gewidmet), vol. 2 (Berlin 1986); I. Hadot, 'Les introductions aux commentaires exégétiques chez les auteurs néoplatoniciens et les auteurs chrétiens', forthcoming. These topics will be treated, and a bibliography supplied, in a collection of articles on the commentators in general.

3. Anthony Kenny, *The Aristotelian Ethics* (Oxford 1978), 37, n.3; Paul Moraux, *Der Aristotelismus bei den Griechen*, vol. 2 (Berlin 1984), 323–30.

edge of space is conceptually problematic.[4] Themistius (*fl.* late 340s to 384 or 385) saw himself as the inventor of paraphrase, wrongly thinking that the job of commentary was completed.[5] In fact, the Neoplatonists were to introduce new dimensions into commentary. Themistius' own relation to the Neoplatonist as opposed to the Aristotelian tradition is a matter of controversy,[6] but it would be agreed that his commentaries show far less bias than the full-blown Neoplatonist ones. They are also far more informative than the designation 'paraphrase' might suggest, and it has been estimated that Philoponus' *Physics* commentary draws silently on Themistius six hundred times.[7] The pseudo-Alexandrian commentary on *Metaphysics* 6–14, of unknown authorship, has been placed by some in the same group of commentaries as being earlier than the fifth century.[8]

By far the largest group of extant commentaries is that of the Neoplatonists up to the sixth century A.D. Nearly all the major Neoplatonists, apart from Plotinus (the founder of Neoplatonism), wrote commentaries on Aristotle, although those of Iamblichus (*c.* 250 – *c.* 325) survive only in fragments, and those of three Athenians, Plutarchus (died 432), his pupil Proclus (410–485) and the Athenian Damascius (*c.* 462 – after 538), are

4. Alexander, *Quaestiones* 3.12, to be discussed in my *Matter, Space and Motion*, forthcoming. For Alexander see R. W. Sharples, 'Alexander of Aphrodisias: scholasticism and innovation', in W. Haase (ed.), *Aufstieg und Niedergang der römischen Welt*, part 2 *Principat*, vol.36.1, *Philosophie und Wissenschaften* (1987).

5. Themistius *in An. Post.* 1,2–12. See H. J. Blumenthal, 'Photius on Themistius (Cod.74): did Themistius write commentaries on Aristotle?' *Hermes* 107 (1979), 168–82.

6. For different views, see H. J. Blumenthal, 'Themistius, the last Peripatetic commentator on Aristotle?', in Glen W. Bowersock, Walter Burkert, Michael C. J. Putnam, *Arktouros*, Hellenic Studies Presented to Bernard M. W. Knox, (Berlin and N.Y., 1979), 391–400; E. P. Mahoney, 'Themistius and the agent intellect in James of Viterbo and other thirteenth-century philosophers: (Saint Thomas Aquinas, Siger of Brabant and Henry Bate)', *Augustiniana* 23 (1973), 422–67, at 428–31; id., 'Neoplatonism, the Greek commentators and Renaissance Aristotelianism', in D. J. O'Meara (ed.), *Neoplatonism and Christian Thought* (Albany N.Y. 1982), 169–77 and 264–82, esp. n. 1, 264–6; Robert Todd, introduction to translation of Themistius *in DA 3,4–8*, forthcoming in a collection of translations by Frederick Schroeder and Robert Todd of material in the commentators relating to the intellect.

7. H. Vitelli, *CAG* 17, p. 992, s. v. Themistius.

8. The similarities to Syrianus (died *c.*437) have suggested to some that it predates Syrianus (most recently Leonardo Tarán, review of Paul Moraux, *Der Aristotelismus*, vol. 1, in *Gnomon* 46 (1981), 721–50 at 750), to others that it draws on him (most recently P. Thillet, in the Budé edition of Alexander *de Fato*, p. lvii). Praechter ascribed it to Michael of Ephesus (eleventh or twelfth century), in his review of *CAG* 22.2, in *Göttingische Gelehrte Anzeiger 168* (1906), 861–907.

lost.[9] As a result of these losses, most of the extant Neoplatonist commentaries come from the late fifth and the sixth centuries and a good proportion from Alexandria. There are commentaries by Plotinus' disciple and editor Porphyry (232 – 309), by Iamblichus' pupil Dexippus (*c.* 330), by Proclus' teacher Syrianus (died *c.* 437), by Proclus' pupil Ammonius (435/445 – 517/526), by Ammonius' three pupils Philoponus (*c.* 490 to 570s), Simplicius (wrote after 532, probably after 538) and Asclepius (sixth century), by Ammonius' next but one successor Olympiodorus (495/505 – after 565), by Elias (*fl.* 541?), by David (second half of the sixth century, or beginning of the seventh) and by Stephanus (took the chair in Constantinople *c.* 610). Further, a commentary on the *Nicomachean Ethics* has been ascribed speculatively to Ammonius' brother Heliodorus, and there is a commentary by Simplicius' colleague Priscian of Lydia on Aristotle's successor Theophrastus. Of these commentators some of the last were Christians (Philoponus, Elias, David and Stephanus), but they were Christians writing in the Neoplatonist tradition, as was also Boethius who produced a number of commentaries in Latin before his death in 525 or 526.

The third group comes from a much later period in Byzantium. The Berlin edition includes only three out of more than a dozen commentators described in Hunger's *Byzantinisches Handbuch.*[10] The two most important are Eustratius (1050/1060 – *c.*1120), and Michael of Ephesus. It has been suggested that these two belong to a circle organised by the princess Anna Comnena in the twelfth century, and accordingly the completion of Michael's commentaries has been redated from 1040 to 1138.[11] His commentaries include areas where gaps had been left. Not all of these gap-fillers are extant, but we have commentaries on the neglected biological works, on the *Sophistici Elenchi*, and a small fragment of one on the *Politics*. The lost *Rhetoric* commentary had a few antecedents,

9. The Iamblichus fragments are collected in Greek by Bent Dalsgaard Larsen, *Jamblique de Chalcis, Exégète et Philosophe* (Aarhus 1972), vol.2. Most are taken from Simplicius, and will accordingly be translated in due course. The evidence on Damascius' commentaries is given in L. G. Westerink, *The Greek Commentaries on Plato's Phaedo*, vol.2., Damascius (Amsterdam 1977), 11–12; on Proclus' in L. G. Westerink, *Anonymous Prolegomena to Platonic Philosophy* (Amsterdam 1962), xii, n. 22; on Plutarchus' in H. J. Blumenthal, 'Neoplatonic elements in the de Anima commentaries', *Phronesis* 21 (1976), 75.

10. Herbert Hunger, *Die hochsprachliche profane Literatur der Byzantiner*, vol.1 (= *Byzantinisches Handbuch*, part 5, vol.1) (Munich 1978), 25–41. See also B. N. Tatakis, *La Philosophie Byzantine* (Paris 1949).

11. R. Browning, 'An unpublished funeral oration on Anna Comnena', *Proceedings of the Cambridge Philological Society* n.s. 8 (1962), 1–12, esp. 6–7.

but the *Rhetoric* too had been comparatively neglected. Another product of this period may have been the composite commentary on the *Nicomachean Ethics* (*CAG* 20) by various hands, including Eustratius and Michael, along with some earlier commentators, and an improvisation for Book 7. Whereas Michael follows Alexander and the conventional Aristotelian tradition, Eustratius' commentary introduces Platonist, Christian, and anti-Islamic elements.[12]

The composite commentary was to be translated into Latin in the next century by Robert Grosseteste in England. But Latin translations of various logical commentaries were made from the Greek still earlier by James of Venice (*fl. c.* 1130), a contemporary of Michael of Ephesus, who may have known him in Constantinople. And later in that century other commentaries and works by commentators were being translated from Arabic versions by Gerard of Cremona (died 1187).[13] So the twelfth century resumed the transmission to the Latin world of commentary material, a transmission which had been interrupted at Boethius' death in the sixth century.

The Neoplatonist commentaries of the main group were initiated by Porphyry. His master Plotinus had discussed Aristotle, but in a very independent way, devoting three whole treatises (*Enneads* 6.1–3) to attacking Aristotle's classification of the things in the universe into categories. These categories took no account of Plato's world of Ideas, were inferior to Plato's classifications in the *Sophist*

12. R. Browning, op.cit., p.7, H. D. P. Mercken, *The Greek Commentaries of the Nicomachean Ethics of Aristotle in the Latin Translation of Grosseteste, Corpus Latinum Commentariorum in Aristotelem Graecorum* VI 1 (Leiden 1973), ch.1, 'The compilation of Greek commentaries on Aristotle's Nicomachean Ethics'. Sten Ebbesen, 'Anonymi Aurelianensis I Commentarium in *Sophisticos Elenchos*', *Cahiers de l'Institut Moyen Age Grecque et Latin* 34 (1979), 'Boethius, Jacobus Veneticus, Michael Ephesius and "Alexander" ', pp. v–xiii; id., *Commentators and Commentaries on Aristotle's Sophistici Elenchi*, 3 parts, Corpus Latinum Commentariorum in Aristotelem Graecorum, vol. 7 (Leiden 1981); A. Preus, *Aristotle and Michael of Ephesus on the Movement and Progression of Animals* (Hildesheim 1981), introduction.

13. For Grosseteste, see Mercken as in n. 12. For James of Venice, see Ebbesen as in n. 12, and L. Minio-Paluello, 'Jacobus Veneticus Grecus', *Traditio* 8 (1952), 265–304; id., 'Giacomo Veneto e l'Aristotelismo Latino', in Pertusi (ed.), *Venezia e l'Oriente fra tardo Medioevo e Rinascimento* (Florence 1966), 53–74, both reprinted in his *Opuscula* (1972). For Gerard of Cremona, see M. Steinschneider, *Die europäischen Übersetzungen aus dem arabischen bis Mitte des 17. Jahrhunderts* (repr. Graz 1956); E. Gilson, *History of Christian Philosophy in the Middle Ages* (London 1955), 235–6 and more generally 181–246. For the translators in general, see Bernard G. Dod, 'Aristoteles Latinus', in N. Kretzmann, A. Kenny, J. Pinborg (eds.), *The Cambridge History of Latin Medieval Philosophy* (Cambridge 1982).

and could anyhow be collapsed, some of them into others. Porphyry replied that Aristotle's categories could apply perfectly well to the world of intelligibles and he took them as in general defensible.[14] He wrote two commentaries on the *Categories*, one lost, and an introduction to it, the *Isagôgê*, as well as commentaries, now lost, on a number of other Aristotelian works. This proved decisive in making Aristotle a necessary subject for Neoplatonist lectures and commentary. Proclus, who was an exceptionally quick student, is said to have taken two years over his Aristotle studies, which were called the Lesser Mysteries, and which preceded the Greater Mysteries of Plato.[15] By the time of Ammonius, the commentaries reflect a teaching curriculum which begins with Porphyry's *Isagôgê* and Aristotle's *Categories*, and is explicitly said to have as its final goal a (mystical) ascent to the supreme Neoplatonist deity, the One.[16] The curriculum would have progressed from Aristotle to Plato, and would have culminated in Plato's *Timaeus* and *Parmenides*. The latter was read as being about the One, and both works were established in this place in the curriculum at least by the time of Iamblichus, if not earlier.[17]

Before Porphyry, it had been undecided how far a Platonist should accept Aristotle's scheme of categories. But now the proposition began to gain force that there was a harmony between Plato and Aristotle on most things.[18] Not for the only time in the history of philosophy, a perfectly crazy proposition proved philosophically fruitful. The views of Plato and of Aristotle had both to be trans-

14. See P. Hadot, 'L'harmonie des philosophies de Plotin et d'Aristote selon Porphyre dans le commentaire de Dexippe sur les Catégories', in *Plotino e il neoplatonismo in Oriente e in Occidente* (Rome 1974), 31–47; A. C. Lloyd, 'Neoplatonic logic and Aristotelian logic', *Phronesis* 1 (1955–6), 58–79 and 146–60.

15. Marinus, *Life of Proclus* ch.13, 157,41 (Boissonade).

16. The introductions to the *Isagôgê* by Ammonius, Elias and David, and to the *Categories* by Ammonius, Simplicius, Philoponus, Olympiodorus and Elias are discussed by L. G. Westerink, *Anonymous Prolegomena* and I. Hadot, 'Les Introductions', see n. 2. above.

17. Proclus *in Alcibiadem 1* p.11 (Creuzer); Westerink, *Anonymous Prolegomena*, ch. 26, 12f. For the Neoplatonist curriculum see Westerink, Festugière, P. Hadot and I. Hadot in n. 2.

18. See e.g. P. Hadot (1974), as in n. 14 above; H. J. Blumenthal, 'Neoplatonic elements in the de Anima commentaries', *Phronesis* 21 (1976), 64–87; H. A. Davidson, 'The principle that a finite body can contain only finite power', in S. Stein and R. Loewe (eds.), *Studies in Jewish Religious and Intellectual History presented to A. Altmann* (Alabama 1979), 75–92; Carlos Steel, 'Proclus et Aristote', Proceedings of the Congrès Proclus held in Paris 1985, J. Pépin and H. D. Saffrey (eds.), forthcoming; Koenraad Verrycken, *God en Wereld in de Wijsbegeerte van Ioannes Philoponus*, Ph.D. Diss. (Louvain 1985).

muted into a new Neoplatonist philosophy in order to exhibit the supposed harmony. Iamblichus denied that Aristotle contradicted Plato on the theory of Ideas.[19] This was too much for Syrianus and his pupil Proclus. While accepting harmony in many areas,[20] they could see that there was disagreement on this issue and also on the issue of whether God was causally responsible for the existence of the ordered physical cosmos, which Aristotle denied. But even on these issues, Proclus' pupil Ammonius was to claim harmony, and, though the debate was not clear cut,[21] his claim was on the whole to prevail. Aristotle, he maintained, accepted Plato's Ideas,[22] at least in the form of principles (*logoi*) in the divine Intellect, and these principles were in turn causally responsible for the beginningless existence of the physical universe. Ammonius wrote a whole book to show that Aristotle's God was thus an efficient cause, and though the book is lost, some of its principal arguments are preserved by Simplicius.[23] This tradition helped to make it possible for Aquinas to claim Aristotle's God as a Creator, albeit not in the sense of giving the universe a beginning, but in the sense of being causally responsible for its beginningless existence.[24] Thus what started as a desire to harmonise Aristotle with Plato finished by making Aristotle safe for Christianity. In Simplicius, who goes further than anyone,[25] it is a formally stated duty of the commentator to display the harmony of Plato and Aristotle in most things.[26] Philoponus, who with his independent mind had thought better of his earlier belief in harmony, is castigated by Simplicius for neglecting this duty.[27]

19. Iamblichus ap. Elian *in Cat.* 123,1–3.

20. Syrianus *in Metaph.* 80,4–7; Proclus *in Tim.* 1. 6,21–7,16.

21. Asclepius sometimes accepts Syrianus' interpretation (*in Metaph.* 433,9–436,6); which is, however, qualified, since Syrianus thinks Aristotle is really committed willy-nilly to much of Plato's view (*in Metaph.* 117,25–118,11; ap. Asclepium *in Metaph.* 433,16; 450,22); Philoponus repents of his early claim that Plato is not the target of Aristotle's attack, and accepts that Plato is rightly attacked for treating ideas as independent entities outside the divine Intellect (*in DA* 37,18–31; *in Phys.* 225,4–226,11; *contra Procl.* 26,24–32,13; *in An. Post.* 242,14–243,25).

22. Asclepius *in Metaph.* from the voice of (i.e. from the lectures of) Ammonius 69,17–21; 71,28; cf. Zacharias *Ammonius, Patrologia Graeca* vol. 85, col. 952 (Colonna).

23. Simplicius *in Phys.* 1361,11–1363,12. See H. A. Davidson; Carlos Steel; Koenraad Verrycken in n.18 above.

24. See Richard Sorabji, *Matter, Space and Motion*, ch. 15, forthcoming 1988.

25. See e.g. H. J. Blumenthal in n. 18 above.

26. Simplicius *in Cat.* 7,23–32.

27. Simplicius *in Cael.* 84,11–14; 159,2–9. On Philoponus' *volte face* see n. 21 above.

The idea of harmony was extended beyond Plato and Aristotle to Plato and the Presocratics. Plato's pupils Speusippus and Xenocrates saw Plato as being in the Pythagorean tradition.[28] From the third to first centuries B.C., pseudo-Pythagorean writings present Platonic and Aristotelian doctrines as if they were the ideas of Pythagoras and his pupils,[29] and these forgeries were later taken by the Neoplatonists as genuine. Plotinus saw the Presocratics as precursors of his own views,[30] but Iamblichus went far beyond him by writing ten volumes on Pythagorean philosophy.[31] Thereafter Proclus sought to unify the whole of Greek philosophy by presenting it as a continuous clarification of divine revelation,[32] and Simplicius argued for the same general unity in order to rebut Christian charges of contradictions in pagan philosophy.[33]

Later Neoplatonist commentaries tend to reflect their origin in a teaching curriculum:[34] from the time of Philoponus, the discussion is often divided up into lectures, which are subdivided into studies of doctrine and of text. A general account of Aristotle's philosophy is prefixed to the *Categories* commentaries and divided, according to a formula of Proclus,[35] into ten questions. It is here that commentators explain the eventual purpose of studying Aristotle (ascent to the One) and state (if they do) the requirement of displaying the harmony of Plato and Aristotle. After the ten-point introduction to Aristotle, the *Categories* is given a six-point introduction, whose antecedents go back earlier than Neoplatonism, and which requires the commentator to find a unitary theme or scope (*skopos*) for the treatise. The arrangements for late commentaries on Plato are similar. Since the Plato commentaries form part of a single curriculum they should be studied alongside those on Aristotle. Here the situation is easier, not only because the extant corpus is

28. See e.g. Walter Burkert, *Weisheit und Wissenschaft* (Nürnberg 1962), translated as *Lore and Science in Ancient Pythagoreanism* (Cambridge Mass. 1972), 83–96.

29. See Holger Thesleff, *An Introduction to the Pythagorean writings of the Hellenistic Period* (Åbo 1961); Thomas Alexander Szlezák, *Pseudo-Archytas über die Kategorien*, Peripatoi vol. 4 (Berlin and New York 1972).

30. Plotinus e.g. 4.8.1; 5.1.8 (10–27); 5.1.9.

31. See Dominic O'Meara, *Pythagoras Revived: Mathematics and Philosophy in late Antiquity*, forthcoming.

32. See Christian Guérard, 'Parménide d'Elée selon les Néoplatoniciens', forthcoming.

33. Simplicius *in Phys.* 28,32–29,5; 640,12–18. Such thinkers as Epicurus and the Sceptics, however, were not subject to harmonisation.

34. See the literature in n. 2 above.

35. ap. Elian *in Cat.* 107,24–6.

very much smaller, but also because it has been comparatively well served by French and English translators.[36]

Given the theological motive of the curriculum and the pressure to harmonise Plato with Aristotle, it can be seen how these commentaries are a major source for Neoplatonist ideas. This in turn means that it is not safe to extract from them the fragments of the Presocratics, or of other authors, without making allowance for the Neoplatonist background against which the fragments were originally selected for discussion. For different reasons, analogous warnings apply to fragments preserved by the pre-Neoplatonist commentator Alexander.[37] It will be another advantage of the present translations that they will make it easier to check the distorting effect of a commentator's background.

Although the Neoplatonist commentators conflate the views of Aristotle with those of Neoplatonism, Philoponus alludes to a certain convention when he quotes Plutarchus expressing disapproval of Alexander for expounding his own philosophical doctrines in a commentary on Aristotle.[38] But this does not stop Philoponus from later inserting into his own commentaries on the *Physics* and *Meteorology* his arguments in favour of the Christian view of Creation. Of course, the commentators also wrote independent works of their own, in which their views are expressed independently of the exegesis of Aristotle. Some of these independent works will be included in the present series of translations.

The distorting Neoplatonist context does not prevent the commentaries from being incomparable guides to Aristotle. The introductions to Aristotle's philosophy insist that commentators must have a minutely detailed knowledge of the entire Aristotelian corpus, and this they certainly have. Commentators are also enjoined neither to accept nor to reject what Aristotle says too readily, but to consider it in depth and without partiality. The commentaries draw one's attention to hundreds of phrases,

36. English: Calcidius *in Tim.* (parts by van Winden; den Boeft); Iamblichus fragments (Dillon); Proclus *in Tim.* (Thomas Taylor); Proclus *in Parm.* (Dillon); Proclus *in Parm.*, end of 7th book, from the Latin (Klibansky, Labowsky, Anscombe); Proclus *in Alcib. 1* (O'Neill); Olympiodorus and Damascius *in Phaedonem* (Westerink); Damascius *in Philebum* (Westerink); *Anonymous Prolegomena to Platonic Philosophy* (Westerink). See also extracts in Thomas Taylor, *The Works of Plato*, 5 vols. (1804). French: Proclus *in Tim.* and *in Rempublicam.* (Festugière); *in Parm.* (Chaignet); Anon. *in Parm.* (P. Hadot); Damascius *in Parm.* (Chaignet).

37. For Alexander's treatment of the Stoics, see Robert B. Todd, *Alexander of Aphrodisias on Stoic Physics* (Leiden 1976), 24–9.

38. Philoponus *in DA* 21,20–3.

sentences and ideas in Aristotle, which one could easily have passed over, however often one read him. The scholar who makes the right allowance for the distorting context will learn far more about Aristotle than he would be likely to on his own.

The relations of Neoplatonist commentators to the Christians were subtle. Porphyry wrote a treatise explicitly against the Christians in 15 books, but an order to burn it was issued in 448, and later Neoplatonists were more circumspect. Among the last commentators in the main group, we have noted several Christians. Of these the most important were Boethius and Philoponus. It was Boethius' programme to transmit Greek learning to Latin-speakers. By the time of his premature death by execution, he had provided Latin translations of Aristotle's logical works, together with commentaries in Latin but in the Neoplatonist style on Porphyry's *Isagôgê* and on Aristotle's *Categories* and *de Interpretatione*, and interpretations of the *Prior* and *Posterior Analytics, Topics* and *Sophistici Elenchi*. The interruption of his work meant that knowledge of Aristotle among Latin-speakers was confined for many centuries to the logical works. Philoponus is important both for his proofs of the Creation and for his progressive replacement of Aristotelian science with rival theories, which were taken up at first by the Arabs and came fully into their own in the West only in the sixteenth century.

Recent work has rejected the idea that in Alexandria the Neoplatonists compromised with Christian monotheism by collapsing the distinction between their two highest deities, the One and the Intellect. Simplicius (who left Alexandria for Athens) and the Alexandrians Ammonius and Asclepius appear to have acknowledged their beliefs quite openly, as later did the Alexandrian Olympiodorus, despite the presence of Christian students in their classes.[39]

The teaching of Simplicius in Athens and that of the whole pagan Neoplatonist school there was stopped by the Christian Emperor Justinian in 529. This was the very year in which the Christian Philoponus in Alexandria issued his proofs of Creation against the earlier Athenian Neoplatonist Proclus. Archaeological evidence has been offered that, after their temporary stay in Ctesiphon (in present-day Iraq), the Athenian Neoplatonists did not return to

39. For Simplicius, see I. Hadot, *Le Problème du Néoplatonisme Alexandrin: Hiéroclès et Simplicius* (Paris 1978); for Ammonius and Asclepius, Koenraad Verrycken, *God en Wereld in de Wijsbegeerte van Ioannes Philoponus*, Ph.D. Diss. (Louvain 1985); for Olympiodorus, L. G. Westerink, *Anonymous Prolegomena to Platonic Philosophy* (Amsterdam 1962).

their house in Athens, and further evidence has been offered that Simplicius went to Ḥarrān (Carrhae), in present-day Turkey near the Iraq border.[40] Wherever he went, his commentaries are a treasure house of information about the preceding thousand years of Greek philosophy, information which he painstakingly recorded after the closure in Athens, and which would otherwise have been lost. He had every reason to feel bitter about Christianity, and in fact he sees it and Philoponus, its representative, as irreverent. They deny the divinity of the heavens and prefer the physical relics of dead martyrs.[41] His own commentaries by contrast culminate in devout prayers.

Two collections of articles by various hands are planned, to make the work of the commentators better known. The first is devoted to Philoponus;[42] the second will be about the commentators in general, and will go into greater detail on some of the issues briefly mentioned here.

What follows is a list of the commentaries in the Berlin edition, with standard abbreviations, and a list of the very few English translations that are currently available.

Berlin edition (*CAG*)

I Alexander *in Metaphysica* (*in Metaph.*) 1–5 and ps.-Alexander *in Metaph. 6–14*, M. Hayduck, 1891.

II 1 Alexander *in Analytica Priora* (*in An. Pr.*), M. Wallies, 1883.

2 Alexander *in Topica* (*in Top.*), M. Wallies, 1891.

3 ps.-Alexander (Michael of Ephesus) *in Sophisticos Elenchos* (*in SE*), M. Wallies, 1898. (But see S.

40. Alison Frantz, 'Pagan philosphers in Christian Athens', *Proceedings of the American Philosophical Society* 119 (1975), 29–38; M. Tardieu, 'Témoins orientaux du *Premier Alcibiade* à Ḥarrān et à Nag 'Hammādi', *Journal Asiatique* 274 (1986); id., 'Les calendriers en usage à Ḥarrān d'après les sources arabes et le commentaire de Simplicius à la *Physique* d'Aristote', in I. Hadot (ed.), *Actes du Colloque Simplicius*, Peripatoi (Berlin forthcoming); id., 'Une coutume nautique assyrien chez Simplicius', *Revue Française d'Assyriologie* (forthcoming). The opposing view that Simplicius returned to Athens is most fully argued by Alan Cameron, 'The last days of the Academy at Athens', *Proceedings of the Cambridge Philological Society* 195, n.s.15 (1969), 7–29.

41. Simplicius *in Cael.* 26,4–7; 70,16–18; 90,1–18; 370,29–371,4. See on his whole attitude Philippe Hoffmann, 'Simplicius' polemics', in Richard Sorabji (ed.), *Philoponus and the Rejection of Aristotelian Science* (London and Ithaca, N.Y. 1987).

42. Richard Sorabji (ed.), *Philoponus and the Rejection of Aristotelian Science* (London and Ithaca, N.Y. 1987).

Ebbesen's edition in *Corpus Latinum Commentariorum in Aristotelem Graecorum* 7.2, 153–199, of an earlier version also by Michael.)

III 1 Alexander *in de Sensu* (*in Sens.*), P. Wendland, 1901.

2 Alexander *in Meteorologica* (*in Meteor.*), M. Hayduck, 1899.

Fragments of Alexander's commentaries have now been collected as follows:

Alexander on the intellect from *in de Anima* (*in DA*), in Paul Moraux, *Alexandre d'Aphrodise, Exégète de la Noétique d'Aristote*, Liège and Paris 1942, 203–21.

Alexander *in Analytica Posteriora* (*in An. Post.*), in Paul Moraux, *Le Commentaire d'Alexandre d'Aphrodise aux Secondes Analytiques*, Peripatoi 13, Berlin 1979.

IV 1 Porphyry *Isagôgê* (*Isag.*) and *in Categorias* (*in Cat.*), A. Busse, 1887.

2 Dexippus *in Cat.*, A. Busse, 1888.

3 Ammonius *in Porphyrii Isagôgên* (*in Isag.*), A. Busse, 1891.

4 Ammonius *in Cat.*, A. Busse, 1895.

5 Ammonius *in de Interpretatione* (*in Int.*), A. Busse, 1897.

6 Ammonius *in An. Pr.*, M. Wallies, 1899.

V 1 Themistius *in Analytica Posteriora* (*in An. Post.*), M. Wallies, 1900.

2 Themistius *in Physica* (*in Phys.*), H. Schenkl, 1900.

3 Themistius *in de Anima* (*in DA*), R. Heinze, 1899.

4 Themistius *in de Caelo* (*in Cael.*), Latin and Hebrew, S. Landauer, 1902.

5 Themistius *in Metaph. 12*, Latin and Hebrew, S. Landauer, 1903.

6 ps.-Themistius (Sophonias) *in Parva Naturalia* (*in PN*), P. Wendland, 1903.

VI 1 Syrianus *in Metaph. 3, 4, 13, 14*, W. Kroll, 1902.

2 Asclepius *in Metaph. 1–7*, M. Hayduck, 1888.

VII 1 Simplicius *in Cael.*, J. L. Heiberg, 1894. (New edition in preparation, P. Hoffmann.)

VIII Simplicius *in Cat.*, C. Kalbfleisch, 1907.

IX Simplicius *in Phys. 1–4*, H. Diels, 1882. (New edition in preparation, L. Tarán.)

X Simplicius *in Phys. 5–8*, H. Diels, 1895. (New edition in preparation, L. Tarán.)

XI Simplicius (?) *in DA* M. Hayduck, 1882.

XII 1 Olympiodorus *Prolegomena* (*Proleg.*) and *in Cat.*, A. Busse, 1902.
2 Olympiodorus *in Meteor.*, W. Stüve, 1900.
XIII 1 Philoponus *in Cat.*, A. Busse, 1898.
2 Philoponus *in An. Pr. 1*, Philoponus (?) *in An. Pr. 2*, M. Wallies, 1905.
3 Philoponus *in An. Post. 1*, Philoponus (?) *in An. Post. 2*, Anon. *in An. Post. 2*, M. Wallies, 1909.
XIV 1 Philoponus *in Meteor.*, M. Hayduck, 1901.
2 Philoponus *in de Generatione et Corruptione* (*in GC*), H. Vitelli, 1897.
3 ps.-Philoponus (Michael of Ephesus) *in de Generatione Animalium* (*in GA*), M. Hayduck, 1903.
XV Philoponus *in DA 1–2*, Philoponus (?) *in DA 3*, M. Hayduck 1897.
XVI Philoponus *in Phys. 1–3*, H. Vitelli, 1887.
XVII Philoponus *in Phys. 4* and fragments, H. Vitelli, 1888.
XVIII 1 Elias *in Isag.* and *in Cat.*, A. Busse, 1900.
2 David *Proleg.* and *in Isag.*, A. Busse, 1904.
3 Stephanus *in Int.*, M. Hayduck, 1885.
XIX 1 Aspasius *in Ethica Nicomachea* (*in EN*), G. Heylbut, 1889.
2 Heliodorus (?) *in EN*, G. Heylbut, 1889.
XX Composite commentary on *EN*, G. Heylbut, 1892:
Eustratius *in EN 1,6*.
Adrastus (?) *in EN 2–5*.
Anon. *in EN 7*.
Aspasius *in EN 8* is printed in XIX,1.
Michael of Ephesus *in EN 9–10*.
XXI 1 Eustratius *in An. Post. 2*, M. Hayduck, 1907.
2 Anonymus Neobarii and Stephanus *in Rhetorica* (*in Rhet.*), H. Rabe, 1896.
XXII 1 Michael of Ephesus *in PN*, P. Wendland, 1903.
2 Michael of Ephesus *in de Partibus Animalium* (*in PA*), *in de Motu Animalium* (*in MA*), *in de Incessu Animalium* (*in IA*), M. Hayduck, 1904.
3 Michael of Ephesus, *in EN 5*, M. Hayduck, 1901.
XXIII 1 Sophonias paraphrase *in DA*, M. Hayduck, 1883.
2 Anon. paraphrase *in Cat.*, M. Hayduck, 1883.
3 Incert. paraphrase *in An. Pr.*, M. Wallies, 1884.
4 Anon. paraphrase *in SE*, M. Hayduck, 1884.

Suppl. I 2 Priscian of Lydia *Metaphrasis in Theophrastum* (*in Theophr.*) and *Solutiones ad Chosroem* (*Chosr.*), I. Bywater, 1886.

Suppl. II 1 Alexander *de Anima* (*DA*) and *Mantissa* (*Mant.*), I. Bruns, 1887.

2 Alexander *Quaestiones* (*Quaest.*), *de Fato* (*Fat.*), and *de Mixtione* (*Mixt.*), I. Bruns, 1892.

English translations

Only those that give the whole, or a substantial proportion, of extant works or fragments are listed.

Commentaries

1. Philoponus, Prooemium of *in DA*, John Dudley, *Bulletin de la Société Internationale pour l'Étude de la Philosophie Médiévale* 16–17 (1974–5), 62–85.

2. Porphyry *Isag.*

(i) O. F. Owen, in *Aristotle, The Organon or Logical Treatises of Aristotle, with the Introduction of Porphyry. Literally Translated*, Bohn's Classical Library, 2 vols., London 1853.

(ii) Edward W. Warren, *Porphyry Isagôgê*, translation and notes, Toronto 1975.

3. Michael of Ephesus *in MA*, *in IA*, Anthony Preus, *Aristotle and Michael of Ephesus, On the Movement and Progression of Animals*, Hildesheim 1981.

4. David *Proleg.*, from the Armenian, Bridget Kendall and Robert W. Thomson, *David the Invincible Philosopher, Definitions and Divisions of Philosophy*, Armenian Texts and Studies, vol. 5, Chico, California 1983.

5. Heliodorus (?) *in EN*, Walter Hatch, *The Moral Philosophy of Aristotle*, London 1879.

6. Michael of Ephesus *in Politica* (*in Pol.*) fragments, Ernest Barker, *Social and Political Thought in Byzantium from Justinian to the Last Palaeologus*, Oxford 1957.

7. Alexander *in Meteor. 4*, Victor C. Coutant, *Alexander of Aphrodisias, Commentary on Book IV of Aristotle's Meteorologica*, Diss., Columbia University N.Y. 1936, privately printed.

8. Simplicius, portions of *Corollary on Place* and *Corollary on Time*, from *in Phys.*, in S. Sambursky and S. Pines, *The Concept of Time in Late Neoplatonism*, Jerusalem 1971; and S. Sambursky,

The Concept of Place in Late Neoplatonism, Jerusalem and Leiden 1982.

9. Ammonius *in Int.*, selections, in H. Arens, *Aristotle's Theory of Language and its Tradition*, Amsterdam Studies in the Theory and History of Linguistic Science, series 3, Studies in the History of Linguistics vol. 29, Amsterdam 1984.

10. See also selections in Thomas Taylor, *The Works of Aristotle, translated from the Greek, with copious elucidations from the best of his Greek commentators, viz. Alexander Aphrodisiensis, Syrianus, Ammonius Hermaeus, Priscianus, Olympiodorus, Simplicius, etc.*, 10 vols., London 1806–1812, and in Thomas Taylor, *The Treatises of Aristotle on the Heavens, on Generation and Corruption and on Meteors, translated from the Greek with copious elucidations from the commentaries of Simplicius and Olympiodorus*, London 1807.

Other related works (for Plato commentaries, see above, n.36)

1. Alexander *Fat.*, with portions of *Mant.*, R. W. Sharples, *Alexander of Aphrodisias on Fate*, London and Ithaca, N.Y. 1983. This replaces the unrevised and posthumously published translation of the *de Fato* by A. Fitzgerald, Scholartis Press, London 1931.

2. Alexander *DA*, with omissions, and *de Intellectu* (= *Mant.* 106–113), A. P. Fotinis, *The de Anima of Alexander of Aphrodisias*, Washington 1980.

3. Alexander *Mixt.*, Robert B. Todd, *Alexander of Aphrodisias on Stoic Physics*, Leiden 1976.

4. Proclus, summary of *de Aeternitate Mundi* (*Aet.*), in Thomas Taylor, *The Fragments that Remain of the Lost Writings of Proclus, Surnamed the Platonic Successor*, London 1825.

5. Philoponus, Arabic summary of a lost work on the eternity of the world, S. Pines, 'An Arabic summary of a lost work of John Philoponus', *Israel Oriental Studies* 2 (1972), 320–52, repr. in *Studies in Arabic Versions of Greek Texts and in Mediaeval Science, The Collected Works of Shlomo Pines*, 2 (*Studies* 2), Jerusalem and Leiden 1986.

6. Alexander *On Time* (*Temp.*), from the Latin, R. W. Sharples, 'Alexander of Aphrodisias *On Time*', *Phronesis* 27 (1982), 58–81.

7. Alexander *Against Galen on Motion*, from the Arabic, N. Rescher and M. Marmura, *Alexander of Aphrodisias: the Refutation of Galen's Treatise on the Theory of Motion*, Islamabad 1969.

8. Alexander *Against Xenocrates on Species and Genus*, from the Arabic, S. Pines, 'A new fragment of Xenocrates and its impli-

cations', *Transactions of the American Philosophical Society* 51 (1961), 3–4.

9. Simplicius *in Epicteti Enchiridion* (*in Epict.*), George Stanhope, in *Epictetus his Morals with Simplicius his comment. Made English from the Greek*, London 1694 (six editions).

Acknowledgments

The present translations have been made possible by generous and imaginative funding from the following sources: The National Endowment for the Humanities, Division of Research Programs, an independent federal agency of the U.S.A.; The British Academy; The Jowett Copyright Trustees; The Royal Society (U.K.); Centro Internazionale A. Beltrame di Storia dello Spazio e del Tempo (Padua); Liverpool University; and by the collaboration of I. Hadot (Paris), C.N.R.S. (Paris), and The Institute of Classical Studies (London). I further wish to thank Eric Lewis and Harry Ide for proof-reading and commenting on the whole of volume 1. For comments on the General Introduction I am grateful to Henry Blumenthal, Victor Caston, I. Hadot, Alain Segonds, Robert Sharples, Robert Todd, L. G. Westerink and Christian Wildberg. Comments on 'Purpose, context and significance' are gratefully acknowledged ad loc., n. 39.

The contra Aristotelem

(i) Purpose, context and significance *Richard Sorabji*

Philoponus' *de Aeternitate Mundi contra Aristotelem (Against Aristotle, on the Eternity of the World)* exercised great influence on Islamic, Jewish, Greek and Latin mediaeval thought, but the extent of that influence has not been evident, because the fragmentary contents of the treatise itself have never previously been assembled. Christian Wildberg has now collected the fragments and translated them for the first time. He has also provided summaries which make coherent sense of the six surviving books. In addition, he is also the first to study and translate a Syriac fragment (134), which reveals that there were originally at least two more books than the six previously recognised. He has argued elsewhere that these books were concerned *inter alia* with the Christian expectation of a new heaven and a new earth. Not only is this expectation mentioned in fragment 134, but in fragment 132, Simplicius says of Philoponus: 'He declares that this world changes into another world which is more divine – a proposition he elaborates in the following books'.[1]

There are 129 Greek fragments, all but one from Simplicius' commentaries, four Arabic fragments and the one Syriac fragment. It is difficult to decide where quotations from Philoponus begin and end, and how the fragments are to be allocated among the original books, but Wildberg's suggestions are persuasive. The *contra Aristotelem* is not a commentary, but an independent treatise. Philoponus refers forward to it in his earlier *contra Proclum* and speaks of it as 'replies to Aristotle on the eternity of the world'.[2] The first five books are concerned with a particular reason for the belief in eternity, namely, the view that the heavens are made of an eternal

1. Christian Wildberg, 'Prolegomena to the study of Philoponus' *contra Aristotelem*', in Richard Sorabji (ed.), *Philoponus and the Rejection of Aristotelian Science* (London and Ithaca N.Y. 1987). See fr. 134 and Simplicius *in Phys.* 1177,38–1178,5 in fr. 132.

2. Philoponus *contra Proclum* 258,22–6.

fifth element different from any found elsewhere in the universe and with a special propensity for rotation. It is supposed to be eternal in the sense that neither the whole nor any part of it can ever begin or end. Aristotle's arguments for its eternity are of special concern to Philoponus as a Christian. In books I to III, he attacks the general case in Aristotle's *de Caelo* for the existence of the fifth element, along with some relevant considerations in Aristotle's *Meteorology*, and in books IV and V he begins to attack the arguments for its eternity. In book VI he moves on to rebut the more general arguments for the eternity of motion and time offered in Aristotle's *Physics* 8.1. Philoponus' discussion in his book VIII of the new heaven expected by Christians reveals a belief in something which will begin but never end. Elsewhere he maintains that such a thing can be achieved only through God overriding nature.[3]

The significance of the *contra Aristotelem* lies only partly in the question of eternity. Certainly, Christians must deny Aristotle's affirmation that there is an eternal element, if they are to uphold their view that the physical universe had a beginning. But another significance is that by denying the fifth element, Philoponus rejects the divinity of the heavens, and thus supports Christian monotheism.[4] A third consequence of denying the fifth element with its special propensity for rotation is that he paves the way for his suggestion in a later work that it was God at the time of creation who implanted an impetus (*entheinai kinêtikên dunamin*) in the heavens, to set them moving.[5] This represents an extension of his impetus theory from the case of projectiles to other parts of dynamics. As Philoponus knew, the pagan Proclus had already suggested that God implanted a certain power in the heavens, in order to extend their duration and motion infinitely, but I do not believe that this was the source of Philoponus' idea.[6] Philoponus' denial of the fifth element and his extension of impetus theory to all parts of dynamics represents part of a wider attack on Aristotelian physics. The rival hypotheses at which he gradually arrived were to influence first Islamic thought and later the sixteenth-century

3. See Lindsay Judson, 'God or nature? Philoponus on generability and perishability', in Richard Sorabji (ed.), op. cit. (1987).

4. Simplicius *in Cael.* 370,29–371,4; cf. 26,4–7; 70,16–18; 90,1–18.

5. Philoponus *de Opificio Mundi* 28,20–29,9.

6. Proclus *in Tim.* 1. 260,14–15; 267,16–268,6; 278,20–1; 279,11; 295,3–12; 473,25–7 (=schol.); 2. 100,18–29; 131,3; 3. 220,1–3; and ap. Philoponum *contra Proclum* 238,3–240,9; 297,21–300,2; 626,1–627,20. I argue that this was not the source of Philoponus' idea in *Matter, Space and Motion*, ch. 15, forthcoming.

Latin West. The General Introduction has already pointed to Galileo's respect for Philoponus' physical theories.

Philoponus was steeped in pagan Neoplatonism, but was independent in more ways than one. He had a knack of turning the pagans' arguments against them on behalf of Christianity. Arguably the best instances are those in which he exploits the pagan conception of infinity to show that Christianity must be right after all in believing that the universe had a beginning. Otherwise, the universe would have passed through a more than finite number of years, and the impossibility of traversing a more than finite number had been universally accepted from Aristotle by the pagan Neoplatonists. Moreover, if the past years up to the present were infinite, their number would soon be greater than infinity, and if some planets had revolved infinitely often, the revolutions of others would be many times infinity. These arguments are presented in various works, but the arguments on exceeding infinity are included in the *contra Aristotelem* and there receive their most graphic formulation.[7]

Nowadays we are likely to find the *contra Aristotelem* less interesting than the earlier *contra Proclum*. For although both are directed against the pagan belief in the eternity of the physical world, the *contra Aristotelem* depends heavily on the outmoded belief in a geocentric universe. But to Simplicius the *contra Aristotelem* is the important work; he tells us that he had not read the *contra Proclum*.[8] In subsequent Islamic thought, it is known to Farabi (*c.* 873–950), to the Christian philosophical school of Baghdad in the tenth and eleventh centuries and to Avicenna (980–1037).[9] Farabi attacks it in at least four works. Surprisingly, he thinks that Philoponus is wrong to ascribe to Aristotle belief in the eternity of the physical world. Farabi's interpretation of Aristotle is derived from the spurious *Theology of Aristotle*, an Arabic version of texts by Alexander, Plotinus and Proclus, distorted so as to present God as creating out of nothing, in the sense of giving the universe a beginning.[10]

7. e.g. ap. Simplicium *in Phys.* 1179,12–26 (fr. VI/132). See Richard Sorabji, *Time, Creation and the Continuum* (London and Ithaca N.Y. 1983) ch. 14.

8. Simplicius *in Cael.* 135, 27–31.

9. Details from Muhsin Mahdi, 'Alfarabi against Philoponus', *Journal of Near Eastern Studies* 26 (1967) 233–60.

10. This is the interpretation of Fritz Zimmermann, 'The origins of the so-called *Theology of Aristotle*', in Charles Schmitt, Will Ryan and Jill Kraye (eds.), *pseudo-Aristotle in the Middle Ages* (London 1986). There is an English translation by G. Lewis of the portions relating to Plotinus in P. Henry and H.-R. Schwyzer's edition of Plotinus *Enneads* vol. 2, (Paris, Brussels, 1959).

The *contra Aristotelem* was known not only in the Islamic world, but eventually in every quarter. In the Latin West, Bonaventure (*c.* 1217–1274) seems to be influenced by the *contra Aristotelem* version of the infinity arguments,[11] and Thomas Aquinas (*c.* 1224–1274) addresses the work in passages to which Christian Wildberg has drawn my attention.[12] Among Jewish thinkers Gersonides (1288–1344) defends the idea of the universe beginning in his *Milḥamot Hashem* (*Wars of the Lord*) with arguments that strongly suggest the ultimate influence of the *contra Aristotelem.*[13] In the Byzantine world, Gemistos Plethon (*c.* 1355–1452), writing in Greek, knows Philoponus as one for whom the heavens are made of fire, not of a fifth element.[14] It might be expected that belief in a rotating fifth element would not survive the thesis of Copernicus (1473–1543) that it is the earth which rotates around the sun, not the sun around the earth. But in 1616 Cremonini was still defending Aristotle's fifth element against Philoponus (John, the Grammarian), in his *Apologia dictorum Aristotelis de quinta caeli substantia. Adversus Xenarchum, Ioannem Grammaticum et alios* (Venice). It has been estimated that belief in the fifth element lasted until 1630.[15]

Philoponus was not the first to attack Aristotle's fifth element. Theophrastus, Aristotle's immediate successor, already raised some doubts about it,[16] although he seems to have accepted it.[17] His successor Strato, however, rejected it,[18] and Xenarchus, an Aristotelian of the first century B.C., wrote a whole work against the fifth substance, *pros tên pemptên ousian.*[19] Simplicius accuses Philoponus

11. See Richard Sorabji, *Time, Creation and the Cotninuum*, 202.

12. Philoponus is referred to as 'Philoponus' in Aquinas' *in de Caelo et Mundo* I.6. 3/9 and I.6. 6/47. He is called 'Grammaticus' at op. cit. I.6. 3/8; I.6. 10/2; I.8. 5/26; I.8. 7/1; I.8. 9/1; I.8. 13/1; I.8. 15/1. There is another reference at *in Int.* I.6. 4/41. Aquinas repeats Simplicius' polemic against Philoponus.

13. The relevant arguments are summarised in Seymour Feldman, 'Gersonides' proofs for the creation of the universe', *American Academy for Jewish Research* 35 (1967), 113–37. Cf. *contra Aristotelem* ap. Simplicium *in Cael.* 84,15–91,19; 121,4–136,1; *in Phys.* 1166,32–1169,5; 1179,15–21.

14. Gemistos Plethon, *contra Scholarii defensionem Aristotelis, Patrologia Graeca* vol. 160, col. 1002; cf. 909.

15. William H. Donahue, *The Dissolution of the Celestial Spheres*, Ph.D. Diss. (Cambridge 1973), 188–9, and Arno Press, N.Y. 1981.

16. Theophrastus *de Igne* 4–6; see for discussion R.W. Sharples, 'Theophrastus on the heavens', in J. Wiesner (ed.), *Aristoteles Werk und Wirkung*, vol. 1 (Berlin 1985).

17. ap. Philoponum *contra Proclum* 520,18–20.

18. Strato fr. 84 Wehrli.

19. Fragments summarised by Paul Moraux, 'Xenarchos (5)', in Pauly's *Real-Encyclopädie der classischen Altertumswissenschaft* (*RE*) IX A^2, 1423ff.; *Der Aristo-*

of stealing his arguments from Xenarchus.[20] But however much Philoponus may have benefited from earlier arguments, the context of his work is new: a defence of Christianity and denial of eternity. He also exploits the theory of epicycles, worked out by Hipparchus and Ptolemy, to argue that since they make celestial motions eccentric and complex, the case for the fifth element, with its simple rotation, is already refuted. Ptolemy himself had not allowed epicycles to weaken his acceptance of Aristotle's aether.[21]

Simplicius' own view is one that harmonises Plato (who spoke in the *Timaeus* only of four elements) with Aristotle. There is indeed a fifth element, but it is composed of the purest parts of the four elements.[22] Moreover, although Plato's *Timaeus* speaks of the heavens as having a beginning, Neoplatonists other than Philoponus follow the tradition according to which this is not meant literally, but is said for paedagogic purposes, as a mathematician uses diagrams, to make things easier to understand.[23] Simplicius criticises Philoponus for misunderstanding Plato,[24] and for failing to maintain the harmony of Plato and Aristotle.[25] The General Introduction has already explained that he construes Philoponus' views on the heavens as an irreverent downgrading of them. He knows that the intention of the Christian monotheists is to reserve all glory for the one God, but he views their denial of the divinity of the heavens as atheistical.[26] He had suffered personally from the Christian authorities, since the Christian Emperor Justinian had stopped his teaching in Athens, along with that of the other pagan Neoplatonists there, in 529. And Philoponus had chosen that very year to attack the earlier Athenian Neoplatonist Proclus, the teacher of their common teacher Ammonius, in the work Simplicius says he had not read, the *contra Proclum*. The view has already been cited that, in replying to Philoponus' next attack, the *contra*

telismus bei den Griechen, vol. 1, (Berlin, New York 1973), 198ff. Discussion in Christian Wildberg, *John Philoponus' Criticisms of Aristotle's Theory of Ether*, Ph.D. Diss. (Cambridge 1984), 138–9.

20. Simplicius *in Cael.* 25,22–4; 26,31–3.

21. Ptolemy *Almagest* 1.3; discussion in Wildberg, op.cit., 153–5.

22. Simplicius *in Cael.* 12,28–30; 16,20–1; 66,33–67,5; 85,7–15; 130,31–131,1; 360,33–361,2; 379,5–6; 435,32–436,1.

23. M. Baltes, *Die Weltentstehung des platonischen Timaios nach den antiken Interpreten*, vol. 1 (Leiden 1976); Sorabji, *Time, Creation and the Continuum*, 268–72.

24. Simplicius *in Cael.* 66,33–67,5. See Philippe Hoffmann on Simplicius' attitude to Philoponus, 'Simplicius' polemics', in Richard Sorabji (ed.), *Philoponus and the Rejection of Aristotelian Science*.

25. Simplicius *in Cael.* 84,11–14; 159,2–9.

26. Simplicius *in Cael.* 26,4–7; 70,16–18; 90,1–18; 370,29–371,4.

Aristotelem, Simplicius may well have been residing away from Athens in the East. He comforts himself with the thought that Philoponus' arguments are ephemeral.[27] It is because Simplicius felt such a strong duty to expose Philoponus that we are fortunate enough to have the fragments from which Philoponus' treatise can be reconstructed.

Philoponus for his part, though a Christian from the start, had begun as a comparatively orthodox follower of the pagan Ammonius. But in his commentaries on the *Physics* and *Posterior Analytics* and in the *contra Proclum*, he was to break away from his initial acceptance in the *de Anima* commentary of the harmony of Plato and Aristotle.[28] He also began to argue, some time later than that commentary, for the Christian belief in the beginning of the physical universe. This had been rejected by the entire pagan tradition, for it was a belief in the beginning of matter itself, not merely of its present orderly arrangement. Philoponus was to write four or five whole books on the subject, first the *contra Proclum*, then the *contra Aristotelem*, then one or two independent treatises,[29] and finally the *de Opificio Mundi*, which treats the Biblical account of Creation.[30] In addition, Philoponus argues on the same subject in his commentaries on the *Physics* and *Meteorology*, and in an unspecified discussion of 'theorems' to which the *Physics* commentary refers back.[31]

As regards place and date, Philoponus lived in Alexandria from around 490 to at least 574. Simplicius claims never to have met him,[32] despite his having studied in Alexandria too. The *contra*

27. Simplicius *in Cael.* 25,34–6.

28. Koenraad Verrycken, *God en Wereld in de Wijsbegeerte van Ioannes Philoponus*, Ph.D. Diss. (Louvain 1985); on harmony in General Introduction, n. 18.

29. Represented by excerpts in Simplicius *in Phys.* 1326–1336 and by an Arabic summary of a work (which I am inclined to think distinct from the former) which is translated into English by S. Pines, 'An Arabic summary of a lost work of John Philoponus', *Israel Oriental Studies*, 2,320–52 (repr. in his *Studies*, 2), and into French by G. Troupeau, 'Un epitome arabe du *de Contingentia Mundi* de Jean Philopon', in *Memorial A.-J. Festugière – Cahiers d'orientalisme* 10 (Geneva 1984), 77–88. The work translated by Pines starts off by referring back to the *contra Proclum* and the *contra Aristotelem*.

30. The date of the *de Opificio Mundi* is still disputed. É. Evrard supports 557–60, in 'Les convictions religieuses de Jean Philopon et la date de son commentaire aux Météorologiques', *Bulletin de l'académie royal de Belgique*, classe des lettres, 5 (1953), 299–357. But W. Wolska reaffirms Reichardt's date of 546–9 in *La Topographie Chrétienne de Cosmas Indicopleustes* (Paris 1962), 163–5.

31. Philoponus *in Phys.* 55, 24–6.

32. Simplicius *in Cael.* 26, 17–19.

Proclum can be dated by an astronomical reference to 529.[33] The *contra Aristotelem* is proved to be later by cross-references between the two treatises,[34] although it is hard to say more than that it was produced in the 530s. Until recently, the commentary on the *Physics* was dated to 517,[35] and it was taken that all commentaries, except the *Meteorology* commentary, were completed by 529. The unspecified 'theorems' were identified with the lost *Summikta Theôrêmata*.[36] Recently, however, it has been suggested that revisions were made after 529 to the commentaries on the *Physics* and the *Posterior Analytics*, and that Philoponus' new ideas on the harmony of Plato and Aristotle and on the beginning of the universe were added after that date. The *contra Proclum* could then mark the beginning of Philoponus' new thinking and be the work referred to for the discussion of 'theorems'.[37] On the alternative chronology, by contrast, Philoponus' new ideas would have been introduced by 517.

In a final period, which lasted from the Council of Constantinople in 553 to at least 574, Philoponus devoted himself to theological controversies within the Christian Church.[38] But this development may be foreshadowed, if already in the 530s the lost books VII and VIII of the *contra Aristotelem* were concerned with the expected new heaven and new earth, and if the *de Opificio Mundi* was written in the 540s.[39]

(ii) Sources, structure and authenticity *Christian Wildberg*

The sources

The present reconstruction of the *de Aeternitate Mundi contra Aristotelem* draws from three different sources: the extant Greek frag-

33. Philoponus *contra Proclum* 579,14–17.

34. *contra Proclum* 134,17; 155,19–24; 258,22–6; 396,24; 399,20–4; 461,1–2; 483,20; *contra Aristotelem* ap. Simplicium *in Cael.* 135,27–8; 136,17; ap. Simplicium *in Phys.* 1141,9; 1142,1–2; 1159,2.

35. By a reference at Philoponus *in Phys.* 703,16–17.

36. This chronology was largely due to the valuable work of Evrard, cited in note 30. On the order of the *contra Aristotelem* and the *Meteorology* commentary, see Wildberg's reply to Evrard in his 'Prolegomena', in Richard Sorabji (ed.), *Philoponus and the Rejection of Aristotelian Science*, 202–9.

37. Koenraad Verrycken, as in n. 28 above. He will expound his views in the second of the collections of articles on the commentators.

38. Henry Chadwick, 'Philoponus the Christian theologian', in Richard Sorabji (ed.), *Philoponus and the Rejection of Aristotelian Science*.

39. I am very grateful to Alain Segonds, Robert Sharples and Christian Wildberg for their comments.

ments, already published Arabic fragments, and one Syriac fragment. By far the most substantial source is the commentaries of the Athenian Neoplatonist Simplicius, the only source to have had direct access to the original treatise. The main evidence for the first five books of the *contra Aristotelem* (fr. 1–107) stems from Simplicius' commentary on Aristotle's treatise *de Caelo*.[40] The fragments of the sixth book (fr. 108–33) stem from his comments on the eighth book of Aristotle's *Physics*.[41] Since Simplicius' attitude to Philoponus' work is highly critical, he sets out the arguments only in order to refute them. In the course of his criticism, Simplicius occasionally repeats particular arguments brought forward by Philoponus, sometimes using slightly different words. In order not to lengthen the present collection unduly, each argument is reproduced only once, though important variants have been taken into account and the reader is always referred to the respective parallel passage in a footnote. Another, less valuable fragment in Greek comes from a treatise entitled *Conspectus Rerum Naturalium* written in the eleventh century by the Byzantine scholar Symeon Seth.[41a]

Further fragments, deriving mainly from Arabic versions, have been included at appropriate places in the first and fourth sections of this collection. Three fragments stem from Farabi's polemical treatise *Against John the Grammarian*[42] (tenth century), one fragment from an anonymous recension of Abū Sulaimān as-Sijistānī's treatise *Ṣiwān al-Ḥikmah*, entitled *Muntakhab Ṣiwān al-Ḥikmah* and written in the twelfth century.[43] The original translations of the Arabic fragments offered by Mahdi and Kraemer have been slightly revised in order to harmonise them with my translation of the Greek fragments. I am indebted to Dr Larry Schrenk and Dr Maknun Gemaledin Ashami for their expert advice.

40. I.L. Heiberg, *Simplicii in Aristotelis de Caelo commentaria, CAG* 7.

41. H. Diels, *Simplicii in Aristotelis Physicorum libros quattuor posteriores commentaria, CAG* 10.

41a. The treatise has been edited by A. Delatte, *Anecdota Atheniensia et alia, tome II. Textes grecs relatifs à l'histoire des sciences* (Paris 1939), 41.

42. The title is not to be found in the Arabic manuscript but has been supplied by M. Mahdi, 'Alfarabi against Philoponus', *Journal of Near Eastern Studies* 26(4) (1967), 233–60 in his translation of the text.

43. The relevant fragment has been published and translated by J.L. Kraemer, 'A lost passage from Philoponus' *contra Aristotelem* in Arabic translation', *Journal of the American Oriental Society* 85 (1965), 318–37; the Arabic text of the whole manuscript of the *Muntakhab* is edited by D.M. Dunlop, *The Muntakhab Ṣiwān al-Ḥikmah of Abū Sulaimān As-Sijistānī*. Arabic text, translation and indexes (The Hague, Paris and New York 1979).

It is commonly believed that Philoponus' treatise *contra Aristotelem* consisted of six books against Aristotle's theory of aether and against his arguments for the eternity of motion and time. The reason for this belief is that Simplicius discusses the arguments of six books only, and that Arabic bibliographers like Ibn Abī Uṣaybi'a, Ibn al-Nadīm, and Ibn al-Qifṭi list the *contra Aristotelem* as a treatise in six books.[44] However, although to my knowledge no fragments of the seventh book survive, the existence of an eighth book is established by a fragment in Syriac (fr. 134), which appears in an anonymous manuscript of the British Library.[45] The manuscript dates from the seventh century and contains extracts from the writings of the Church Fathers.[46] In spite of the Arabic evidence, there are no good reasons for doubting the authenticity of fragment 134.[47] It ought to be accepted that the *contra Aristotelem* consisted of more than six and of at least eight books.

The structure of the treatise

In this reconstruction of the *contra Aristotelem*, the collected fragments have been divided into sections (books) which are believed to correspond to the original division of the treatise. This arrangement of the surviving fragments has to be justified in the light of the evidence.

In general, there can be no doubt that the treatise, like the polemic against Proclus, was divided into 'books' (*biblia*), the exact number of which was equal to or greater than eight. Several citations are preceded by a reference to the book and chapter from which they derive. Moreover, the fragments found in Simplicius can be arranged in groups forming sets of arguments on particular topics. A general impression is created that in the first five books of the *contra Aristotelem* Philoponus followed Aristotle's argument in *de Caelo* 1.2–4 fairly closely (with a digression on *Meteorology* 1.3

44. See M. Steinschneider, 'Johannes Philoponus bei den Arabern', in *Al-Farabi, – Alpharabius – des arabischen Philosophen Leben und Schriften*. Mémoires de l'académie imperiale des sciences de Saint Petersbourg VII 13(4) (1869), 162: '11. Widerlegung des Aristoteles, 6 Tractate.' For further references see M. Mahdi, 'The Arabic text of Alfarabi's *Against John the Grammarian*', in S.A. Hanna (ed.), *Medieval and Middle Eastern Studies in Honour of A.S. Atiya* (Leiden 1972), 269 n.1.

45. British Library MS Add. 17 214 fol. 72vb–73ra.

46. See W. Wright, *Catalogue of Syriac Manuscripts in the British Museum acquired since the year 1838* (London 1871), 915–17.

47. I have argued this elsewhere: see C. Wildberg, 'Prolegomena to the study of Philoponus' *contra Aristotelem*', in Richard Sorabji (ed.), *Philoponus and the Rejection of Aristotelian Science*.

in the third book), and that in the sixth book he followed the argument of *Physics* 8.1. Because of this arrangement, Simplicius was able to integrate Philoponus' criticism into his running commentaries on Aristotle. Nothing is known about book VII of the *contra Aristotelem*, but it seems likely that like book VIII it treated the creation and destruction of the universe from the point of view of Christian theology.[48] The proposed division of the collection of fragments is based on the following evidence. Simplicius says, in a prologue to his discussion of Philoponus' criticism of Aristotle's arguments for the eternity of motion and time, *in Phys.* 1117,15–1118,9:

> One of our contemporaries <i.e. the Grammarian> . . . has written five long books (*polustikha biblia*) against what has been shown <by Aristotle> in *On the Heavens* <*de Caelo*> concerning their eternity. In my exegesis of the first book of the treatise *On the Heavens* I have tried to point out that these <writings> are rotten and have stood up only against stupid pupils. His sixth book takes up arms against the eternal motion and eternal time established in this treatise <i.e. the *Physics*>. . . . For these reasons I thought it right in going through this book, to point out . . . what the objections <he> raises against it are like and from what state of mind they have issued.

These remarks indicate that the fragments found in Simplicius' *Physics* commentary stem from book VI of the *contra Aristotelem*,[49] while the material found in the *de Caelo* commentary originally belonged to books I-V. In that last commentary one can distinguish four long and clearly separated sections which Simplicius, digressing from the commentary proper, dedicates to the refutation of 'the Grammarian': (1) *in de Caelo* 26–59; (2) *in de Caelo* 66–91; (3) *in de Caelo* 119–142; (4) *in de Caelo* 156–199.

In the first of these sections Simplicius concerns himself with Philoponus' criticism of the central Aristotelian assumption that 'nature is a principle of motion' used in *de Caelo* 1.2. Simplicius states once that he is citing 'the seventh chapter' of the *contra Aristotelem*,[50] and in a fragment which parallels Simplicius' first quotation, Farabi says that he is citing 'chapter 2'. These are proper references only if one understands them to mean, for example,

48. See fr. 134 and cf. fr. 132: Simpl. *in Phys.* 1178,2–5.
49. See *in Phys.* 1129–1182. The passages cited at *in Phys.* 1326–1336 belong to a separate treatise.
50. See fr. I/7: *in Cael.* 32,1.

chapter *x* of the whole treatise or of the first book.[51] At any rate, in the second section on Philoponus, Simplicius makes it clear that he is now citing the second and the third books of the treatise.[52] The main subject-matter of the second book is Aristotle's claim regarding the absence of the properties 'heavy and light' from the celestial region, whereas the subject-matter of book III is an argument in the *Meteorology*, which is relevant to the question of the eternity of the world.[53] Simplicius' third digression deals predominantly with Philoponus' critique of Aristotle's argument for the eternity of the celestial body in *de Caelo* 1.3. These fragments stem from the fourth book of the *contra Aristotelem*. For in a small, separate treatise, demonstrating *inter alia* that an infinite capacity cannot reside in a finite body, which was written not long after the polemic against Aristotle, Philoponus refers back to the fourth book of that work. Fragments of the latter treatise can be found in Simplicius' commentary on the *Physics*, 1326–1336. According to the first reference there, Philoponus claims to have shown in book IV of the *contra Aristotelem* that one and the same prime matter belongs to the celestial and the sublunary regions. This is indeed the argument of fr. IV/70–72. Likewise, at *in Phys.* 1333,30ff. and 1335,1 Philoponus is quoted as having said that in book IV of the *contra Aristotelem* he showed that it is false to regard things as imperishable simply because their decay is not perceived or experienced. This may be taken as a reference to the line of argument of which fr. IV/75, 78, and 80 form a part.[54]

The fourth and last section on Philoponus in Simplicius' *de Caelo* commentary discusses the fifth book of the *contra Aristotelem*. The subject-matter here is the problem of contrariety in circular motion raised by Aristotle in *de Caelo* 1.4. Simplicius says that Philoponus 'spends a whole book, the fifth, striving to refute those propositions which prove that there is no movement contrary to circular movement'.[55] This is discussed at length in the ensuing argument, and Simplicius mentions at a later stage that he is citing the 25th chapter of the fifth book.[56]

51. My own reconstruction of the fragments of the first book of the *contra Aristotelem* agrees largely with the one proposed by É. Evrard, *Philopon, Contre Aristote, livre I*. Mémoire de licence, Université de Liège (unpublished typescript).

52. *in Cael.* 75,16f. (fr. II/47); 78,12f. (fr. II/49); 80,28 (fr. III/52).

53. See *in Cael.* 80,23–29 (fr. III/52). The end of Book III is evidently arrived at in fr. III/61: *in Cael.* 91,3f.

54. Cf. also Farabi's remark in fr. IV/62.

55. See *in Cael.* 157,1–3 (fr. V/81).

56. See *in Cael.* 190,21f. (fr. V/102).

The authenticity of the fragments

Although Simplicius refers to his adversary as *ho Grammatikos* (the Grammarian) or more often simply as *houtos* (this man), it is undisputed that John Philoponus is indeed the target of his polemic and that the arguments cited by him in this context are attributable to Philoponus. Nevertheless, there remains the problem of authenticity. It has to be borne in mind that Simplicius, who may be regarded as a reliable though by no means impartial transmitter of the opinions of earlier philosophers, displays the most hostile and bitter attitude towards his Alexandrian colleague. The question arises, to what extent can the citations found in Simplicius be regarded as communicating an authentic picture of the original treatise? Has Simplicius truncated or even manipulated Philoponus' arguments in order to make his refutation appear all the more devastating? How many arguments did he consider, and how many did he pass over in silence? These and similar questions are of course difficult or impossible to answer. However, in what follows a few points will be raised which suggest that the arguments preserved in the fragments are authentic, and that the extant citations do provide us with a fairly comprehensive impression of the original work.

A fragment (or argument) of a treatise may be said to be authentic in two different senses. The first and stronger sense requires that the fragment be a literal quotation of a passage in the original treatise; the second, weaker sense merely requires that it give an accurate and adequate account (paraphrase) of the original argument. Only very few fragments of the *contra Aristotelem* may be regarded as authentic in the first sense. On ten occasions, at any rate, Simplicius introduces his citation with the explicit remark that he is now quoting Philoponus literally.[57] But in the vast majority of cases Simplicius merely states that 'the Grammarian says (*phêsin, legei, legôn*) the following'. The Greek phrase does not imply that Simplicius is reproducing the sentences as written by Philoponus. Yet, for several reasons, we may assume that he is providing a paraphrase, and he means it to be a valid paraphrase, of the argument. At *in de Caelo* 178,26f., for instance, Simplicius says that he has largely followed the outline of the argument but has abridged the text in order to be concise. The method by which he proceeded can perhaps best be illustrated by a comparison of the

57. See fr. I/5; III/54; (IV/63); IV/65; (IV/71); V/81; V/84; V/94; V/97; V/102: 190,22; VI/121 (see VI/122*: 1159,5ff.).

parallel fragments IV/78 (Greek) and IV/79 (Arabic). The fragments indicate that Philoponus argued that the fact that people assign the highest place to the deity does not entitle one to infer, as Aristotle did, that the heavens must be divine and eternal.[58] Of the two fragments, the Arabic fr. IV/79 is the longer; it is not entirely clear whether or not and to what extent this passage, in particular at the end, has received an arabesque decoration.[59] But even if this is the case, it becomes clear that Simplicius reproduced the gist of Philoponus' argument only in so far as it had a direct bearing on Aristotle or the commentators. This impression is confirmed by the fact that he ignored the Christian-theological arguments forming the essence of the final books of the *contra Aristotelem*.[60] In a third category of fragments Simplicius evidently provides just a rough summary or statement of Philoponus' opinion as he perceives it. These fragments are often elliptical but nevertheless informative; they have been marked with an asterisk, and one would have to decide in individual cases how much emphasis may be laid on them. As regards all three types of citation, there are several reasons for believing that the material in Simplicius is, by and large, authentic in the weaker sense of the word. First, in the case of parallel fragments deriving from different and independent sources, the ideas and arguments attributed to Philoponus are essentially in agreement. Secondly, many of the views expressed in these fragments can be identified as having been put forward by Philoponus in other treatises as well. Thirdly, although Simplicius' attitude may be correctly described as 'hostile', it is important to realise that his blatant hostility is mixed with a strong feeling of intellectual superiority. That is to say, although Simplicius regarded Philoponus as a genuine threat to pagan philosophy and learning, he is nevertheless convinced that the Grammarian's arguments are vacuous and appeal only to the uneducated crowd. Many arguments he did not consider worth setting out at length, though he usually resorts to direct quotation precisely whenever he can hope that Philoponus' embarrassment in the eyes of his own readership is greatest. These points taken together make it seem unlikely that Simplicius deliberately misrepresented arguments on a large scale:

58. Cf. Aristotle *de Caelo* 1.3, 270b5–9.

59. On this point cf. Kraemer, 'A lost passage', 326.

60. In fr. VI/132 Simplicius mentions in passing the existence of further books dealing with the theological topic of a new creation; and in fr. III/60* he indicates that Philoponus showed great respect for David, the alleged author of the Psalms, yet Simplicius gives no evidence anywhere else that Philoponus ever referred to the Old Testament.

after all, he was absolutely confident about his ability to demolish them without so doing.

If it is accepted that the fragments are indeed authentic in the wider sense of the word, the question arises how much of the original treatise has in fact come down to us. Again, this question cannot be answered with certainty, but one may pursue it speculatively. Simplicius emphasises now and again that the treatise before him is extraordinarily lengthy and repetitive. The second book had more than thirteen subdivisions, the fifth book at least twenty-five.[61] These figures and the general similarity between the *contra Aristotelem* and the *contra Proclum* suggest that the two treatises were arranged in a similar way. If one further considers that the *contra Aristotelem* consisted of at least eight books, it is reasonable to infer that the work was approximately half as long as the *contra Proclum*.[62] If this is indeed the case, the present collection of fragments, in purely quantitative terms, amounts to approximately 30 per cent of the original treatise.[63] However, although we possess good evidence of perhaps most of the philosophical arguments directed against Aristotle, we are almost entirely ignorant of the content of the seventh and eighth books as well as of the theological import in general.

In the translation below, the bare structure of the argument is outlined in paragraphs in smaller type. Footnotes offer some further explanations, propose textual emendations, and provide necessary cross-references.[64]

I wish to express my gratitude to many people who have helped me at various stages in the work on this book: Richard Sorabji, Geoffrey Lloyd, David Sedley, Gwil Owen, Robert Wardy, Charles Brink, Larry Schrenk, John Snaith, Maknun Gemaledin Ashami, Andrew Kopkin, Harry Ide and Eric Lewis. The translation is gratefully dedicated to my parents.

61. Cf. fr. II/47: *in Cael.* 75,16f. and fr. V/102: 190,21f.

62. The *contra Proclum* is divided into eighteen books with an average number of 10.4 subdivisions. The whole treatise covers just over 269 folio pages.

63. The length of the *contra Proclum* is about 160,000 words; the length of the *contra Aristotelem* may therefore be estimated at 80,000 words. The material assembled here adds up to *c.* 26,000 words.

64. Further relevant bibliography: Richard Sorabji, *Time, Creation and the Continuum: theories in antiquity and the early middle ages* (London 1983); id. (ed.), *Philoponus and the Rejection of Aristotelian Science*.

Conventions and textual emendations

Conventions

In the translation, the following conventions have been used:

* A fragment supplied with an asterisk is believed *not* to include any direct citation or paraphrase of an original argument in the *contra Aristotelem*. The fragment nevertheless contributes to an understanding of Philoponus' position.

" " Double quotation marks signify that the passage in question may – with some degree of certainty – be regarded as a valid representation (paraphrase) of Philoponus. In some cases, for instance where this is explicitly stated by Simplicius, the passage may be considered as a direct citation. The quotation marks do not always agree with the marks as set in the Greek text.

' ' Single quotation marks have been used to denote quotations from authors other than Philoponus.

( ) Round brackets enclose the usual parentheses and agree, by and large, with the brackets as set in the Greek editions.

< > Pointed brackets enclose words and phrases not in the original text but added to the translation which may help to clarify the meaning of the text.

[ ] Square brackets indicate that words or phrases have been omitted in the translation. If lines m to n of text have been omitted, the denotation is [m . . . n].

Passages in smaller type have been added by the translator.

Textual emendations

The following textual changes have been adopted in the translation:

Simplicius *in Cael.* (ed. Heiberg):

28,8 διάφορον for διάφορα with MS A
32,1 αὑτοῦ for αὐτοῦ
67,16 ὁλότητες for ὁλότητος
126,12 comma after μαρτυρίαν, not after ἀγνοῶν
171,24 comma after κἀνταῦθα, not after φησί
173,9 ἀσυμμετρία for συμμετρία
185,24 διεστὸς for διεστὼς with MS B
187,16 ἐννοήσας for ἐννοήτας
190,23 ἀπ' αὐτῶν ἐπ' ἐναντίας for ἀπ' αὐτῶν ἀπ' ἐναντίας
194,23 move colon to after ζητῶν
197,2 ἡ ἀρχὴ with MSS A + B

Simplicius *in Phys.* (ed. Diels):

1118,1 αὐτοῦ for αὑτοῦ
1133,20 οὐ before ἐφαρμόσει
1135,8 μένον for μόνον with 1138,22
1135,13 ἐπὶ τῶν μὴ for μὴ ἐπὶ τῶν
1141,26 δημιουργήσῃ for δομιουργήσῃ
1148,21 καὶ γράφειν with Diels
1157,13 τοῦ νοῦ for τοῦ νῦν
1178,17 omit καὶ with editio Aldina
1178,32 οὗ for οὐ
1179,6 τοῦ ἐνεργείᾳ for τοῦ ἐνεργεία

Brit. Mus. MS Add. 17 214:

73 r a 17 lacuna; read *ms<tryn>*

Abbreviations

Commentaries on and paraphrases of a work are indicated by the preposition *in* followed by the name of the work in question, often abbreviated. Thus *in An. Post.* abbreviates a commentary or paraphrase of the *Posterior Analytics*.

Works of Aristotle

An. Pr.	*Analytica Priora*
An. Post.	*Analytica Posteriora*
Ath. Resp.	*Atheniensium Respublica*
Cael.	*de Caelo*
Cat.	*Categoriae*
DA	*de Anima*
Div.	*de Divinatione per Somnum*
EE	*Ethica Eudemia*
EN	*Ethica Nicomachea*
GA	*de Generatione Animalium*
GC	*de Generatione et Corruptione*
HA	*Historia Animalium*
IA	*de Incessu Animalium*
Id.	*de Ideis*
Insom.	*de Insomniis*
Int.	*de Interpretatione*
Iuv.	*de Iuventute et Senectute, de Vita et Morte*
Lin. Insec.	*de Lineis Insecabilibus*
Long.	*de Longitudine et Brevitate Vitae*
MA	*de Motu Animalium*
Mem.	*de Memoria et Reminiscientia*
Metaph.	*Metaphysica*
Meteor.	*Meteorologica*
MM	*Magna Moralia*
PA	*de Partibus Animalium*

Phys.	*Physica*
Poet.	*Poetica*
Pol.	*Politica*
Probl.	*Problemata*
Protr.	*Protrepticus*
Respir.	*de Respiratione*
Rhet.	*Rhetorica*
SE	*de Sophisticis Elenchis*
Sens.	*de Sensu et Sensibili*
Som.	*de Somno et Vigilia*
Top.	*Topica*

Other works

Aet.	*de Aeternitate Mundi*
Alcib.	*Alcibiades*
in Epict.	*in Epicteti Enchiridion*
Fat.	*de Fato*
Isag.	*Isagoge*
Mant.	*de Anima Mantissa*
Mixt.	*de Mixtione*
Parm.	*Parmenides*
P. Eth.	*Problemata Ethica*
Proleg.	*Prolegomena*
Quaest.	*Quaestiones*
Temp.	*de Tempore*
Tim.	*Timaeus*

Philoponus *contra Aristotelem*

Translation

PROLOGUE

In the Prologue, Simplicius explains why he decided to refute the arguments of the *contra Aristotelem*. Since Philoponus' work is so long, it has remained unexamined, and only because of its length has the author received a high reputation. Philoponus' arguments would not trouble any educated man, but the uneducated Christians, who know nothing about Aristotle and philosophy in general, value them as support for their own religious convictions. Simplicius sets out to repudiate the arguments of the *contra Aristotelem*, first in order to defend Aristotle and the other philosophers against its unjust attack, and secondly in order to help those who have been misguided by Philoponus' work.

Prologue Simpl. *in Aristotelis de Caelo* 25,22–26,31: These are the objections Xenarchus has raised against the hypotheses handed down from Aristotle.[1] But one of our <contemporaries, i.e. the Grammarian>, a hunter for fame, as it seems, who has passed off some of Xenarchus' objections as his own and collected other, similar ones, has sprung up to criticise Aristotle, aiming at the objective, as he says, of proving the whole world perishable, as if he would receive a big reward from the Creator if he proved him <to be> a creator of perishable things only, but of nothing imperishable. Because of this desire he proposes to contradict the arguments of Aristotle before us in books of enormous length, not only hoping to intimidate fools by quantity but also deterring, I should think, the majority – in particular men of higher respectability (*tous kathariôterous*) – from studying this extraordinary nonsense. As a consequence, <his> writings have remained unexamined, <and> just from the fact of his having written so many pages against Aristotle they have earned the author a reputation for wisdom. But I know that exploits of this kind, just like the so-called gardens of Adonis, are believed by fools to blossom, yet they wither in a few days. And as for me, in setting myself to elucidate Aristotle's treatise *On the Heavens* <*de Caelo*> to the best of <my> ability, I thought I should not pass over this man's objections, which address no educated man but rather the uneducated, in particular those who always take pleasure in unusual things and begrudge the high reputation of antiquity, and still more those who think they serve God if they believe that the heavens, which came into existence for the service

1. On the objections referred to, see Paul Moraux, *Der Aristolelismus bei den Griechen I* (Berlin and N.Y. 1973), 197–214.

of man, as they say, possess nothing exceptional in comparison with the things below the moon, and if they take the heavens to be perishable like them. For in the belief that these objections support their opinion about God they hold them in great esteem, although they know nothing about these <things> and still less about <the writings> of Aristotle, against which they dare to raise the <objections>, but chatter to each other and brag to us that the doctrines of the philosophers have been overturned. Thus, for the sake of these <philosophers> and of those who are readier to listen, and so that Aristotle's treatise *On the Heavens* and <his> reverential conception of the universe should keep their ancient glory undisputed, I decided to set forth these objections and to refute <them> to the best of my ability. For it appeared <to be> more suitable to combine the objections and their refutation with the comments on the treatise. However, if at times I seem to utter a harsher word against this man, no one should be offended. For I feel no hostility towards the man whom, to my knowledge, I have never seen. But it is appropriate first to inflict a reasonable penalty upon him who has learned from Aristotle and his commentators – if indeed he has learned anything about these things. For from Menander and Herodian and the like no one has come to us with learning superior to Aristotle's as regards the nature of the things that exist. And yet, he <sc. the Grammarian> does not hesitate to write about Aristotle – whom one would not go wrong in calling the model, or better, the father of intelligence itself – both that he has been clever enough to obscure the truth by the mist of his fallacies, and that the shrewd Aristotle has obscured the truth by the complexity of the composition; and in many instances he ostentatiously presents himself as being wiser than <Aristotle> and his commentators. Furthermore I thought that it would be good too to help in this way those who have, as a result of this man's recklessness, been led into a disparagement of Aristotle's <writings> by showing them that his vainglorious ignorance is entirely despicable.

BOOK I

The first book of the *contra Aristotelem* deals with central arguments of Aristotle's *de Caelo* 1.2. There, and in the following two chapters of the *de Caelo*, Aristotle develops his famous theory of aether. He argues that the universe does not consist just of four concentric spheres (or regions) of earth, water, air and fire (in that order, earth occupying the centre of the universe, which is equated with the downward direction), but that there must be a fifth element, the first body (*prôton sôma*) or aether (*aithêr*) as he calls it, which is the element of the heavens. This forms a fifth sphere, or rather (see introduction to fragments 6 to 8) a set of spheres surrounding the other four. Aether is prior to and more divine than the other four elements (the sublunary ones, as they are called because of their position below the moon), and above all imperishable. The main reason Aristotle gives for the theory is that the heavens have a circular motion which is natural to them, whereas the four elements below the moon are seen to move by nature upwards and downwards in a straight line.

Philoponus first criticises Aristotle's conception of the relation between nature and motion in elementary bodies. He points out that the movement of the sphere of fire (firesphere) is circular too, and proposes his own solution: he agrees with Aristotle that cosmological movements are due to 'nature' as a principle of motion, but claims that it is in fact not necessary to assume a fifth sort of primary body. Circular motion must be regarded as one of the natural motions of fire and air, and it is not at all prior to rectilinear motion, as Aristotle supposed. In consequence, it is not necessary to postulate the existence of a distinct celestial element.

Fragments 1*–5

Philoponus begins with a criticism of Aristotle's thesis that in the case of simple physical bodies (that is, the elementary bodies earth, water, air, fire and aether) nature is a principle of a single motion, *de Caelo* 1.2, 268b14–16. He adduces two main objections. First, if different natures generate different movements, the same movements ought to be generated by the same natures. But this is not the case. Earth and water, for instance, move with the same movement, but their natures are different. Secondly, if it is true that bodies which are different in nature (e.g. water and earth) *can* move with the same movement, then, by contraposition, it should also be true that bodies which move with different movements *can* be of the same nature, i.e. it is not impossible that the heavens are of the same nature as the sublunary bodies although they move with a different movement. Philoponus' second argument is formally invalid.

1* Simpl. *in de Caelo* 26,31–27,4: The first objection, then, against the aforementioned hypotheses of Aristotle[2] <the Grammarian> has taken in debased form from the <arguments> of Xenarchus as follows: if different movements are generated by different natures, it would be arbitrary (*apoklêrôtikon*) if the nature <generating> the same movements is not one and the same. Therefore, since both earth and water move towards the centre, they should be of the same nature and the same species, and similarly fire and air, moving towards the upper region. And accordingly, a syllogism is formed by <the Grammarian> as follows:

<If> earth and water are simple bodies and both move towards the centre, they should be moved, according to Aristotle, by the same nature; but <bodies> moved by the same nature *are* of the same nature and of the same species; therefore, as a consequence of this, earth and water are of the same species, which <the Grammarian> says to be evidently absurd, if indeed the one is dry and the other wet.

2* Symeon Seth, *Conspectus* (36). [Delatte, *Anecdota*, 41,1–14]

What is the Substance of the Heavens?

Aristotle said that the heavens <are> a fifth body and different from the four elements, which he has shown on the basis of <an argument on> motion as follows: <bodies> with different movements also <possess> different natures. The movements of the elements are different from the movement of the heavens; the former move in a straight <line>, but the heavens <move> in a circle, so therefore they are different in kind. Objecting to this proof John Philoponus says:

Well Aristotle, if <it were true that bodies with> different movements also <possessed> different natures, then <it would also be true that bodies with> the same movements <possessed> the same natures. However, we see that the movement of earth is downward, and so is the <movement> of water; therefore both <would have> the same nature. Similarly, air and fire move upwards, but they are different in nature.

2. It seems that Simplicius is referring back to *in de Caelo* 12,6–11 where he summarised six hypotheses he thinks Aristotle uses in *de Caelo* 1.2: (1) There are two simple movements: movement in a circle and movement in a straight line. (2) A simple movement is the movement of a simple body. (3) The movement of a simple body is simple. (4) There is only one movement natural for each simple body. (5) A single thing possesses only a single contrary. (6) The heavens move in a circle.

3 Farabi, *Against Philoponus* (9)-(15). [Mahdi, *Alfarabi*, 257–9]: (9) His <sc. Philoponus'> statement in[3] <book I,> chapter 2 that "it is not fair to argue that bodies whose movements are different in species possess different natures and to disregard the argument that bodies which move with one and the same movement possess one and the same nature" is valid, provided by "bodies" he means simple bodies. However, he must explain to us that the simple bodies which are different in species move with one and the same movement.

(10) Hence he said: "If water and earth are simple, and each of them moves by nature towards the middle <of the world>, it is evident then that he <sc. Aristotle> means that the nature by which they move is the same; this same argument applies to air and fire, for both of these move away from the middle. The answer is this: if earth and water move with a movement that is one in species, *then* their natures by which they move are one in species." This <conditional> is correct. But it remains to be shown that their movement is one in species.

(11) <Hence he said>: "There are two simple magnitudes, the magnitude of the circle and the magnitude of the straight line. Therefore, locomotion is of two kinds: movement in a straight line and movement in a circle. Since the straight line has two ends, the things that move away from them must necessarily consist of only two relations (their locomotions in a straight line take place in opposite directions); for, of the two things that move in a line, the starting-point of the one is the goal of the other. Simple, rectilinear, natural movements are of two species: the movement of heavy bodies towards the centre of the universe and the movement of light bodies away from the centre and the middle; for movements to the right and the left, and forward and backward are not simple, because they share in the upward and the downward movement.

(12) Then he stated that both earth and water move towards the centre of the universe; therefore their movement becomes one in species. For, even though earth moves faster than water, fastness and slowness do not change the species <of a movement>, just as a large clod falls down faster than a small one, and its movement is not changed by this. This is true, similarly, of fire and air; for, even though fire moves faster, they both move away from the centre.

3. Mahdi translates the Arabic *fī* with 'on' instead of 'in', thus suggesting that Farabi does not say that he is referring to the first book, chapter 2, of Philoponus' *contra Aristotelem*, but that Philoponus is commenting on a passage from book 1, chapter 2 of the *de Caelo*, i.e. 268b26–269a2.

This, then, makes it evident that the movement of water and earth is one in species and, similarly, the movement of fire and air.

(13) Then he sought to explain afterwards that earth and water are not one in species, nor air and fire: for whoever says this reduces the elements to two rather than four; and one need not argue further about this point, since it is admitted by Aristotle and his followers.

(14) Then, after that, he said: "If, then, the simple bodies whose nature is not one in species <move with a movement that is one in species>." He considers that it must follow from this that there are <simple> bodies <which are one in species> which move with movements that are different in species. Therefore he claimed that it does not follow that that which moves in a circle and that which moves in a straight line should possess different natures, but they can possess the same nature, even though their movements are different in species.

(15) This, then, is a synopsis of what he says. He bases himself on <the assumption> that water and earth are different yet have a movement that is one in species.

4 Simpl. *in de Caelo* 28,1–11: But this man <sc. the Grammarian> takes it for granted <first> that water and earth are different in nature, the one being moist, the other dry (even though at this point nature is actually not being assessed in these <terms>), and <secondly> that they move towards the lower region with the same movement (even though again they do not do this in the same <manner>). He then adduces a second syllogism which he has put to illegitimate use (*katakekhrêtai*) in later arguments too; <it runs> as follows:

"If <bodies> that are different in nature like earth and water can move with the same movement, <then,> converting with negation (*sun antithesei antistrephôn*),[4] he says, you will say: there is nothing to prevent <bodies> which move with a different[5] and not the same movement from being of the same nature,[6] so that,

4. i.e. 'forming the contrapositive', or, in propositional logic, transposition. Transposition is a valid immediate inference stating that a hypothetical proposition is equivalent to another hypothetical proposition whose antecedent is the denial of the consequent of the first hypothetical, and whose consequent is the denial of the antecedent of the first hypothetical, $(p \rightarrow q) \equiv (\sim q \rightarrow \sim p)$.

5. Read *diaphoron* with MS A.

6. In lines 16–18 Simplicius repeats the argument as follows: 'If things different in nature can (*endekhetai*) move with the same movement, <then> nothing prevents (*ouden kôluei*) – which is the same as 'can' – things not moving with the same movement from being not different (*adiaphora*) in nature.'

even if the heavens move in a circle but the <bodies> below the moon <move> in a straight <line>, still there is nothing to prevent the heavens from being of the same nature as the sublunary <bodies> and perishable like them."

5 Simpl. *in de Caelo* 30,26–34: Next, although <the Grammarian> agrees that the heavens possess neither weight nor lightness, he attempts to prove that there is nothing to prevent them from possessing heat and cold. This is the way he writes, for I too <sc. Simplicius> am forced to speak nonsense:

"For even if light bodies always happen to be hot, and equally, if heavy ones are always cold, it will not necessarily follow that those <bodies> which are neither light nor heavy are devoid of coldness and heat. For the conversion from the antecedent (*hê ek tou hêgoumenon antistrophê*) is not valid. Look: if someone is a man, he is also always an animal; but it is not true <to say> that if someone is not a man, <then> he is also not an animal."

Fragments 6–8

In *de Caelo* 1.2, 268b26–269a2 Aristotle establishes a correlation between simple bodies, i.e. the elements, and simple motions, and between composite bodies and composite motions. Philoponus objects that although Aristotle distinguishes between upward and downward motion, i.e. motion away from and towards the centre of the universe, he fails to distinguish, in the case of the heavens, between eastward and westward motion and disregards the differences in speed of the various celestial bodies.

Furthermore, Aristotle's supposition that the movement of the celestial bodies is strictly circular conflicts with the astronomical theories of eccentrics and epicycles. Greek astronomical theory attempted to explain the phenomenon of the complex movements of the planets by a theory, both mathematical and physical, that heaven consisted of a set of transparent spheres (the heavens) which carried the heavenly bodies round on distinct courses. So far Aristotle agreed. But it was later added that the spheres revolved at different speeds around points which did not coincide with the centre of the universe (hence eccentrics). The stars and planets were supposedly attached to these spheres, sometimes by means of a further, much smaller rotating sphere (the epicycle), if the apparent irregularity of a planet's motion required this.

Finally, Philoponus objects that circular and rectilinear cosmological motion cannot be compared because in the former case one is speaking of the movement of a whole, in the latter case of the movement of parts.

6 Simpl. *in de Caelo* 31,6–16: And he adduces another <objection against> the propositions on simple movements as follows:

"Just as in the case of the four elements: even if rectilinear movement is one in genus, there still exists, since the <movement> away from the centre is different in species from the <movement> towards the centre, a difference in species between fire and earth because of this; in the same way, since there is a difference in species between westward and eastward movement, the moving <bodies> will also be different. And the planets, if they indeed differ naturally in speed from one another, as earth and water do although they possess the same downward momentum (*rhopê*), differ in species because of being faster and slower."

Therefore, he says that the simple bodies are not five only but equal in number to the spheres plus the four elements.

7 Simpl. *in de Caelo* 32,1–11: In his[7] seventh chapter this man <sc. the Grammarian> says:

"If Alexander <sc. of Aphrodisias> was correct in pointing out that Aristotle defined that kind of movement as circular in the proper sense which takes place around the centre of the universe, but if those <kinds of movement> which do not take place around the centre of the universe are neither strictly circular nor simple, and if the stars too – which move with <their> own movement along the spheres, as the astronomers hold – revolve around distinct centres of their own which do not coincide with the centre of the universe, then it is evident that neither the stars themselves nor their epicycles nor the so-called eccentric spheres (*hai ekkentroi sphairai*) carry out a proper circular or simple movement, because both downward <movement> and upward <movement> are observed. For, even if this conflicts with Aristotle's hypotheses," he says, "the stars are clearly seen to reach a perigee and apogee."

8 Simpl. *in de Caelo* 33,17–20: "Besides," he says, "Aristotle did not make the comparison between the elements and the heavens on the same <assumptions>, <because> in one case he took the whole as moving in its proper place, but in the other case <he took> a part as having abandoned its proper places and to have come to be in its counternatural place."

Fragments 9–17*

In an Aristotelian universe, the outer shell of the sublunary region is supposedly constituted by 'the firesphere'. Aristotle's position on the ques-

7. Read *hautou* and cf. below fr. II/47: 75,16; fr. III/52: 80,28; fr. V/86: 165,31 with the apparatus.

tion of the movement of this sphere of fire is contradictory. In *de Caelo* 1.2, 269a7–18 he argues explicitly that none of the four sublunary elements can move in a circle, either naturally or counternaturally (i.e. by virtue of an external force). However, in *Meteorology* 1.3, 340b32–341a3; 1.4, 341b22–24; 344a11–13 he supposes that the firesphere revolves in a circle. In order to evade this difficulty, Damascius, Simplicius and Olympiodorus, for instance, argued that the movement of the firesphere is neither natural nor counternatural, but supernatural, cf. ap. Philoponum *in Meteor.* 97,20f.; Simplicius *in de Caelo* 21,1–25; 35,12–20; 51,5–28; Olympiodorus *in Meteor.* 2,21–29. Philoponus attempts to show (fr. 9–17*) that the movement of the firesphere must be natural, and that fire and air possess two natural and simple movements, upwards and in a circle, just as earth and water are by nature at rest or in downward motion. In these arguments Philoponus both rejects indirectly the theory of supernatural motion and suggests that the heavens are of the same nature as the sublunary elements. In Philoponus' view, circular motion too is a natural motion of sublunary elements.

9 Simpl. *in de Caelo* 34,5–11: Because he wants the heavens to be perishable, <the Grammarian> is eager to show that they are of the same nature as the elements also on the basis of the <argument> that they move with the same movement.

"For", he says, "both the firesphere (*to hupekkauma*) and the air move in a circle, <and they possess> this movement by virtue of their own nature – just like the heavens. For <the movement> is either according to nature or forced and contrary to nature, and it is better not to be at all than always to be in <a state> contrary to nature. But the whole will also be contrary to nature if its parts are contrary to nature."[8]

10* Simpl. *in de Caelo* 34,21–24 + 30–32: <The Grammarian> further objects to the <following> proposition[9] that 'as a result of force it is possible that the movement is of another and different <body>, but it is impossible <for this to happen> naturally'. For the movement towards the centre of the universe is natural for

8. The argument is elliptical. Philoponus aims to show that the circular movement of the firesphere is a natural motion (and not a supernatural one, as Damascius, Simplicius and Olympiodorus supposed). The starting point is the (exhaustive) Aristotelian dichotomy according to which a movement is either natural or counternatural. Given that the natural motion of a part of fire is upward to the circumference, then, if circular motion were contrary to its nature, the circular movement of the whole firesphere would be counternatural to fire as well because the same account applies to the part and the whole. But since it would be better not to be at all than to be permanently in a state contrary to nature, and since the firesphere and its motion exist, it follows that circular motion must belong to it naturally.

9. See *de Caelo* 1.2, 269a7f.

earth and water. [24 . . . 30] But if, as this man believes, movement towards the centre of the universe is natural for either <body>,[10] it does not after all move with a movement of a different <body>, but with its own individual <movement> according to nature.

11* Simpl. *in de Caelo* 34,33–35,8: After quoting the sentence which reads[11] 'further, if the <movement> contrary to nature is contrary to <the movement> according to nature' and the following <arguments> by which Aristotle proves not only that circular movement is not natural for any of the elements, but also <that it is> not counternatural either, <the Grammarian> in my opinion utters a lot of nonsense (*polla lêrôn*) when he tries to show that circular movement is not contrary to <the nature> of fire. Aristotle says this as well, except that he says that it is neither according to nor contrary to nature, but this man wants <circular movement> to exist according to nature, <and> to begin with he shows that it is not contrary to nature, for the purpose of which he uses the Aristotelian proof. For if a single thing possesses a single contrary, <and if> the movement downwards is contrary to the natural movement of fire, then circular movement will not be contrary to it as well. In consequence, <circular movement> is not counternatural <for fire>. For the counternatural is the contrary. Therefore, circular movement belongs to fire naturally when it is in its proper place.

12* Simpl. *in de Caelo* 35,12–20: But as I <sc. Simplicius> said,[12] how can one maintain that the <circular movement> which is not proper <to fire> is natural? If indeed <the movement> is completely simple it is better to say that it is supernatural (*huper phusin*), in order that again one natural <movement> belongs to one <elementary body>. He debases (*parakharattei*) this too by saying that fire has two natural movements, the one in an upward direction <which belongs to> the parts of <fire> which have become detached from the totality, the other, a circular one, <which belongs to> the totality <itself>, so that there is nothing to prevent the revolving heaven itself from consisting of fire, and the movement will not be contrary to its nature. And it is clear that in all these <arguments> he led himself astray into thinking that the

10. i.e. water and earth.
11. See *de Caelo* 1.2, 269a9–18.
12. Cf. *in de Caelo* 34,20f.

circular motion, which is the celestial <motion>, belongs to fire – not supernaturally, but naturally.

13* Simpl. *in de Caelo* 35,28–33: But this man continues to prove contentiously that simple circular movement is proper to the totality of the firesphere, when previously he did not <even> concede that this kind of movement belonged to the things in heaven.[13] But the reason is that <he> thinks to infer from this that, even if the heavens move with a circular and simple movement, nothing prevents them – since they are of the same nature as the <bodies> below the moon – from being perishable like them.

14 Simpl. *in de Caelo* 36,9–18: Since he has argued a lot against Alexander <of Aphrodisias>, who showed that the movement of the firesphere is not simple but composite, a few of these <arguments> ought to be put to the test. <The Grammarian> says:

"Even though some <parts> of the firesphere and of the air rise and other <parts> descend, and some are condensed (*puknoutai*) whereas others are rarefied (*mainoutai*), and <although> it is evident that one <part> moves faster, the other more slowly, still, the circular movement of the whole is simple. For it is possible that, when fire is carried upwards and water downwards, some of their parts are hurled here, others there, by <the agency of> some kind of wind, but the whole nevertheless moves with a simple <movement> away from or towards the middle."

15 Simpl. *in de Caelo* 36,21–25: "And as the sphere of the morning star rotates", he says, "the morning star itself, moving on its own epicycle, is sometimes more in perigee and sometimes more in apogee, and the same <is true> of the other planets. But still, the heavens as a whole move with a single and simple movement."

16 Simpl. *in de Caelo* 37,3–12: "But", he says, "if some part of the air or of the firesphere is rarefied or condensed, this does not render the movement of the whole non-simple. For rarefaction and condensation are in fact changes of quality, and not spatial movements. For if in falling towards the centre a lump of earth happens to heat up or cool down, this too does not render the movement non-simple."

Notice, how in his witless sentences he fails to realise that what is rarefied becomes lighter but what is condensed heavier, and in

13. Cf. above fr. I/7.

this way also the spatial movements of the parts become unequal in speed (*anisotakheis*). But when water turns into hail as it falls downwards, it will not possess a simple locomotion downwards, as he believes.

17* Simpl. *in de Caelo* 37,12–29: But again he cites a passage from Alexander <of Aphrodisias> which reads: 'For at the same time when <an elementary body>[14] is carried round it necessarily moves according to its proper momentum (*kata tên oikeian rhopên*) as well, either upwards if it belongs to the light <bodies>, or downwards if it belongs to the heavy ones. Therefore its movement comes to be compounded of rectilinear and circular <motion>.'

<The Grammarian> mischievously distorts the <passage> because he understands 'upwards' and 'downwards' to refer to the whole, and he tries to show that the firesphere can move neither upwards, because it touches the lunary sphere, nor downwards by nature. But it is clear that <Alexander> says that although the whole <firesphere> is moved in a circle by <the agency of> the heavens, some of its *parts* move upwards, others downwards, as the passage from Alexander cited by him earlier indicates. 'For,' <Alexander> says, 'fire and air move neither simply with this circular movement nor <with a movement> in a straight <line>, but <they move> with a composite <movement>. For some of their <parts> proceed to the heights and some come down to the lower <region> in <the course of> this revolution; in addition, they are rarefied and condensed.' Consequently, <Alexander> said that some and not all of their <parts> are rarefied and condensed, in view of which, since they account for the variation of spatial motion, he does not agree that the <circular> movement in space remains simple. Yet <the Grammarian> frequently brings in the <argument> that if circular movement did not belong to the firesphere and the air by nature, they would not last for a long <time> because <the movement> would be contrary to nature. For also Aristotle says that what is contrary to nature is destroyed very quickly.

Fragments 18–32

In *de Caelo* 1.2, 269a18–28 Aristotle argues that the circle is prior to the straight line, that circular motion is in consequence prior to rectilinear

14. The argument in fact only applies to fire and air.

motion, and that the celestial body is therefore prior to the sublunary bodies.

Philoponus first objects that the inference from the priority of motion to the priority of body is unjustified because sublunary bodies move in a circle as well (fr. 18). He then sets out to refute Aristotle's argument in detail, first conceding that the circle is prior to the straight line (fr. 19–24), then rejecting this crucial assumption (fr. 25–32).

Fragments 19–24: Philoponus accepts, for the sake of the argument, Alexander's (and Simplicius') definition of the complete as that which has a beginning, a middle, and an end (on the origin of this obscure definition see fr. 32). He argues that if the circle is complete in this sense, circular motion will be incomplete because it has no limits, but rectilinear motion will be complete because all rectilinear movements possess a beginning, a middle, and an end. So either the celestial motion is eternal and incomplete, or it is complete and limited, i.e. not eternal (fr. 22). He further attempts to reject Aristotle's argument on formal grounds (fr. 23).

Fragments 25–32: Aristotle's assumption that the circle is complete and therefore prior to the straight line, which is incomplete, is indefensible if one accepts the given definition of completeness. Philoponus claims that the contrary is the case: the circle is incomplete because no two-dimensional circle possesses a beginning, a middle, and an end. But every straight line is complete because the longest straight line, the diameter of the universe, is limited. Moreover, it is not true that a (natural) circle cannot be increased, as Aristotle argued.

Philoponus finally dismisses the given definition of completeness as useless (fr. 29*–32). Aristotle should have given a proper, universal definition of completeness.

18 Simpl. *in de Caelo* 42,17–22: But he, our young crow – a jackdaw rather – who 'chatters in vain against the sacred bird of Zeus', according to the magniloquent Pindar,[15] and sneaks out (*parekduomenos*) against what has been said by Aristotle in the present <passage>,[16] adduces a first objection whereby he plagiarises the third <argument> of Xenarchus.[17]

"Even if", he says, "the <body> moving in a circle may be primary, it does not follow that it is different from the four elements,

15. Cf. Pindar, *Olympian Odes* 2. 87f.

16. i.e. *de Caelo* 1.2, 269a18–28.

17. In *in de Caelo* 42,6–14 Simplicius has summarised three of Xenarchus' objections to the primacy of the circular movement of the heavens. The third objection reads (42,10–14): 'Thirdly, that even if there is something which moves in a circle, it is not different from the four <elements>, if indeed some of the elements too are at rest while others move in a circle when they are complete <i.e. when they are in their proper places>; above all, this applies to fire. For the <parts> which are still incomplete move with a <movement> in a straight <line>, which – as Aristotle thought as well – is an incomplete <movement>.' Cf. also the argument cited by Simplicius at *in de Caelo* 21,33–22,17.

as in fact rest and circular movement belong to these as well when they are complete (*teleios*)."

19 Simpl. *in de Caelo* 42,27–31: Then, in conceding for the time being that a circle is complete because it has a beginning, a middle, and an end, <the Grammarian> says:

"What necessitates that the *movement* taking place in a <circle> is complete as well? If it is for the reason that it has a beginning, a middle, and an end, as Alexander said but not Aristotle, then the <movement> in a limited straight <line> possesses the same properties."

20 Simpl. *in de Caelo* 43,8–12: Further he says: "Precisely because they suppose circular movement, which possesses neither a beginning nor a limit, to be eternal, it is evident that it should be incomplete (*atelês*) because it is unlimited (*apeiros*), whereas the <movement> in a limited straight <line> should be complete. For they say that an unlimited straight <line> is incomplete because it does not have a beginning, a middle, and an end, and yet it is not subject to further increase (*prosauxêsis*)."

21 Simpl. *in de Caelo* 43,22–25: "But since in reality", he says, "a straight <line> is never unlimited, it is evident that every movement in a straight <line> will have a beginning, a limit and what <is> between these. Surely then, <rectilinear movement is> also complete, at least in terms of the definition of 'complete'."

22 Simpl. *in de Caelo* 44,15–18: "Furthermore," he says, "if the movement of the heavens and the time capable of measuring it are complete, <then> they possess a beginning, a middle, and an end, and they will not be unlimited or unceasing (*anekleipta*), as Aristotle believes. But if unceasing, then they are not complete. For they do not possess a beginning, a middle, and an end."

23 Simpl. *in de Caelo* 45,2–7: However, the proof[18] is not circular (*diallêlos*), as <the Grammarian> believes.

"For if", he says, "it is because the circle is complete that <Aristotle> also thought the movement in it to be complete, and if the movement <takes place> in a physical circle,[19] and if this <phys-

18. i.e. the proof in *de Caelo* 1.2, 269a18–28.
19. As opposed to a mathematical (geometrical) circle, cf. fr. I/25: 46,9; I/26: 46,22f.

ical circle> is the celestial body, and again, if it is because circular movement is complete that <he also took> the body moving with this <movement>, i.e. the heavens, to be complete, then the argument is circular and not a proof."

24 Simpl. *in de Caelo* 45,27–29: "But if", he says, "the celestial <body> is complete because it is spherical, then in this respect, at any rate, it will not be different from the other elements, the totalities of which even Aristotle himself wants to be spherical."

25 Simpl. *in de Caelo* 46,4–11: But again, as if <the Grammarian> regrets that he has conceded that the circle is complete rather than the straight <line>, he attempts to prove the opposite:

"For if", he says, "the circle were assumed to be a plane surface,[20] as Alexander thinks, <then> it would not have a centre in actuality, in order that it may escape being divided there and so losing its continuity (*mêketi esti sunekhês*). In consequence, it does not have a beginning. The limited line, however, whether natural or mathematical, does have actual extremes. Then, in so far as the actual is complete rather than the potential, the straight <line> will be complete rather than the circle."

26 Simpl. *in de Caelo* 46,17–25: But the reason why <the Grammarian> preferred to say these things exposes his foolishness even more. For he says that the centre of the circle is not actual, in order that the continuity of the <circle> may not be disrupted (*diakoptetai*). However, if it is indeed continuous in virtue of the given definition of the continuous, <i.e. that> of which the extremes are one,[21] <and if> the centre, being one, is common to all straight <lines> drawn from <the centre> to the circumference, how would the <centre> being actual destroy the continuity? "But if", he says, "the circle is linear (*grammikos*), then first it would be mathematical and not natural, and secondly, it would not be <possible> to take as actual either the centre of such a circle, or the <region> between the circumference and the centre."

27* Simpl. *in de Caelo* 46,29–47,3: <The Grammarian> then, by a reference to the diameter of the world, objects even to the <opinion> that it is possible to increase a limited straight <line>, and

20. i.e. as opposed to a *kuklos grammikos*, i.e. a circle which consists merely of the line of the circumference, see fr. I/26: 46,22f.

21. Cf. *Physics* 6.1, 231a22; also 5.3, 227a11f.

<he objects> to the interpretation of Alexander which says that in theory nothing prevents any <given> limited straight <line> from being increased, and he defends himself by vacuous considerations. I <sc. Simplicius> said that Aristotle looked at the nature of the straight <line> as not linking up with itself like the circle, but, so far as depends on it, as extending indefinitely – just like this man's argument. For <the Grammarian> also says <that> in the case of a circle, if it should be a body, or in the case of a sphere, a body poured round it equally from all directions and attached to it will make <the circle or sphere> larger.

28 Simpl. *in de Caelo* 47,10–13: "But many circular and spherical <things>", he says, "in living bodies increase by food taken in, like the head of a human being and the circle of the cornea in the eye."

29* Simpl. *in de Caelo* 47,27–30: But because he finds fault with the given definition of 'complete' he also says that one wastes one's labour[22] when one tries to divide a hand or a tongue or earth or fire or any other part into a beginning, a middle, and a last.

30* Simpl. *in de Caelo* 48,5–11: And in the case of the three-dimensional body we shall not be at a loss, as this man believes, <over the question> of which <dimension> has the definition of a beginning, which of a mean, <and> which <the definition> of an end. For it is evident that the <dimension> of line and length is the beginning, the <dimension> of the plane surface the middle, and that of depth is the end. But if the cube makes one wonder which <dimension> is the beginning, which the middle, and which the end because the three dimensions are equal, I <sc. Simplicius> will again reply that we will take the beginning to be defined as length, even though it makes no difference from where one begins.

31 Simpl. *in de Caelo* 48,14–22: For instance, the gentleman has thought of a further cleverness:

If "the linear circle", he says, "is complete in so far as it has a beginning, a middle, and an end, it will still be incomplete in so far as it does not possess the three dimensions, so that in one sense it is complete, but in another it is incomplete. Then, if circular movement takes place along a circular line and not in the three

22. Literally: 'one falls into extreme coldness (*psukhrotês*)'. In Greek, 'coldness' is a metaphor for fruitlessness.

dimensions, it is also incomplete. So if <Aristotle> intended to demonstrate from the <premise> that circular movement is complete that it is also prior to rectilinear <movement>, he should have defined the notion of 'completeness' universally and <should have> shown that the definition applies to every circle, but does not <apply> to any straight <line>."

32 Simpl. *in de Caelo* 48,35–49,12: And it is remarkable that although he hears Aristotle saying[23] 'for end, middle and beginning possess the number of the universe, but the universe and the complete do not differ in form from one another', and although he himself uses the word 'complete' in this sense up to this point, and although in what immediately follows he objects to <Aristotle's> conception when he says "Just why is that which possesses a beginning and a limit and something between these complete?", he none the less still demands that Aristotle should define the concept of 'complete' universally. <This is remarkable>, unless we are to conclude that by universal he means not that which is common, but that which is collected from all the particulars by reference to their differentiae – which was impossible. But he asks:

"Just why is that which possesses a beginning and a limit, and something between these complete, and not rather that which has neither a beginning nor a limit, like the infinite line? For <the infinite line> does not admit of theoretical addition or increase."

And it is remarkable that although <the Grammarian> has written works on grammar as well, he nowhere inquires into the etymology of 'the complete' (*to teleion*), which wholly derives from 'the end' (*to telos*).

Fragments 33–36*

Philoponus points out the well-known contradiction in *de Caelo* 1.2 that Aristotle first argues explicitly (269a9–18) that circular motion is neither natural nor counternatural for the four sublunary elements, but later in the chapter (269a32–b6) assumes that circular motion is indeed counternatural for them, and therefore natural for some other element.

At the end of book I Philoponus seems to have shown that other philosophers before him had also argued against Aristotle's fifth element (fr. 36*).

23. Cf. *de Caelo* 1.1, 268a11–13 and 20f.

33 Simpl. *in de Caelo* 56,26–57,8: But here the Grammarian has not shrunk from describing his own lack of intelligence and hastiness as a piece of ignorance and a contradiction in the arguments of Aristotle, for he says:

"In the second proof, when <Aristotle> wanted to show that that which moves in a circle is none of the four elements, he said that circular movement is neither natural nor counternatural for the four elements, because the <movement> which is contrary to their nature is straight,[24] and a single thing <can only have> a single contrary. Here,[25] when he wanted to show in turn that circular movement is necessarily natural for some <element> other than the four elements, he took it for granted that circular movement belongs to the four <elements> contrary to nature, but since it is a natural and simple movement it must be entirely natural for some <element>. But if circular movement is counternatural for them, it will <follow> on this hypothesis too that one <thing> possesses two contraries, since there is also a counternatural movement for them in a straight <line>, <i.e.> the one opposite to <their> natural <movement>. So either<Aristotle> made a false assumption in the former passage, i.e. that the heavens cannot be one of the four elements moving in a circle contrary to nature; or he wrongly supposed now that circular movement is counternatural for the four elements. For what he said would be an absurd consequence of the former hypothesis, <namely> that two are contrary to one, is precisely what has been shown to result from the <hypothesis> laid down now."

34 Simpl. *in de Caelo* 58,1–10: "Although <Aristotle> believes", <the Grammarian> says, "that none of the elements can move even counternaturally in a circle, he nevertheless says that circular movement is counternatural for them, and this way there will again be two contrary to one." [4 . . . 5] "But there is nothing to prevent us", he says, "from converting the proposition and saying that movements in a straight <line> are counternatural for Aristotle's fifth <and> revolving body, even though it never moves counternaturally with these <rectilinear movements>. For they are simple as well. Therefore, there will again be two rectilinear movements, which belong to <the fifth body> counternaturally, contrary to the one circular movement, which it <executes> naturally."

24. Philoponus is referring to the argument of *de Caelo* 1.2, 269a9–18.
25. i.e. *de Caelo* 1.2, 269a32–b6.

35 Simpl. *in de Caelo* 58,14–22: Unable to look away from the madness of his counter-argument towards truth, <the Grammarian> brings into action the following, believing that Aristotle regarded <movement> in a straight <line> as contrary to circular movement, although somewhat later[26] <Aristotle> produced very long arguments – as <Philoponus himself> says – in which he attempts to show that there is no movement contrary to circular movement.

"For rectilinear movements", he says, "are natural and simple, and they do not belong to the fifth body by nature. Therefore, they will necessarily be counternatural for it. But 'counternatural' is the contrary of 'natural'. Rectilinear movements, being simple, are therefore contrary to circular <movement>."

36* Simpl. *in de Caelo* 59,6–10: He considers himself to have won an important point in showing that other <philosophers> as well have argued against the fifth substance, but he does not notice that none of these wrote their replies in the belief that the eternity of the world was being shaken, but they were engaging in practice arguments which, in comparison to the teachings of earlier philosophers, contained something novel.

26. i.e. in *de Caelo* 1.4.

BOOK II

The second book focuses mainly on Aristotle's argument that the heavens are neither heavy nor light, *de Caelo* 1.3, 269b18–270a12, i.e. that the heavens lack those properties which essentially belong to sublunary elements. Philoponus attempts to show that it is not true that weight and lightness belong to the elements as such, that the totalities of the sublunary elements are neither heavy nor light, and that the celestial body would not be able to move upwards or downwards even if it were e.g. a light body. He makes the final claim that the circular movement of the things in heaven is both natural and psychical.

Fragments 37–44*

Philoponus first rejects the conclusion of Aristotle's argument that the heavens are neither heavy nor light. After all, the celestial body is located in the place above and should be light because of this (fr. 37–39). Yet Philoponus is far from endorsing the view that the celestial body is light. He agrees with Aristotle that the heavens are neither heavy nor light, only for a different reason. His reason is that the totality of each element, even the whole earth or the whole world, possesses neither weight nor lightness. These properties belong only to parts of elementary bodies which have become detached from the totality and are in a counternatural place (fr. 40*–44*). In these arguments Philoponus not only relies on the authority of Plato and Themistius, but also adduces some original thought experiments.

37 Simpl. *in de Caelo* 66,8–14: But since – regardless of whether one falls into the open sea or into a bath, but especially if <one falls> into a filthy puddle – it is necessary to swim,[27] let us turn aside again in order to look at the words of the Telkhin.[28] He further says:

"If <Aristotle> demonstrated that the celestial <body> is neither heavy nor light, using the <argument> that it is not one of the four elements, <and if> the arguments that proved this have

27. Simplicius is alluding to Plato *Republic* 5, 453D5–7.

28. i.e. the Grammarian. Simplicius uses the word *telkhinos* with reference to Philoponus also elsewhere, cf. *in Phys.* 1117,15ff. (= Prologue VI). In Antiquity, this derogatory term denoted malicious and envious people; hence, in the passage of the *Physics* commentary mentioned, Simplicius continues to speak of the Grammarian's *baskania* (slander). On the complex origin and meaning of the word *telkhinos* see H. Herter, 'Telchinen', in G. Wissowa, W. Kroll and K. Mittelhaus (eds.), *Real-Encyclopädie der Classischen Altertumswissenschaft* V^{A} (Stuttgart 1934) 197–224, esp. 206–11. Apart from this, it is not impossible that 'Telchin' was also a sobriquet for 'Christian'.

been refuted, <then> it is evident that the point proved by them, <namely> that it is neither heavy nor light, is refuted as well."

38 Simpl. *in de Caelo* 66,17–24: <The Grammarian> continues: "If <Aristotle> correctly defined the lightest as that which rises to the top (*to epipolazon*) of all ascending bodies,[29] <and if> the heavens float on top (*epipolazein*)[30] of everything, then they should be the lightest body of all," not having paid any attention to what the expression 'ascending bodies' (*tois anô pheromenois*) and <the expression> 'floating on top' (*epipolazein*) stand for, regarding <both> as meaning the same as 'to be located <on top>'.

He says that 'light' means away from the centre, which is the same as moving upwards; lightness, he says, is that which ascends most, which, after having risen from below, floats on top of everything.

"For olive oil, too, floats on top of water after it has relinquished the place below to <water>."

39 Simpl. *in de Caelo* 70,34–71,6: The Grammarian says: "But since there are according to Aristotle only two differences and oppo- 71, 1
sitions of place, 'above' and 'below',[31] each body therefore is – because it exists in a place – either in the upper or in the lower region. Then, since the spheres of the heavens, with the exception of the fixed, each has as its place the boundary of the surrounding sphere – the lunary sphere having as its place the boundary of the sphere of Venus, and this sphere the <boundary of> the sphere of Mercury, and so forth – <then> these <spheres> are necessarily in the upper region and certainly not in the lower. In consequence, they partake of lightness."

40* Simpl. *in de Caelo* 66,33–67,19: Now this man <sc. the Gram-
marian> seems to follow Plato who says that the heavens consist 67, 1
of fire, not knowing what Plato means by fire, and that it is not the same as what Aristotle says moves upwards and is therefore light and rises to the top of all <bodies> which move upwards and is the lightest because of this, but this kind of fire, the celestial, Plato

29. See *de Caelo* 1.3, 269b25f.

30. The verb is in both cases *epipolazein*, which can mean both 'to rise to the top' and 'to float on top', i.e. it possesses a dynamic as well as a static sense. Philoponus seems to make deliberate use of this ambiguity.

31. See *de Caelo* 1.8, 277a22f.

wants to be pure light (*phôs*), <for he> defines light too as one form of fire.

But again, <the Grammarian> prolongs many an argument as he is trying to show that the totalities of the elements do not move in a straight <line>. Now, above all it ought to be understood that something which desires (*to ephiemenon*)[32] inclines in all circumstances towards the desired object (*to epheton*), and, given that both are bodies, the inclination they have remains, even if they have contact with each other, as a consequence of which they are not simply contiguous but are contiguous while holding on to the desired objects and approaching them as much as possible. So equally, also the totality of the firesphere, in striving to approach the heavens even more than any part of it, always retains its inclination towards them, so that it would follow if someone – let this be supposed for the sake of the argument – removed the heavens.[33] Now, above all, as I <sc. Simplicius> have said, this was necessary to understand. But if this is above this man's head, who is blinded by the aim of <his> writings, none the less it is still clear than even if the totalities[34] of the elements do not possess an inclination, and the heavens, as he believes, are not different from them in this respect, the parts of the elements, at least, move in a straight <line>, whereas the <parts> of the heavens do not suffer anything of this sort, and in this respect, at any rate, the difference between them is well defined.

41* Simpl. *in de Caelo* 68,6–10: But since he did not understand the Platonic <arguments> this man cites Themistius in support, quoting a long passage from his paraphrase of the fourth book of *On the Heavens*, in the attempt to show that <Themistius>, too, objected with Plato to the <tenet> that something is light or heavy in its proper place (*en tôi oikeiôi topôi*);[35] but I <sc. Simplicius> do not think Plato says this directly, but that 'heavy' and 'light' are not natural.[36]

32. *to ephiemenon*. The 'desire' of an elementary body is of course neither conscious nor in any way psychological.

33. Lines 7–14 contain Simplicius' argument. In contrast to Philoponus (see lines 5–7), he contends that the total sphere of an elementary body as a whole possesses an inclination (*rhopê*) despite the fact that it is in its proper place.

34. Read *holotêtes*.

35. Cf. Plato *Timaeus* 62C1–63E7.

36. i.e. 'heavy and light' do not belong to bodies by nature.

42* Simpl. *in de Caelo* 70,2–8: But Themistius himself, whom <the Grammarian> cites as evidence, although he denies 'heavy' and 'light' most certainly of <elements> that are in <their> proper places, none the less says that the inclination does belong to those elements which are in places foreign <to them>. He <sc. Themistius> says: 'It would be more reasonable and in agreement with the phenomena concerning these <matters>, if the inclinations were rather assigned to the elements <which are> in places foreign <to them>.'[37] Wherefore he, too, clearly admits that no <inclination> belongs to the heavens.

43 Simpl. *in de Caelo* 71,19–33: And yet, <the Grammarian> spins out many words, thinking that Themistius bears witness in his support that when the elements are in their proper places, they do not partake of weight or lightness, but that <these properties> accrue to them through their removal to a counternatural <place>; and he further thinks to infer from this that the totality of fire – though, he would say, of the other elements as well – does not partake of weight or lightness any more than the heavens, so that it ought to be of the same nature.

"But because the earth, if it were hypothetically removed from <its> proper place and released, would return to <that place>, one must not think because of this," he says, "that the whole earth possesses weight. For if under a similar hypothesis someone removed the whole world, it would also return to its own place once it was released. And yet, the whole world cannot possess weight or lightness because it embraces all <things> inside itself. But perhaps nothing prevents <the world> from moving according to the prevalence of the <things> inside it, but there is no one to say whether it is carried upwards or downwards, because 'up' and 'down' are inside it."

44* Simpl. *in de Caelo* 72,10–16: The following I <sc. Simplicius> <have to> say against the articulate Themistius.[38] For from him <the Grammarian> has provided himself with this support which he puts to a worse purpose. <The Grammarian> says that even if one does not allow that the world is hypothetically assumed to be removed, still, what prevents one from assuming stars falling down from <their> proper abode towards the inner <region>? If this <star> were imagined returning again to <its> natural place, it

37. Cf. Themistius *in de Caelo* 221,28–30.
38. Simplicius' direct criticism of Themistius follows in lines 16ff.

would move in a straight <line>. But Aristotle nevertheless wants none of the things in heaven to partake of weight or lightness.

Fragments 45*–46

Philoponus has to face an obvious objection: Why does no part of the celestial body become separated from it in the same way as parts become separated from the totalities of the sublunary elements? Philoponus' answer to this problem is that the heavens are the most important physical part of the universe. They are an analogue of the heart in living beings, and less corruptible than the other parts of the world. In fr. 46 Philoponus argues that weight and lightness are not properties which belong to the elements as such, but depend on the relative location of the elementary body in question. In their proper places the elements are not heavy or light.

45* Simpl. *in de Caelo* 73,4–15: The dissimilarity deriving from the parts is a ready objection to those who say that the heavens are of the same nature as the sublunary elements, given that the parts of the elements clearly become detached from the whole and are generated and destroyed, but according to true reports handed down <to us> in the whole of the past no part of the heavens seems to have become detached or to have changed.[39] <Consequently,> in order to refute, as be believes, this objection, the Grammarian says that the more important and principal parts in living beings are less affected, like the heart, and nevertheless they consist of the same elements. And as he agrees that the heavens are more important than the other bodies inside the world[40] he says that above all they are affected to the least <degree> of all, and because of this its parts evidently do not suffer the same as the parts of the elements.

46 Simpl. *in de Caelo* 74,16–26: <The Grammarian> also quotes Aristotle who says in the fourth <book> of this treatise[41] that fire is light everywhere and earth is heavy everywhere, but that water is heavy in other elements and light when it is in earth, and that air is light in water and earth, but outside of these it is heavy, <which> he makes plain <by the example> that an inflated bladder weighs more than an empty one. And from this <the Grammarian> infers that heaviness and lightness do not belong to the elements as such.

39. Cf. Aristotle *de Caelo* 1.3, 270b11–16.
40. Cf. also below fr. IV/75: 138,32–34; fr. IV/80: 142,7–25.
41. See *de Caelo* 4.4, 311b6ff.

"For <otherwise> it would not be the case", he says, "that the same <elements>, <endowed> with the same capacities (*dunameis*) and having received nothing in addition from outside, are in fact light in one place and heavy in another only because of their relation towards each other, and <that they are> light in relation to one, but heavy in relation to another <element>. 'White' at least, and 'black' and 'hot' are not displaced in their arrangement, regardless of how they relate to other <things>."

Fragments 47–48

In order to refute Aristotle's position entirely, Philoponus concedes that the elements are heavy and light in their proper places. Aristotle argued that the heavens cannot move in a straight line naturally or counternaturally because they consist of aether, and are therefore neither heavy nor light. Philoponus shows that the heavens could not move in a straight line even if one supposed that they do consist of heavy or light bodies. For first, there is no space above or below for them to move to as a whole, and secondly no part of the celestial body can become detached without the whole sphere being destroyed, for the heavens, Philoponus argues, are a solid body.

47 Simpl. *in de Caelo* 75,16–76,29: In the thirteenth chapter of his second book <the Grammarian> argues as follows:

"But let it be agreed not only that the elements possess weight or lightness in places that are foreign <to them> (*en tois allotriois topois*), but that they are characterised by capacities of this kind even when they are in <their> proper <places>. For not even in this way, I think, will there be any argument which is able to show that the celestial body alone is devoid of these capacities, seeing that Aristotle inferred that <the heavens> do not partake of weight or lightness from the fact that they do not move in a straight <line> naturally. For in order to prove that <the heavens> do not move in a straight <line> naturally he assumed that the heavens are different from the substance of the bodies which move in a straight <line>; and from <the proposition that> they do not move in a straight <line> <he then inferred> that they do not partake of weight or lightness. Therefore, if there were some argument to show that even if the heavens partook of weight or lightness or were a compound of heavy and light bodies, it would nevertheless be impossible for them to move in a straight <line>, then it would surely be evident that they are not necessarily devoid of weight and lightness simply because they do not move in a straight line. Let this be the starting point of the proof."

Next he assumes that the heavens are a solid and rigid body (*sterron kai antitupon sôma*) which cannot give way like water and air, and that, if any part of them becomes detached, they do not remain continuous by closing up[42] as they <do>, and he says that
76, 1 the spherical shape is the cause of the solidity.

"Therefore," he says, "if the heavens were light, they would not move in a straight <line> because of this since they <already> occupy their proper place – the extremity, just as the whole earth, too, cannot possibly move downwards as it <already> occupies the natural <place>. But if <the heavens> were heavy, again, they could not possibly move outside <their place> in a straight <line>. For outside there is no empty space (*to kenon*), and besides, <movement> towards the centre is the natural movement for heavy bodies. But they could not move towards the centre (i) because there is no empty space in between, and if there were, the smaller place would not be able to contain the larger body; and (ii) because <the heavens> are held together by their parts on every side in the shape of a sphere and are indivisible or difficult to divide. For in the case of liquids and easily divisible <substances> which yield to the onset of others – if any part of the whole escapes, the remaining parts will close up to each other and make the whole continuous again; this is <true of> the other elements apart from earth. But in the case of solids and <substances> that are difficult to divide – if any part <of these> becomes detached the shape of the whole will perish. Thence, as long as it is necessary that the heavens remain in <their> natural shape and the whole world exist, it is impossible that any one of the parts of the heavens become deprived of the continuity of the whole. Accordingly, we shall not ask why the parts of the other elements become detached, though <the parts> of the heavens do not. For if some parts of the former become detached, the continuity and natural shape will nevertheless be preserved because of the closing-up of the remaining parts, and for the whole no damage will result because of this, but it is impossible for this to happen in the case of the heavens. Consequently, as long as they and the universe must be preserved no part of them may become detached. The fact that the heavens behave in this way demonstrates that they have received

42. More literally: 'by replacing reciprocally' (*antiperiistamenon*).

some other form which is different from the simple <forms>,[43] but it does not <demonstrate> that <the heavens> are also different from the elements in nature. For equally, when water freezes it may turn into hail or snowflakes, but they are not because of this considered to be bodies of a fifth nature."

Concluding the passage he says:

"Surely then, if, even on the assumption that <the heavens> partake of weight and lightness, we discovered that straight movement cannot possibly belong to them, it follows that it is not <correct to infer> that they are free from lightness and weight merely because they do not move in a straight <line>."

48 Simpl. *in de Caelo* 77,23–27: From the solidity of the heavens <the Grammarian> derives a remarkable explanation of the fact that no part of the heavens becomes detached although <the heavens> are of the same nature as the sublunary elements:

"For <the parts of the heavens> which have become detached would not conjoin because <the heavens> are rigid (*antitupon*) and hard to divide (*dusdiaireton*); they would have remained incomplete (*atelês*)."

Yet, he also regards earth as rigid; in which way, then, do the parts of <earth> become detached?

Fragments 49–51*

Philoponus finally argues, in agreement with Plato, that the movements of the celestial bodies are both natural and psychical. He also points to the fact that Aristotle's position on this issue could well be regarded as contradictory.

49 Simpl. *in de Caelo* 78,12–79,14: In the following <arguments> until the end of the second book <the Grammarian> does not seem to say anything concerning the present <problems>[44] and nothing which might <serve> his own immediate aim; instead, he is merely eager to entangle Aristotle in contradictions. [15 . . . 17] <First> he shows by means of many arguments which, as he says, are in agreement with Plato, that the circular movement of the heavens is natural *and* imparted by a soul because the heavens are a living

43. Or: <bodies>?

44. i.e. why the parts of the other elements become detached though the parts of the heavens do not, despite the fact that the heavens are, according to the Grammarian, perishable and passive like the other elements; see *in de Caelo* 78,10–12.

being (*zôion*), and although < he says this> in more <words> than are necessary, I <sc. Simplicius> still think this is said correctly. But <then> he finds fault with Aristotle for supposedly rejecting in the second book of this treatise[45] <the claim> that circular movement is <imparted by> a soul, as Plato held, and for saying that on this account <the movement> would be contrary to nature and in need of rest (*anapaula*) and resistance (*antereisis*),[46] as are other living beings.

25 "Yet, the same Aristotle", <the Grammarian> claims, "also says about it:[47] 'The heavens are animate and contain a principle of motion,' and as regards the stars he <says> that they should not be conceived as mere bodies and monads which possess an arrangement but are entirely inanimate, but that it is necessary to assume that they participate in activity and life.[48] And yet," he says, "if <the heavens> contain a soul and a principle of motion, what kind
79, 1 of motion other than local will <the heavens> carry out by the agency of this principle, if indeed they are not generated or destroyed, and do not increase, diminish, or change qualitatively? And if <Aristotle> proved in the eighth book of the *Physics* that the heavens are a limited body,[49] <and that> a limited body has limited capacity (*dunamis*),[50] and that circular movement is
5 unlimited,[51] then it is necessary that <the rotation> is provided by a cause of unlimited capacity (*hupo apeirodunamon aition*). However, the nature in a limited substrate is limited itself. According to <Aristotle>, therefore, that which moves the heavens with a circular movement is something essentially different. So how can he think <it right> to explain the <motion> as <deriving> merely from nature?"

Then, having made the above accusations in these <arguments>, he says that it is not impossible for the same movement to be caused
10 by a soul and by nature at the same time.

"For example, if one imagined", he says, "one of the birds making

45. See *de Caelo* 2.1, 284a27–35.

46. The passage in the *de Caelo* referred to in the previous note does not mention *antereisis* (resistance), but in *MA* 2, 698b9–18 Aristotle states that in the case of both the animals and the universe there cannot be progression and motion unless there is some ground or medium offering resistance.

47. Cf. *de Caelo* 2.2, 285a29f.

48. Cf. *de Caelo* 2.12, 292a18–21.

49. That there is no infinite sensible body is in fact proved in *Physics* 3.5 and *de Caelo* 1.5–7.

50. Cf. *Physics* 8.10, 266a23–b6.

51. Cf. *Physics* 8.8, 261b27ff.

a straight flight towards the centre: the impulse of the soul thus coincides with the natural inclination (*phusikê rhopê*) of the body."[52]

He thinks that Aristotle does not allow this in the passage concerned,[53] and he rejects the exegesis of Alexander which states this.[54]

50* Simpl. *in de Caelo* 199,27–35: But since he added an <argument> of the following kind too, that if the celestial body moves with a circular locomotion not by nature but by the agency of a soul (*hupo psuchês*), as is the case in living beings, or by the agency of some other superior force (*hupo allês tinos huperteras dunameôs*), it is not possible to infer from its motion either that heaven is generated or that it is ungenerated – and he invokes Aristotle as witness who says in the eighth book of the *Physics* that the heavens are moved by a superior cause (*ex huperteras aitias*) – he evidently does not understand that the same motion can be accomplished by different causes and that in one way the heavens *qua* natural body are moved in a circle by nature, in another way *qua* animate being (*hôs empsukhon*) by soul, and again *qua* intelligent being (*hôs ennoun*) by mind.

51* Simpl. *in de Caelo* 80,13–23: Remarkably, this man is as stuffed with the <arguments> of Plato as he is with those of Aristotle.

For although Plato explained the circular movement of the heavens before he attributed a soul to it, <the Grammarian> none the less defends Plato <on the ground> that he spoke <of the movement of the heavens> as solely psychical; <and the Grammarian> says that <circular movement> is not counternatural for the body because it does not possess any other <movement> naturally, just as no spatial movement is counternatural for the whole world since it does not move in space naturally. The same

52. Note that in the *contra Aristotelem* Philoponus regarded the heavens as animate; cf. Simplicius' remark fr. III/61: 91,17f: 'It is worth knowing that <the Grammarian> wants the heavens to be animate . . .'

53. The passage in question is again *de Caelo* 2.1, 284a27–35; cf. Simplicius *in de Caelo* 79,14–20.

54. Philoponus understands *de Caelo* 2.1, 284a27–35 as a denial of the psychical origin of the celestial motion, and although he himself proposes that this motion is generated both by nature and by soul, he rejects Alexander's attempt to interpret *Aristotle* in this way. On Alexander's statement of the identity of psychical and natural motion, see ap. Simplicium *in de Caelo* 377,20–381,18; 387,5–24.

<point>,[55] then, must also be made against him when he asks about the firesphere as a whole whether circular movement belongs to it naturally or counternaturally: if <the firesphere> does not possess this <movement naturally>, it does not possess any <movement> naturally, and <in that case> we must not say that <circular movement> belongs to it either naturally or counternaturally, but <only> supernaturally, as has been said.

55. The '*same*' point is that where no motion is natural, none is counternatural. Philoponus had said this about the heavens and Simplicius now applies the point to the firesphere, stating against Philoponus that circular motion cannot belong to it counternaturally, since no motion belongs to it naturally. Simplicius' reply starts in line 22 after the colon.

BOOK III

In the third book of the *contra Aristotelem* Philoponus turns his attention away from the *de Caelo* and discusses an argument in Aristotle's *Meteorology* 1.3, 340a1–3. Here Aristotle argues that the heavens cannot consist of fire because in that case each of the other elements would have been destroyed long ago. Philoponus shows that this argument is false, and he advocates Plato's position according to which the celestial body consists for the most part of fire. Having done this, Philoponus proceeds to assimilate the celestial and the sublunary regions by a comparison of the qualities of their respective substances. He claims that both regions are essentially of the same nature.

Fragments 52–55

Philoponus adduces first that the firesphere involves the same difficulty, i.e. that the massive presence of fire in that region should by now have destroyed the other elements. But Aristotle's argument is in fact not sound because the celestial fire, just like the fire of the firesphere, is incapable of burning. Even if it were capable of burning, this would not make any difference. For first, it is not true that the active intensity of a quality changes proportionally with the quality of the underlying body. Secondly, the remoteness of the things in heaven greatly reduces the heat generated by them for the things here, and thirdly, the celestial fire would not affect the sublunary elements because it does not even affect the firesphere: like is not affected by like. Finally, he attacks Alexander's supposition that the elements must have equal capacities.

52 Simpl. *in de Caelo* 80,23–81,11: But since it is his aim, as he himself admits, to defy the propositions on the eternity of the heavens, <the Grammarian> has not been content with objecting to what has been written in the <treatise> *On The Heavens*, but has in addition spent his third book objecting to what has been said by Aristotle in the *Meteorology*,[56] <i.e.> that the heavens are not fiery. There is nothing to prevent us from showing the rottenness of these arguments as well, especially since it will result in our learning what sort of fire Aristotle denies the heavens to be, what sort of thing Plato declares the fiery <substance> of the heavens to be, and what sort of thing this man asserts it to be, in unwitting agreement with Plato. And so, when Aristotle says in the first

56. See *Meteor.* 1.3, 339b16–340a3.

<book> of the *Meteorology*[57] that 'if the whole heavens together with the stars consisted of fire, each of the other elements would have vanished long ago,' this man first replies that the firesphere causes the same difficulty because it is larger than the <things> surrounded by it.

"But neither", he says, "the <fire> of the firesphere nor the celestial fire are capable of burning (*kaustikon*), but what is capable of burning is the <fire> in our region, which is excess of fire (*huperbolê puros*), according to Aristotle."

As regards these <sentences>, it must be understood that in his <opinion> the whole argument is concerned to show, again, that the celestial body is of the same nature as the sublunary <bodies>, so that it is demonstrated that it is also perishable like them.

53* Simpl. *in de Caelo* 81,22–26: And in these <arguments> he has spent many words in vain in order to show that the qualities of the elements do not increase in proportion (*ou pros analogian epauxontai*) to the mass of the bodies in which they exist. For ten thousand times more water, as it were, is not ten thousand times colder, but a measure of seawater is as cold as the whole sea.

54 Simpl. *in de Caelo* 82,8–83,30: This man has been content with <the explanation> that this sort of fire is not capable of burning; he gives no further thought to the identity of nature and the interchange between elements. These are the kind of <comments> which our unlucky student of philosophical arguments has put forward. But since I <sc. Simplicius> suppose some <readers> will not believe that any would-be author could be so illiterate as to be ignorant of these matters, I am forced again to cite what he has said.

"The remoteness (*diastasis*) of the things in heaven and especially of the stars – which the older <philosophers> thought to consist mainly of the substance of fire – reduces the heat generated by them for the things here; this the sun clearly shows because it warms those things most to which it has come nearer. And so, what kind of qualitative <effect> would the heat inside the fixed sphere, supposing that it is of a thermal nature (*thermê phusis*), have on the <spheres> surrounding the earth, which are so far away? For the ultimate <sphere> could not possibly act qualitatively upon the subsequent spheres because they are like it, nor could these

57. See *Meteor.* 1.3, 340a1–3.

<act upon> the firesphere. For like is not naturally affected by like.[58] The firesphere, therefore, would retain its own nature because it would not admit of any of the heat within the spheres, and the firesphere itself would not have any greater <effect> on the things inside than <it does have> now, even if all things around were fiery, and <this is true> above all because this kind of fire is not assumed to be a burning flame (*phloga kaustikon*), as we have pointed out frequently."

In these <sentences> it is evident that this man thinks that the sun warms us more during the summer because it is nearer to us then; it is also clear that he thinks that the <sun> is nearer to us at noon than <at the time> when it is rising or setting, since it warms us more at noon. And he is ignorant of the fact that the earth in comparison with the sphere of the sun possesses virtually the ratio of a point, so that the parallax of the exact position of the <sun> in comparison with the <position> as seen by us is most minute because of this. How, then, <is it possible> that <the sun> approaches us and recedes further away from us over such a distance that thereupon such a difference of heat is generated in the summer as opposed to the winter?[59] But <the Grammarian> is also ignorant of the following: just as the sun in any position <in the zodiac> warms us on each day more at noon (although its distance from us is the same) because of the more <direct> reflection of the rays <of the sun> upon themselves,[60] in the same way <the sun> generates the difference of heat and cold over the seasons, because in the summer it comes nearer, not to *us*, but to the point of our zenith, and in the winter it departs from it again. But one hears that <the Grammarian>, who regards the celestial

58. For *in de Caelo* 82,21f. cf. also 83,15f. The quotation there is incorrectly extended to line 18. See also 83,21.

59. Solar parallax is the apparent change of position of the sun due to changes of position of the observer on the surface of the earth. Simplicius argues, on the basis of astronomical theory, that the distance between the sun and the earth is so vast that the earth is a mere point when compared to the sphere of the sun. For this reason, solar parallax is most minute and is negligible in astronomical observation. Simplicius objects to Philoponus that since the distance of the sun is so vast, one would have to assume an enormous variation of this distance during the year in order to be able to explain the great variation of heat generated by the sun in the sublunary world. Such an observation contradicts astronomical theory, and hence the generation of heat by the sun cannot be caused by the sun coming closer, as Philoponus suggested.

60. The meaning of this remark is that the angle between the incoming and the reflected ray is smallest at noon; they will therefore traverse some portion of air twice and thus generate more heat.

body as hot and <endowed> with the same kind of heat as the sublunary fire, says that it is the only one of the bodies in the world which is inactive. For neither does the fixed <sphere> act upon the celestial spheres below it, nor does the whole of the heavens act upon the firesphere.

"For by nature", he says, "like is not affected by like, but it is only the case that the firesphere acts upon the things below it."[61]

And it is evident that although the heat of the heavens is something vital (*zôtikê tis*), as this man claims, they do not transmit the <heat> to the things below the moon. But how can he, who assumes that the fixed heaven is hot, say on the one hand that it is entirely inactive, and on the other hand that the sun warms us? For according to his argument the <fixed sphere> has no influence on the <other> celestial spheres:

"For by nature, as he says, like is not affected by like."

Nor does it <act upon> the firesphere, so that it does not <act upon> the things here either. But now, do the heavens, by virtue of their qualities, act at all upon the sublunary things and suffer from them, or does this worthy fellow maintain that they neither act nor suffer because they possess the same qualities and the same nature as the <sublunary bodies>? Yet it is clear that according to the arguments brought forward by him the firesphere does not act at all upon the air except for its outermost part which is contiguous to the air, and again, the air <does not act> except for its outermost <part>. But how can someone who has conceded earlier that the heavens are more solid, more powerful, and more important, declare now that they are less efficacious than anything else?

55 Simpl. *in de Caelo* 83,30–84,4: But Alexander said that the reason why the elements are preserved, stay together and are not mutually destroyed is the equality of their capacities, but air would exceed <them> by far if it reached into the heavens,[62] and against this <the Grammarian> objects:

"A small <quantity of> air can be cooled down or heated up to a very high <degree>, and a large <quantity> to a gentler <degree>."

And it is clear that nothing prevents qualities which are added from outside from being more excessive in a small <quantity>, as

61. End of citation here.

62. On Alexander's argument cf. his commentary *in Meteor.* 12,9–20.

has been said,[63] and <from being> more gentle in a large <quan- 84, 1
tity>; yet, the <qualities> which belong to the air *by nature* necessarily coextend with its magnitude, and natural capacities are understood in terms of these <qualities>, but not in terms of the <qualities> which are added from outside, and one must understand the equality as being <the equality> of these capacities.

Fragments 56–61*

In these fragments the substance and qualities of the heavens are discussed. Philoponus relies on Plato in arguing that the heavens consist for the most part not only of fire, but also of the purest parts of all four elements. As opposed to Aristotle's position that the celestial body is devoid of any quality Philoponus holds that virtually all qualities can be found in the celestial and the sublunary regions alike. In short, the substances of both regions are wholly alike in nature.

56 Simpl. *in de Caelo* 84,15–22: "Plato", he says, "held that the heavenly bodies are not <composed> of fire alone, but that they partake above all of that sort of fire which produces a better mixture of the other elements.[64] All the fine and purest substance of all elements," he says, "which also possesses the relation of form to the other <elements>, has been chosen for the composition of the celestial bodies, while the more material and so to speak sludgy portion of these <elements> exists here below. This <i.e. the former> is the sort of fire Plato wants the stars and sun to be composed of."

57* Simpl. *in de Caelo* 87,29–88,2: In reply to <the Grammarian> who is campaigning to place heat and coldness, dryness and wetness, softness and hardness as well as the other tangible and perceptible qualities (*haptas kai pathêtikas poiotêtas*) in the
heavens, one must say: if such qualities of the heavens act upon 88, 1
and suffer from the things here by nature, why is it that until now clearly no qualitative change which is due to the things here has taken place in <the heavens>?

58* Simpl. *in de Caelo* 88,8–14: But how does he think <to infer> from the fact that the sun warms the things here that it is qualitatively warm <and> partakes of a huge fire, which he infers from the

63. Cf. Simplicius *in de Caelo* 81,26–82,4.
64. Cf. Plato *Timaeus* 31B4ff.; 40A2f.; 58C.

colour as well? Look: although the other stars are said to partake of a huge fire and to possess a fiery colour, as he says, Saturn[65] is believed to cool and to combine things down here, and it is evident that by virtue of the same argument it ought to be cold as well, and not fiery, but rather watery.

59 Simpl. *in de Caelo* 88,28–89,26: But further, as <the Grammarian> does not scruple to blaspheme heaven outright – insanely rather – and evidently <blaspheme> God who had given and gives substance (*hupostêsantos kai huphistôntos theou*) to the heavens, he openly proclaims that the things in heaven do not <possess> any other nature than the elements in this world. "For there is", he says, "perhaps no <quality> observed in the things there that does not also belong to the terrestrial bodies." And he brings in transparency (*to diaphanes*) which is observed alike in the heavens and in air, water, glass, and certain stones.[66] He did not refrain from adding the <word> 'alike' (*homoiôs*). And the different colours in stars he calls not only alike but even identical (*ta auta*) to the terrestrial ones.

"And the colour called 'brilliance' (*to lampron*)", he says, "and light, and all the qualities which are constant attributes of light belong to numerous terrestrial bodies as well: to fire and to fire-flies, to <the> heads or scales of fish, and to other similar things."[67]

Is it possible that this man is mentally sound when he says that the light and brightness of the things in the heavens belong to fire-flies and scales of fish?

"And spherical shape", he says, "does not belong to the celestial bodies alone but also to all the other elements, and even to some of the compounds; and circular movement belongs to fire as well as to some <parts> of the air."

In this way he shamelessly or carelessly obscured <the fact> that the firesphere moves with the said circular movement by the agency of the heavens, which is evidenced by the comets and the other appearances there that rise and set together with the fixed stars. But after having said other, similar things, he finally adduces that <the heavens>, being visible at all events, are also tangible

65. Literally: 'the star of Kronos'. On the capacities of the planets cf., e.g., Ptolemy *Tetrabiblos* 1.4 and Plotinus *Enneads* 2.3,5.

66. Cf. Aristotle *de Anima* 2.7, 418b4–9.

67. Literally: '<the> heads of certain <animals> or scales of fish, and to other similar things', but cf. Aristotle *de Anima* 2.7, 419a2–6.

(*haptos*),[68] and being tangible they have tactual qualities: hardness, softness, smoothness, roughness, dryness, wetness, and <other> comparable <qualities> as well as heat and cold, which include all these. And that <the heavens> are tangible is evident from what I <sc. Simplicius> have said earlier. Yet, <the Grammarian> is arguing on the assumption that the celestial bodies are also tangible *to us;* this is clear from his frequent appeal to the heat of the sun and his final claim that what is three-dimensional (*to trikhê diastaton*)[68a] is identical in the heavenly bodies and in things in our region. For no three-dimensional thing will differ from another in so far as it is three-dimensional, just as no body will differ from another in so far as it is a body. And it is evident that this proposition makes out not only the heavens <to be> of the same nature as the things in this <world>, but also God himself, if something like that is conceivable.

60* Simpl. *in de Caelo* 90,13–25: Due to his vain contentiousness it escaped <the Grammarian's> notice that even this David, whom he honours so much, teaches the contrary. For <David> discloses that he did not regard the things in heaven <to be> of the same nature as the things below the moon when he says that 'Heaven declares the glory of God and the firmament sheweth his handywork',[69] but not the 'fire-flies' and the 'scales of fish'. But also the saying of Aristotle fits here well, that 'if one absurdity has been granted the others follow.'[70] For how would someone who thinks that God is of the same nature as he himself hesitate to disrespect the most beautiful and noblest of God's creations? <The Grammarian> seems to conclude this argument in anger at those, as he says, who introduce for the celestial bodies a nature which is different from and alien to the elements, and which has nothing in common with them, and this even though all who are talked about in philosophy assume that the heavens <consist> of the four elements.

61* Simpl. *in de Caelo* 91,3–7 + 17–19: At the end of arguments of this sort he says that according to Aristotle, too, the celestial body is a compound because <Aristotle> says in the <treatise>

68. Cf. Plato *Timaeus* 31B4–6.
68a. See below, n. 95a.
69. See Psalms 19:1 (= Psalms 18:2 Septuagint).
70. See *Physics* 1.2, 185a11f.; 1.3, 186a9f.

On the Soul that every animate body is a compound of elements,[71] but here, in the second book <of *On the Heavens*>,[72] he clearly says that the heavens are animate. [7 . . . 17] Yet, it is worth knowing that in contrast to others, his comrades,[73] <the Grammarian> wants the heavens to be animate as well; yet, he nevertheless appears to be no less impious towards <the heavens> than the greatest fools among them.

71. Cf. *de Anima* 2.1, 412a15f.; 2.11, 423a12–15; 3.13, 435a11–14.

72. Cf. *de Caelo* 1.7, 275b26; 2.2, 285a29.

73. i.e. other Christians. Basil, for example, denied that the heavens are animate, see *Hexaemeron* 3.9.

BOOK IV

Returning to the argument of the theory of aether in the *de Caelo*, Philoponus discusses Aristotle's demonstrative argument that the heavens are ungenerated and indestructible as well as the additional, dialectical evidence adduced in support of this tenet. In the course of his refutation Philoponus clarifies what he means by creation *ex nihilo*.

Fragments 62–63

Philoponus sets out to refute Aristotle's argument that the heavens are ungenerated and undestructible, *de Caelo* 1.3, 270a12–22. His main refutation is preceded by a not entirely serious accusation that Aristotle's argument is incoherent because he does not clarify the sense in which he uses the word 'ungenerated' (*agenêtos*).

62 Farabi, *Against Philoponus* (7). [Mahdi, *Alfarabi*, 256]: (7) One must also wonder about <the following>. He <sc. Philoponus> states that in his fourth book he had refuted the proofs by which Aristotle argues that the world was not generated and is incorruptible. When he reached the fourth book he said literally as follows, in the chapter in which he stated Aristotle's proof. He said:

"His proof that the heavens are ungenerated and that they are incorruptible." Then he said: "Examining the proofs that he stated and the explanations of some of those who commented on them."

63 Simpl. *in de Caelo* 119,7–120,12: But again, he who entitles himself 'Grammarian' pursues the clear aim of persuading <people> like himself to suppose that the world is destructible and has been generated at some time; in consequence, he is annoyed with those who prove that the heavens are ungenerated and indestructible, and stirs up a lot of verbal muck against what has been said by Aristotle in these <passages>.[74] Let us invoke an assistant, the great Herakles, <and> descend to the cleansing of the ordure in his words. After having initially outlined the Aristotelian distinction of the senses of 'ungenerated' and 'generated' <drawn> at the

74. Simplicius has just commented on *de Caelo* 1.3, 270a12–b25.

end of the book,[75] he then asks according to which sense Aristotle proves the heavens to be ungenerated now,[76] and he writes as follows:

"Neither the heavens nor the world would be ungenerated <in the sense> that they are in fact impossible to be generated.[77] For they clearly exist and have received the perfection of their nature. Therefore, only one further hypothesis remains, if <the heavens> cannot have been generated <in the sense> of having a beginning of existence, not even a beginning which brought them into existence without a process of generation. Then, since Aristotle, as he wanted to reject this kind of generation of the world, used the axiom that everything generated is generated out of a contrary, one must ask if generation out of a contrary belongs indeed to everything generated in time."

In these <lines the Grammarian> denies that 'ungenerated' <has the sense> of 'impossible to be generated', which is the third sense. For they clearly exist, he says, and have received perfection. Yet, Aristotle too knows perfectly well that <the heavens and the world> exist, but they exist in such a way that they are neither *generated* nor exist at one time and not at another.

"Therefore," he says, "one hypothesis concerning 'ungenerated' remains, if they are not ungenerated as touch (*haphê*),[78] lightning (*astrapê*), and in general instantaneous things (*ta exaiphnês*) are. For these have a beginning of existence although they have not been brought into existence by <a process of> generation.[79] So, which of the three senses of 'ungenerated' specified by Aristotle is the one in question now?"

120, 7 [119,32 . . . 120,7] And it is evident <for Simplicius> that <Aristotle> means that the heavens are ungenerated in the same sense as <something> which cannot be generated, but not as <some-

75. See *de Caelo* 1.11, 280b6–20. In *de Caelo* 1.11, 280b6–14 Aristotle distinguishes between three different senses of *agenêtos* (ungenerated). Something is said to be ungenerated: (1) If it has come to be without a process of generation, for example, being touched or being moved. Touch and motion do not involve a process of generation (b6–9). (2) If it has not yet been generated but possibly will be generated (b9–11). (3) If it is absolutely impossible to be generated (b11–14). The third sense is ambiguous because it can denote either (a) something which does not exist at all and never will exist, or (b) something which has existed from all eternity. Later, at *de Caelo* 1.12, 282a27–29 Aristotle points out that he wants the term to be understood primarily in this last sense.

76. i.e. *de Caelo* 1.3, 270a12–22.

77. i.e. in sense 3(a) in n. 75 above; cf. also *in de Caelo* 120,2f.

78. 'Touch' rather than 'kindling', cf. *de Caelo* 1.11, 280b6–9.

79. Cf. also *in de Caelo* 120,15–19.

thing> which cannot exist at all, as <Philoponus> thought, in the sense that two and two cannot become three. For because this[80] cannot come into existence by a process of generation, it is not true to say that it cannot be generated, but that it does not belong to the things that exist at all.

Fragments 64*–72

Aristotle argued in *de Caelo* 1.3, 270a12–22 that the heavens must be eternal (i.e. ungenerated and imperishable) because (i) all things are generated out of a contrary (*enantion*) and perish into a contrary, but (ii) the celestial body has no contrary because there is no contrary to circular motion. Premise (i) relies on the theory of generation developed by Aristotle in *Physics* 1.7–9. There, the process of generation is explained in terms of a change in a substrate (or subject, *hupokeimenon*, or matter, *hulê*) from a state of privation (*sterêsis*) to a state in which the substrate possesses some definite form (*morphê, eidos*). Aristotle calls form and privation opposites (*antikeimena*) or even contraries (*enantia*) without drawing a clear distinction between cases in which e.g. a cold thing becomes hot and cases in which e.g. some shapeless piece of marble is turned into a statue. Premise (ii) is justified by Aristotle in *de Caelo* 1.4 and examined by Philoponus in book V.

Fragments 64*–72 are a detailed refutation of the first premise. The argument is designed as a dilemma. Philoponus begins with a distinction between the two senses of 'contraries': contraries proper (e.g. hot/cold, wet/dry, black/white, and so forth), and contraries in terms of form (*eidos*) and privation (*sterêsis*) (e.g. musical/unmusical, man/not-man). In fr. 65 he suggests that Aristotle must have used 'contraries' in the former sense because the heavens surely possess *some* privative contrary, e.g. immobility. But then, in fr. 67, he shows that it is not true that all things are generated out of a contrary proper: individual substances (*atomoi ousiai*) are generated, and there is no contrary to substance; the same is true of things falling into the other categories. Therefore Philoponus concludes in fr. 69 that Aristotle must have spoken, contrary to the initial suggestion, of contraries in terms of privation and form, and he refers to Themistius in support of this point. But if one accepts this solution, the heavens will appear to be generated and destructible because they do possess both form and privation as well as a common matter (*hulê*) (fr. 69–72). Hence, if one accepts the one sense of contrariety Aristotle's first premise is false; if one accepts the other sense, the heavens too must be conceived as being generated and destructible.

64* Simpl. *in de Caelo* 121,4–14: And in order to demonstrate this[81] <Aristotle> uses two premises, as has been said before, one

80. i.e. that two and two equals three.
81. i.e. that the heavens are ungenerated and indestructible, cf. *in de Caelo* 121,3.

saying that what is generated is generated out of a contrary (*ex enantiou*) and perishes into a contrary (*eis enantion*), and the other saying that there is no movement contrary to circular movement. So this man sets out to object to these two <premises>, and he begins with the former first. And all I <sc. Simplicius> was able to contribute towards an understanding of Aristotle's ideas on these <matters> has been stated before. On the basis of that, I think, this man's objections are easily refuted. He says, then, that Aristotle and his commentator Alexander <of Aphrodisias> want <the hypothesis> 'contraries are generated out of contraries' to be true of contraries in the proper sense (*epi tôn kuriôn enantiôn*), but others say that the hypothesis is sound for privation (*sterêsis*) and form (*eidos*).

65 Simpl. *in de Caelo* 121,25–122,9: For with a view to showing that Aristotle says that the heavens have no contrary in the proper sense of the word, <the Grammarian> tries to prove this on <the assumption> that the heavens possess an opposing privation. For he says that Aristotle would not have held that the heavens did not possess any contrary <at all>, given that he called 'privation'
122, 1 a contrary.[82] Again I <sc. Simplicius> am compelled to cite his words for the sake of those who cannot believe that someone wrote such arrant nonsense.

"For even if it is agreed", he says, "that no movement is contrary to the movement of the heavens, it is at least not impossible that there is a privation of this movement. For there is some opposing privation of any natural thing that exists in a substrate. But motion is a natural thing. For the immobility (*akinêsia*) before the movement and after the cessation (*paula*) of the movement is in fact the privation of this movement. Therefore, if it is not impossible that there is a privation opposite to the movement of the heavens, it follows that <Aristotle> did not use <the word 'contraries'> in the sense of form and privation, but in the sense of contraries <in the proper sense>."

66 Simpl. *in de Caelo* 123,4–7: He therefore says a little further on: "For white and black and in general all those <properties> of which there is some intermediate (*ti metaxu*) between the opposites (*antikeimena*), these are no doubt contraries anywhere. There is no intermediate, however, between form and privation, for both of

82. See, e.g., *Physics* 1.7, 191a13f.; cf. 190b26.

them exist in matter, and matter is not an intermediate between them."

67 Simpl. *in de Caelo* 123,11–124,17: Having said many things like that <the Grammarian> sets out to prove, first, that it is not true <to say> that things are generated out of contraries in the proper sense, and subsequently <to prove> that <they are not generated> out of privation either. And that <generation> does not involve contraries in the proper sense he thinks to show by means of more <arguments>, the first of which runs as follows:

"If", he says, "not only the attributes (*ta sumbebêkota*) but also the individual substances (*atomoi ousiai*) are generated, and if there is no contrary to substance (*ousia*), as Aristotle himself teaches in the *Categories*,[83] how is everything generated out of a contrary? Secondly, if irrational souls, too, are subject to generation, and if not every form of soul is ungenerated and indestructible, <then> let someone tell us out of what kind of contrary the soul of a horse, a bull, or any other irrational living being is generated, or into what <kind of> contrary they are resolved again when they perish. But further, the falsehood of the argument will appear even more clearly when the forms of the soul are considered. For what is the contrary of the spirited? What is the contrary of <the> generative, of <the> nutritive, of <the> productive,[84] and of <the> appetitive <form of the soul>?[85] Thirdly, not only in the case of substances but also in the case of their attributes the Aristotelian hypothesis clearly does not hold true. For a triangle, a circle and the other shapes are generated, and it is evident that none of these are generated out of a contrary, if indeed no shape is contrary to shape, as <Aristotle> held as well. Fourthly, left comes to be from right. But these are relative terms and not contraries. And plainly, in the case of all those categories which do not involve contraries it is evident that individuals belonging to these <categories> are not subject to generation out of contraries" – this he adds as a fifth <argument>. "Sixthly, <the assumption> is not even universally true of the <category of> quality which most of all <involves> contraries," so he claims, "for instance 'hot' and 'cold', 'dry' and 'moist'. For these are not necessarily in all cases generated out of contraries. For if air", he says, "possesses neither colour nor flavour – as is shown <by the fact> that it is neither visible nor tasteable 124, 1

83. Cf. *Categories* 3b24–32.
84. i.e. productive in terms of growth.
85. For *in de Caelo* 123,17–24 cf. also 129,19–23.

– and if it changes into water, which possesses both colour and flavour, out of what kind of contraries of colour and flavour in air do colour and flavour in water come to be? And if air changes into earth or into fire, the same must be said. But more than that, by the putrefaction of air", he said, "living beings are generated with various colours and differences of flavour. Out of what kind of contraries in the air <do they come to be>, if air does not possess <these qualities>?" But he concedes that it is generated out of the suitable privation, which is the absence of colour in air. As regards fire he asks about its colour, that is <to say> about light (*phôs*),

"whether there is a contrary to light or not. If not, it would not be generated out of a contrary. But if <there is a contrary to light>, what else other than darkness would this be?"

But darkness is the privation of light and not the contrary, as he claims to have shown elsewhere.[86]

"But", he says, "even if one agrees that darkness is contrary to light, in this way too the Aristotelian proposition is equally, not to say more, refuted. For when fire is generated by friction out of air which is illuminated in daytime, it is clear that it is generated out of <the air> not as an illuminated thing but as air. For that reason it is also generated out of the <air> at night. So the light which is in the generated <fire> has not been generated out of a contrary."[87]

68 Simpl. *in de Caelo* 126,5–16: But if this is the case[88] then first, <the Grammarian> is clearly entirely ignorant of what has been said by Aristotle, seeing that he thinks to demonstrate that Aristotle says that generation and destruction are accomplished solely by the antithesis of contraries in the proper sense. Secondly, all his objections made on the grounds of such guesswork, because they are beside the point, have turned out to be in vain, and they do not affect Aristotle's proof. For even he himself <sc. the Grammarian> confirms – though it is worthless as a confirmation,[89] because he does not know what the argument is about – he none the less confirms that generation <occurs> out of privation, just as Aristotle held as well.

86. Cf. Philoponus *in de Anima* 341,10–342,16.

87. For *in de Caelo* 123,34–124,17 cf. also 130,28–131,13.

88. i.e. that, according to Simplicius, Aristotle used the terms 'contrariety' and 'antithesis' in the context of generation and destruction predominantly in the sense of 'form and privation', and not of contraries in the proper sense; cf. *in de Caelo* 125,20–24; 126,2–5.

89. Comma after *maturian*, not after *agnoôn*.

"For the fire that is generated out of air has," he says, "in so far as it has become coloured, received <its> generation not out of a contrary, but out of the corresponding privation alone."

69 Simpl. *in de Caelo* 131,17–132,17: But perhaps there was no need for my arguments[90] because <the Grammarian> clearly agrees in his text that the Aristotelian proposition stating that 'what is generated is generated out of contraries'[91] is true of the most generic <type of> antithesis of form and privation, but by no means <true of> the remaining contrarieties. But what is frivolously said by him in the following brings Themistius into conflict with Aristotle. <The Grammarian> says:

"For by those <sentences> in which he has changed the expression 'contraries' into 'opposites in terms of privation and form', even Themistius himself has shown us quietly that Aristotle's hypothesis is not correct."[92]

Yet, because Themistius knew the passage in the *Physics* Aristotle referred to in this argument,[93] it was reasonable enough of him to say that Aristotle understands the <phrase> 'out of a contrary and into a contrary' universally, taking it as the most generic contrariety of form and privation. But <the Grammarian> knew he was writing for schoolboys, which is why, I believe, he did not read, or else, he did not understand the passage on generation in the *Physics* and spewed out so much arrant nonsense against the word 'contraries', thinking that the length <of his arguments> suffices to perplex his audience. But he says on the basis of empty opinion rather than research:

"Let it be agreed that Aristotle calls form and privation contraries here,[94] and that everything generated is generated out of the corresponding privation, just as that which perishes relapses from form into privation," and, in saying these <things>, he thinks to show from them that according to Aristotle the heavens too will appear to be generated and destructible. Let us look at these remarkable ventures of his as well, to see from what kind of self-evident axioms he derives the propositions he is concerned with.

"Every natural form", he says, "which exists in a substrate and

90. Simplicius is referring to his long refutation at *in de Caelo* 126,16–131,17 of Philoponus' arguments in fr. IV/67.

91. See *de Caelo* 1.3, 270a14f.

92. Cf. Themistius *in de Caelo* 14,24f.

93. See the implicit reference to *Physics* 1.7 in *de Caelo* 1.3, 270a17.

94. i.e. in *de Caelo* 1.3, 270a14f.

<in> matter always possesses an opposing privation out of which it has been generated and into which it resolves when it perishes. But both the heavens and the whole world are characterised by a natural form; in consequence, they too will possess a privation out of which they have been generated and into which they perish. For because man is generated out of not-man and house out of not-house and, speaking generally, any natural and artificial form attains generation out of what is not of its kind, therefore also the heavens – for they are a natural form as well – have been generated out of not-heaven, and world out of not-world. But this argument would perhaps require", he says, "that there exists some substrate and matter prior to the generation of the world in which the privation of the heavens and world existed <and> out of which, when it changed, the heavens and the world were generated. But <the argument> does not strictly imply that the heavens are ungenerated and without a beginning <of existence>, as the Philosopher <sc. Aristotle> intended to show. On the contrary, <it> rather <implies> that <the heavens> are generated and have a beginning of existence."[95]

70 Simpl. *in de Caelo* 133,21–29: At any rate, <the Grammarian> introduces two premises, one saying that the heavens are characterised by a natural form embedded in matter (*phusikôi eidei kai enulôi*), and the other saying that something characterised by a natural form possesses an opposing privation (*sterêsis antikeimenê*). The latter premise, being false, he proffers as evident. The former, which says that the heavens are a natural form embedded in matter (*phusikon kai enulon eidos*), he attempts to prove by many <arguments>, despite the fact that it is not really disputed, thus bringing matters of common agreement into dispute by superfluous reasoning. But perhaps nothing prevents <us> from looking at the things said by him in these <passages>.

"It is quite ridiculous", he says, "to say that the heavens are immaterial. For they are not intelligible, but perceptible."

71 Simpl. *in de Caelo* 134,9–28: It seems that this man regards that body as matter which the Peripatetics called second substrate

95. For *in de Caelo* 132,12–17 cf. also 132,32–133,1.

(*deuteron hupokeimenon*),[95a] for he spends many arguments seriously showing that the heavens possess a body – and therefore also matter. Yet, who would dispute that the heavens possess a body? But if this body is their matter, it is certainly not necessary that <the heavens> possess, as this man believes, an opposing privation as well, and are generated and destructible. For privation is connected with that <kind of> matter[96] which underlies the things that are generated and destroyed. Therefore it is perhaps superfluous to contradict his arguments, except that he seems to think that because the <things> in heaven and the <things> below the moon are both three-dimensional (*trikhê diastata*), nothing distinguishes them from one another, <and> he makes ample use of the ambiguity of words.[97] For who would maintain that the celestial body is of the same nature as the things here? When he writes the following:

"What is surprising about this, then, that just as it is agreed that one and the same matter underlies thousands of forms of the <things> below the moon because it possesses the fitness (*epitêdeiôs*) for receiving all forms – as the process of change of all things into one another shows – so in the same way the same matter is by nature recipient of the forms of the <things> in heaven as well?"

When he writes this, how does he not recognise that if there really exists the same matter for the <things> in heaven and the <things> below the moon, and is recipient of the same forms,

95a. Second substrate: the first substrate would be the most fundamental subject of properties in a body, a subject also known as prime matter (*prôtê hulê*). Philosophers in Late Antiquity considered that, abstractly conceived, it lacked qualities, corporeality and even (on most interpretations) dimensions, for these would be properties or forms superimposed on the first substrate. The *second* substrate would be that substrate viewed less abstractly as having some minimal properties or forms imposed, e.g. the three dimensions of length, depth and breadth, either with exact measurements specified (Simplicius' interpretation of Aristotle) or with measurements not yet specified (Philoponus' interpretation). Philoponus had come to reject what he took to be Aristotle's view, and proposed that the so-called second substrate could really serve as prime matter, being the *first* substrate both for celestial and for sublunary forms. It was not to be viewed as incorporeal or formless, but as already a body and as constituting the form or defining characteristic of body, as well as constituting its prime matter. He called it 'the three-dimensional' (*to trikhê diastaton*), cf. fr. III/59. See Richard Sorabji, 'John Philoponus', in Richard Sorabji (ed.), *Philoponus and the Rejection of Aristotelian Science*, 18–24.

96. With a reference to Aristotle *Metaph.* 8.4, 1044b3–8, Simplicius has just drawn a distinction between celestial matter, which only admits of spatial change, and sublunary matter, which admits of substantial change as well, see *in de Caelo* 134,2–9.

97. Cf. also above fr. III/59: 89,22–25.

then <the things in heaven and the things below the moon> must completely change into one another? Yet, even though he has recklessly and mindlessly uttered all <this>, I <sc. Simplicius> do not believe that he would say that the <things> in the heavens and the things below the moon change into one another.

72 Simpl. *in de Caelo* 135,21–136,1: "But", he says, "if the celestial matter differs from the <matter> below the moon, the <two kinds of> matter will be compounds of their common nature and the differentiae (*diaphorai*) belonging to that <nature>."

But this <the Grammarian> said in the belief that the differentiae occur only in species (*kat' eidos*); he does not take into account the <differentia> corresponding to subordination (*kata huphesin*), in virtue of which the things proceeding from the One differ. And yet, it is by this <subordination> that one achieves the procession (*proodos*) of every individuating quality (*idiotês*) in so far as it individuates.[97a] But since <the Grammarian> is evidently displeased with the <concept of> incorporeal matter (*asômatos hulê*) he claims that in the eleventh section of <his> refutation of the <writings> of Proclus[98] he has proved that it is impossible that the so-called incorporeal and formless matter exists, <and> that instead the bodies are ultimately reduced to the three-dimensional (*to trikhê diastaton*);[99] but neither have I <sc. Simplicius> read his boastings there nor would I be pleased to read shallow nonsense, when even now I do not know how my project of expounding the *de*
136, 1 *Caelo* has made me fall into Augeas' dung.

97a. In Neoplatonic metaphysics the universe is arranged hierarchically, with the supreme deity, the One, at the top, and then the Divine Intellect, the World Soul, the material world, and at the bottom prime matter. Each lower level 'proceeds' from the One, because it owes its beginningless existence ultimately to the One. What Philoponus is said to overlook is that things can be differentiated from each other not only in the way that species within a genus are differentiated by having distinct differentiating characteristics (*differentiae*). They can be differentiated instead by being more or less subordinate (*kata huphesin*) in the order in which they proceed from the One. Matter differentiated in the second way will not be turned into a composite of matter plus *differentia*. On Philoponus' substitution of the three-dimensional for incorporeal and formless matter, see above, n. 95a.

98. See *de Aeternitate Mundi contra Proclum* (ed. H. Rabe), 403ff.

99. The present passage leaves open whether Philoponus' phrase *to trikhê diastaton* denotes (pure) 'tri-dimensionality' or some kind of three-dimensional material substrate, as Simplicius seems to suggest when he alludes to the Peripatetic second substrate, cf. fr. IV/71: 134,9f. and above, n. 96. See also the argument in Philoponus *contra Proclum* 11. 3–6.

Fragments 73–76

Philoponus argues next that it is not true that all things generated require a pre-existing substrate. First, 'nothing' must not be reified. Creation *ex nihilo* means that the necessary condition for the generation of something is generated as well. Form is created together with the substrate. In fr. 76 Aristotle is accused of sophistry, in particular of illicitly changing the subject matter in his argument (*metabasis eis allo genos).*

73 Simpl. *in de Caelo* 136,12–26: But so far, as <the Grammarian> says, he has refuted the arguments of Aristotle which prove that the world is ungenerated – 'refuted', that is, by writing nonsense of this kind. He agrees, however, that by what has been said he has not refuted <the proposition> that <the world> is generated out of a pre-existing substrate. Therefore he wants to show that the world came into existence out of not-being (*ek mê ontos*). And he makes a quick reference to a proof of this in the *contra Proclum*, except that he presents the objection and attempts to invalidate it by saying:

"For if something were generated out of complete not-being, they say, it would follow that not-being exists. For it has changed into being. Now, if someone argues", he says, "that the things generated are generated out of not-being in the same way as a ship <is built> from timber – which means that not-being itself underlies the thing generated and changes into it – <then> it will truly follow that not-being exists. But I do not think that anyone is witless enough to understand generation out of not-being in this way; rather, anything generated is brought into being <only> in so far as it is generated without existing previously."

74* Simpl. *in de Caelo* 137,16–19: He attempts to show by means of many <arguments> that the things immediately generated by God are not generated out of some pre-existing substrate, but the form <is generated together> with the substrate.

75 Simpl. *in de Caelo* 138,32–139,6: "It has been agreed that the heavens as a whole as well as in <their> parts are the most important and essential parts of the world. For by their movement all bodies inside are guided naturally.[100] But in the <parts> below 139, 1
the moon generation and destruction as well as the other <things>

100. Cf. below fr. IV/80: 142,17–20 (also *in de Caelo* 143,6–9 and 172,20–22) where this sentence is cited as well and attributed to Philoponus. Although the argument is not critical of Aristotle, this fragment appears to stem from the *contra Aristotelem*.

laid down by Aristotle occur. For in this world things are formed by transformation, and the things generated are generated out of a substrate and the opposites. And the destruction of one thing is the generation of another, because even in the lowest <regions> of the universe no substance perishes as a whole, but in some sense the change in this world is merely alteration, for no substance perishes."

76 Farabi, *Against Philoponus* (7). [Mahdi, *Alfarabi*, 256]:[101]
(7) [. . .] And he literally says this:

"If the Philosopher wants to demonstrate by these statements, which we stated before, that the *world* is not generated, on what ground did he transfer what he said about the *the heavens* to the *world?* Is it because Aristotle applies <what he says about> the heavens (supposing that they are <ungenerated>) to the entire world?"

For according to John <sc. the Grammarian>, he <sc. Aristotle> had in mind here only the case of <that part of> the world which moves with a circular movement.

"How, then, did he permit himself to speak of the entire world in place of this part of the world (for what is made evident about certain parts of the world, whether a state or anything else, need not necessarily be true of the entire world), and not distinguish between the two, and this either unintentionally, or intentionally as someone who employs sophistry? For to shift one's ground from the particular to the universal and from one particular to another is one of the topics of sophistry, as he explained in *Topics* 2[102] and subsequently in *<On> Sophistical <Refutations>*."[103]

Fragments 77*–80

Aristotle supported his theory of aether and the eternity of the heavens by three *phainomena* (received ideas), see *de Caelo* 1.3, 270b1–25. Philoponus rejects at least two of them. The fact that all men allot the highest place to God is no proof of the eternity and divinity of the celestial region. Similarly, the apparent unchangeability of the heavens is no proof of its eternity either. There are many instances of highly unchangeable things in the sublunary world as well. Heaven, the most important part of

101. This passage belongs to the fourth book; in the Arabic text it immediately follows the passage reproduced as the first fragment of the fourth book, cf. above fr. IV/62. The translation follows Mahdi's.

102. Cf. *Topics* 2.1–5.

103. Cf. *On Sophistical Refutations* 18, 176b20ff.

the universe, remains unchanged for as long as the universe itself exists. But, since the celestial spheres constitute a limited body, they are by definition destructible.

77* Simpl. *in de Caelo* 139,23–27: But since <the Grammarian>, who has challenged what he takes to be the more forceful of Aristotle's arguments concerning the uncreatedness of the world, sets out in the following to undermine the confidence deriving from both the common opinion of men and sense-perception, let us look at his criticism of these arguments as well.

78 Simpl. *in de Caelo* 141,11–19: "Even though people disagree with each other on other topics," as this man says, "all nevertheless agree to this, namely to assigning the place above to God, and because this dogma based on common ideas (*koinai ennoiai*) has been implanted in the souls of men it should be immutable in this respect. But if all assign the place above to God", he says, "this is no infallible proof of the assumption that the heavens are indestructible. For those who believe that sanctuaries and temples are full of deities raise their hands towards them, but no one thinks them to be without a beginning or indestructible. They think rather that one place is more appropriate for God than another."

79 (As-Sijistānī) *Muntakhab Ṣiwān al Ḥikmah* (237):[104] And he[105] said in another chapter that

(1) "if all men allot the highest place to the divine cause, and therefore raise their hands to heaven when they pray on the assumption that the abode of God is in that place, still, this is not proof that all men believe the heavens to be imperishable and ungenerated. For we find that the ancients and the people of our time who clearly assert that they believe the entire world to be generated raise their eyes to heaven when they pray no less than those <others>.

(2) "Furthermore, most of the Greeks and the barbarians believe that their temples and the holy places are dwellings for gods, and they believe that the images and idols < . . . >[106] are fitting for

104. Edited by Dunlop, *The Muntakhab Ṣiwan al Ḥikmah* (The Hague, Paris, N.Y. 1979). The translation follows Kraemer, 'A lost passage from Philoponus' contra Aristotelem in Arabic translation', *Journal of the American Oriental Society* 85 (1969), 326 with minor alterations.

105. Sc. Yaḥyā an-Naḥwī, i.e. the Arabic name for John the Grammarian.

106. Although there is no lacuna in the existing manuscripts, the syntax suggests that something is missing.

their gods, as they claim. Yet, I <sc. Philoponus> do not think that it has dawned on any one of them whose natural reasoning is unimpaired that the temples and idols are imperishable and that there is no beginning to their existence.

(3) "Therefore, if many men believe that the divine cause dwells in heaven, it ought not to be thought that this is proof that they also believe <the heavens> to be imperishable and ungenerated. Rather, they must believe that this place is more illuminated by the light of God than another, just as they believe that one place is more appropriate for God than another, and just as it is thought that one man is closer or more remote from God than another according to the light of God shed upon him as a result of his good behaviour and fine actions. For all things are filled with God, and it is impossible that anything at all be devoid of God. And the light of God is shed upon everything according to its conduct during its life, or according to its nature."

80 Simpl. *in de Caelo* 142,7–25: "But", he says, "the fact that in the entire past the heavens do not seem to have changed either as a whole or in <their> parts must not be taken as a proof that they are completely indestructible and ungenerated. For there are also some animals which live longer than others, and <some> parts of the earth, mountains for example, and stones like the diamonds, exist almost as long as the whole of time, and there is no record that Mount Olympus had a beginning of existence, or <was subject to> increase or diminution. And in the case of mortal animals, for the time that they are to be preserved it is necessary that the most important of their parts retain their proper nature, so that as long as God wants the world to exist it is also necessary that the most important of its parts be preserved. But it has been agreed that the heavens as a whole as well as in <their> parts are the most important and most essential parts of the world. For by their movement all bodies inside are guided naturally.[107] Therefore it is necessary that as long as the world is to be preserved, the heavens will not abandon their proper nature in any respect, neither as a whole nor in <their> parts. But if it has rightly been shown by Aristotle that all bodies have a limited capacity (*dunamis*),[108]<and if> the heavens, too, are a body, <then> it is evident that they are also liable to destruction because the term 'destruction' applies to

107. Cf. above fr. II/45* and fr. IV/75: 138,32–34.
108. See *Physics* 8.10, 266a23–b6.

them, even though so far they clearly have not been affected by anything leading to destruction."

BOOK V

The fragments of the fifth book may be divided into two sections. In the first section Philoponus attacks Aristotle's assumption that the local movements of contrary bodies are contrary as well. In the second and main part of the book Philoponus criticises in detail the arguments of *de Caelo* 1.4 where Aristotle attempts to justify his earlier assumption that no movement is contrary to circular motion. The implication of Aristotle's argument is that the celestial body is eternal. For if the circular motion of the heavens has no contrary, then, Aristotle infers, there exists no body that is contrary to the celestial body, e.g. in the way fire is contrary to water. If there is no such body, the heavens will not be subject to generation and destruction.

Fragments 81–86

Aristotle's supposition that nothing is contrary to the celestial body, *de Caelo* 1.3, 270a18–20, is based on two hypotheses.

(i) The local movements of contrary bodies are contrary as well, 270a17f.

(ii) There is no movement contrary to circular motion, 270a19f. and *de Caelo* 1.4.

In fr. 81–85 Philoponus repudiates the first hypothesis. What does Aristotle mean by contrary bodies? Does he refer to the *substance* or the *qualities* of bodies? If he means 'substance', Aristotle would be contradicting himself, for there is no contrary to substance. Moreover, proposition (i) is not convertible, as Aristotle supposed, i.e. contrariety in locomotion does not presuppose contrariety in the bodies moving (fr. 82–83). If Aristotle thinks, on the other hand, that the qualities of bodies that move with contrary movements are contrary, he faces logical and empirical difficulties (fr. 84–85). Simplicius objects that in his discussion of physical contrariety Philoponus theoretically separates substance and qualities (fr. 86).

81 Simpl. *in de Caelo* 156,25–157,6: Let this be our statement on the <present> issue.[109] But since 'again the swine is raging', as the poet Alcaeus says, it is necessary, again, to turn aside towards this Grammarian who discloses in the <following> arguments – apart from stupidity – <his> gross malignancy as well. At any rate, having said in these <arguments> that Aristotle showed the heavens to be ungenerated and indestructible on the basis of two hypotheses, one saying that everything generated is generated from a contrary, the other assuming that there is no contrary to the

109. Simplicius has commented on the whole chapter *de Caelo* 1.4.

celestial body, he <sc. the Grammarian> continues literally in the following words:

"Although we have conceded the second hypothesis – I mean that there is no contrary to the celestial body because nothing is contrary 157, 1 to substance at all – we have proved the former to be false."

He who says these things spends a whole book, the fifth, striving to refute those propositions which prove that there is no movement contrary to circular movement. He did not realise that if no natural composition (*phusikê sustasis*) is contrary to the substance of the heavens, i.e. to its natural composition, then no natural movement is contrary to the natural movement of <the heavens> either, given that nature is the principle of motion.

82 Simpl. *in de Caelo* 157,21–159,3: Again, since Aristotle set out to show that nothing is contrary to a body moving in a circle on <the basis of> the <two hypotheses> that (i) the local movements of contrary <bodies> are contrary as well, <and> that (ii) there is no movement contrary to circular movement, <the Grammarian> objects to both <hypotheses>, and first to <the proposition that> 'the local movements of contrary <bodies> are contrary as well'. And he asks "whether Aristotle wants the *substances* of those <bodies> of which he says that their local movements are contrary to be contrary, or – given that the substances of bodies are not contrary themselves – <whether he wants> them to partake at any rate of contrary qualities, as <for instance> fire and water, which move in contrary <directions>, partake of the quality 'heat' and the <quality> 'coldness' respectively, and as, for instance, the flesh of an Ethiopian and the flesh of a Scythian, although not contrary in substance, partake at any rate of contrary colours.

"And if Aristotle means indeed that the substances of bodies which move with contrary motions are contrary, <then> he will be caught in contradicting himself. For he himself taught us in the *Categories* that nothing is contrary to substance and especially not to the <compound> of form and matter.[110] There, <in the *Categories*,> he taught that it is the characteristic property of substance to be the same and numerically one, and to be recipient of 158, 1 contraries. In what sense, then, are <bodies> moving with contrary movements contrary? For the same substance which underlies contrary movements, <i.e. a substance> which will become white

110. See *Cat.* 3b24–32. Lines 157,32–35 are identical to 165,32–35. The latter are preceded by the remark that this passage stems from book 5, chapter 3, cf. below fr. V/86, 165,31.

and black, hot and cold, large and small, will be contrary to itself. For it is arbitrary to call those <bodies> contrary which move with contrary movements in space, but not <those that change> in terms of quality, growth and diminution. For nature is the principle of motion and rest not only in terms of place but also of quality and quantity," and evidently also of substance, although this man did not mention it. For change in terms of generation and destruction is also natural.[111]

"And bodies that move in terms of alteration and generation should be <considered> contrary rather than <bodies which move in contrary directions> in space, given that spatial change is merely an accidental property. We observe not only in the case of other species of motion that numerically identical bodies move with contrary movements by nature, but also in the case of local <movements>. For the air possesses not only a principle of upward but also <a principle> of downward movement. For if some <part> of the earth which underlies <air> – or <some part> of the water – is taken away from underneath, <the air> will immediately fill the space (*khôra*), just as it is carried upwards if some <part> of that which lies above it is taken away. But if one takes the force of the vacuum (*hê tou kenou bia*) and not a natural principle to account for the movement downwards, what prevents <us> from saying that the <air's> local movement upwards has the same cause? For it is carried upwards if there happens to be empty space (*kenê khôra*), but otherwise <it is> not. And it is perhaps not only possible but even necessary that the same as is <true of> the other contrary movements is also true of <changes> of place, <i.e.> that there is one genus of them, local movement, and one substrate, <e.g.> air, so that it does not follow that the <bodies> possessing contrary movements are contrary in substance. For nothing is contrary to itself."

Now if this man had put this forward in a spirit of perplexity and inquiry, asking how apparently incompatible propositions of a wise man <sc. Aristotle> will fit together – <i.e.> the <propositions> in the *Categories* saying that nothing is contrary to substance and that the same, numerically identical substance is recipient of contraries, and the present <proposition> which says that the movements of contrary <bodies> are contrary as well – <then> he should rightly be regarded as a lover of learning. For if the <bodies> which possess contrary movements are contrary, as Alex-

111. Lines 7–9 are an interjection by Simplicius.

ander said (for Aristotle did not <claim this>), <then> the same substance appears to be contrary to itself, and substance will not only possess some contrary, but <will possess> *itself* <as a contrary>. But if <the Grammarian> declares in no spirit of inquiry, but in intemperate haste:

"Therefore, either everything shown in the *Categories* must necessarily be rejected as false, or what <is shown> here.[112] If the former <propositions> are true and in agreement with the nature 159, 1
of things, then it is false that the things moving with contrary movements are bodies contrary in substance," – <if this is his position>, I <sc. Simplicius> believe, he will be rightly judged not to be a lover of learning but a man who learns too late.

83* Simpl. *in de Caelo* 162,20–163,3: But the Grammarian says that it is arbitrary to say on the one hand that the things executing contrary changes of place are contrary bodies, and to say on the other hand that the things executing contrary changes in terms of alteration and growth are not at all contrary, supposing, as it seems, that if the local movements of contrary <bodies> are contrary as well, <then it is> also <true> that those <bodies> of which the local movements are contrary are contrary <bodies>. However, if <the two propositions> are not equivalent (*ei mê exisazei*), <then> it is not valid to put the antecedent into the position of the consequent, nor does it follow from what has been said by Aristotle that the things executing contrary changes in terms of alteration or of place – as <the Grammarian> says – are contrary to themselves as the equivalence <of the propositions> has not been demonstrated beforehand. On the other hand, if the <propositions> are equivalent to each other and <it is true> both that the local movements of contrary <bodies> are contrary as well and that those <bodies> of which the local movements are contrary are <indeed> contrary <bodies>, <then> it is evident that the consequent will not be absurd. But what is actually the case I <sc. Simplicius> think I have explained earlier.[113] I have cited the above <argument> now as evidence of <the fact> that this man, who cannot even perceive the entailments of propositions, deceives himself <in thinking>

112. i.e. in *de Caelo* 1.3, 270a12–22.

113. Cf. 161,18–26. Simplicius is defending the position that bodies moving in space in contrary directions can correctly be called contrary in substance, but bodies moving qualitatively or quantitatively cannot. The basis for this position is the distinction between active and passive motions, cf. 159,26ff. Physical bodies possess the active principle of motion in themselves.

that he and the preceding silly presuppositions have said anything. But having forgotten, as it seems, that the argument deals with
163, 1 natural and simple movements, he says that the soul, too, will at the same instant be contrary to itself because it is either moving or capable of moving towards virtue and vice as well as towards false and true judgment.

84 Simpl. *in de Caelo* 163,11–30: Then he writes the <following> (again I am forced to cite more of his <arguments> in order not to appear a denouncer to those in doubt):

"These are <the consequences> if they call the things moving with contrary movements bodies contrary in substance. But suppose someone said that they are not contrary in substance – because absolutely nothing is contrary to substance – but that things moving in contrary directions partake at all events of contrary qualities, as is the case with fire and earth. For the one <element> is in fact hot, the other cold, and the former is light, but the latter is heavy.[114] By conversion with negation (*sun antithesei antistrophê*)[115] it will follow from this that the things which do not partake of contrary qualities do not move with contrary movements, nor does their movement have a contrary movement at all. However, it is not true that if the movement of a body does not possess a contrary movement, this <body> will not partake of a contrary quality. For it is not valid to draw a converse conclusion from the antecedent.[116] Suppose someone held that the <propositions> were equivalent (*exisazei*): so that <it is true> that the <bodies> that possess a movement contrary to their <own> movement partake of contrary qualities as well; and <it is also true> that <bodies> that partake of contrary qualities possess always a movement contrary to their <own> movement. Although he may think that this should be conceded to him as an indemonstrable thesis,[117] he is nevertheless refuted by the facts themselves. For the totalities of the elements clearly partake of contrary qualities, but at least the movement of the firesphere and the <movement> of the air, being circular, do not possess a contrary movement, for the

114. Lines 163,12–17 are identical to 165,17–21.

115. i.e. contraposition or, in propositional logic, transposition, cf. above, n. 4.

116. The conditional in question (lines 14–16) is: 'If bodies possess contrary movements (p), then they possess contrary qualities (q).' Philoponus allows $\sim q \rightarrow \sim p$, but he rejects $\sim p \rightarrow \sim q$ because the terms 'possessing contrary movements' and 'possessing contrary qualities' are not equivalent.

117. Indemonstrable in the sense of being a first principle.

reason for which Aristotle himself holds that circular movement does not possess a contrary movement."

85 Simpl. *in de Caelo* 164,21–27: But this man still carries on striving to show – on the <basis> of facts, as he claims – that the terms are neither equivalent nor convertible (*dunaton antistrephein*). And at this point he again twists and turns in an even more unthinkable manner.

"For both the air and the firesphere, which possess contrary qualities, possess a circular movement. Then, if 'circle' is not contrary to 'circle', <things> which possess contrary qualities do not possess contrary movements."

86 Simpl. *in de Caelo* 165,10–166,13: In these <sentences> cited above he <sc. the Grammarian> puts forward repeatedly that there is nothing contrary to substance, and he thinks that Aristotle is in disagreement with himself because he clearly states this in the *Categories*, whereas here, <in the *de Caelo*>, he says that the local movements of <bodies> contrary in substance are contrary as well;[118] because of this I <sc. Simplicius> think that <the Grammarian> is entirely ignorant of what is meant by saying that nothing is contrary to substance. I am judging from the distinction[119] on which he based his reply, by which he clearly revealed how he thought when he wrote in the passage just set out:

"These are <the consequences> if they call the things moving with contrary movements bodies contrary in substance. But suppose <they are> not contrary in substance – because absolutely nothing is contrary to substance – but that things moving in contrary directions partake at all events of contrary qualities, as is the case with fire and earth. For the one <element> is in fact hot, the other cold, and the former is light, but the latter is heavy."[120]

You notice that he has contrasted contraries in respect of quality with contraries in respect of substance, thinking that the former are clearly different from the latter – and <that they are> not opposites in terms of accidental qualities (*kata tas tukhousas poiotêtas*) but <in terms of> substantial <qualities> (*tas ousiôdeis*), as in the case of fire, he claims, and of earth. For the one <element> is in fact hot, the other cold, and the former is light, but the latter

118. Cf. *de Caelo* 1.3, 270a17f. with *Cat.* 5, 3b24–32.
119. Philoponus draws a distinction between contrariety *qua* substance and contrariety *qua* qualities, see below.
120. Cf. above fr. V/84, 163,12–17.

is heavy. If, then, he does not suppose these and similar <bodies> to be contraries in respect of substance – since every composite substance, which above all he considers not to possess a contrary, is <a compound> of matter and the substantial qualities – what other natural, composite substance remains of which he thinks it is true <to say> that there is no contrary to substance? For he thinks that this is stated in the *Categories* about composite substances, since he clearly wrote in the third chapter of his fifth book:

"If Aristotle means that the substances of all bodies moving with contrary movements are contrary themselves, <then> he will be caught contradicting himself. For he himself taught us in the *Categories* that nothing is contrary to substance and especially not to the compound of matter and form."[121]

166, 1 So what kind of natural body is composed of matter and form but is not characterised by opposite qualities? For even if one assumed it to be the three-dimensional (*to trikhe diastaton*),[121a] this, according to the Grammarian, is <not a composite, but mere> matter and becomes a natural body and composite substance <only> when characterised by opposite qualities. <So substance> characterised by contrary qualities is no different from this <composite substance>. But if the body <in question> is not matter but a compound of matter and form, <then> its form possesses opposite differentiae as well. For there is matter of body, Aristotle says, and this matter <is the matter> of the 'great and small' too.[122] What kind of substance composed of matter and form is there, then, besides the one which is characterised by opposite qualities of hot and cold and light and heavy, <a substance> of which he thinks that <the proposition> that nothing is contrary to substance is true? For it seems he agrees that <this proposition> is not true of this <kind of substance>.[123] For this reason he attempts to pursue the argument in a different way, attacking the figure of the conversion, of which he is manifestly ignorant as well.[124]

121. Cf. above fr. V/82, 157,32–35. 121a. Philoponus cannot present this as a *composite* lacking opposite qualities, because for him it becomes a composite only when it acquires opposite qualities.

122. Simplicius is probably referring to *GC* 1.5, 320b22–24, citing it out of context. Philoponus seems to have claimed, 166,2f., that the three-dimensional substrate (on which see above, n. 95a) is not characterised by opposites. Simplicius assimilates 'the three-dimensional' to 'the great and small', thereby suggesting that it does possess opposite *differentiae*. 'The great and small' played the role of an indeterminate substrate for Platonists.

123. i.e. a substance characterised by the above-mentioned opposite qualities, e.g., an element.

124. Simplicius has criticised Philoponus' logic in the context of an argument of the first book of the *contra Aristotelem*, cf. *in de Caelo* 28,25ff.

Fragments 87–89

Philoponus proceeds to refute Aristotle's second hypothesis, i.e. that no movement is contrary to circular motion.

As a first argument (*de Caelo* 1.4, 270b32–271a5) in support of this thesis, Aristotle, and Alexander of Aphrodisias, held that straight movement is not contrary to circular movement because the two straight movements upwards and downwards are already opposed to one another (cf. fr. 87). Philoponus argues (fr. 88–89) that a single straight movement is contrary both to the opposite straight movement and to circular movement, only in a different respect.

87 Simpl. *in de Caelo* 170,11–171,9: But this worthy man who accuses Aristotle of being clever with words – to some <of which> he is not even faithful, while other matters he presents as exposing <Aristotle's> cleverness – seems to agree with the repudiated <arguments> after a lot of ambitious disagreement, and in the following he writes:

"Even if we agree that it is true that body is contrary to body and furthermore that the local movements of contrary bodies are contrary as well and, in inverse consequence, that, if there is no movement contrary to the movement of a body, <then> there is no body contrary to it, it must of course be shown that no movement is contrary to circular motion. Now if we cite each argument by which Aristotle attempted to prove this and refute it, <then> it is evident that if it has not been shown that no movement is contrary to circular movement, it will not have been shown that no body is contrary to a body moving with <circular motion>."

But see how the man who threatens things like this evidently is not even faithful to what has been written <by Aristotle>. For after citing the Aristotelian passage of the first argument[125] and Alexander's interpretation, he leaves Aristotle and goes off to saying about Alexander that although he professed to show that the straight <line> is not contrary to the curved line, he does not seem to have shown anything. But neither Aristotle nor Alexander professed to show this; on the contrary, this man has failed to recognise the line of the argument which runs as follows: If there is some <movement> contrary to circular movement it is <movement> in a straight <line>. Yet, it is emphatically not <movement> in a straight <line>. Consequently there is no movement contrary to circular <movement>. And <Alexander> establishes the conditional by the fact that the straight <line> is thought

125. Cf. *de Caelo* 1.4, 270b32–271a5.

to be opposed to the curved <line>. But even if the <lines> were opposites, the <movements> along these <lines> would not be contrary because there is not <just> one single <movement> in a straight <line> but two. Each of these <straight movements> is in opposition to the other, and a single thing has a single contrary, as has been pointed out frequently. But when Alexander compares straight movement to circular <movement> in the <sentences> where he says: 'The straight is thought to be contrary to the circular because the latter is thought to be bent everywhere whereas the straight <is thought> to be the most unbent of all lines; hence, if it is not contrary to the circular, neither would be any one of the other <lines> which are thought to be less opposed to it',[126] this man <sc. the Grammarian> thinks that the straight <line> is compared to the circle, and he dared to rewrite Alexander's passage when he wrote:

"In particular the straight is thought to be in opposition *to the circle*"[127] although <Alexander> wrote '*to the circular* <i.e. movement>', as is evident also from what follows.[128]

88 Simpl. *in de Caelo* 171,17–32: Next, <the Grammarian> attempts to show that movement in a straight <line> is contrary to both straight and circular movement, each in virtue of something else, just as 'excess' <is contrary> to 'deficiency' and to 'proportion', and 'arrogance' <contrary> to 'humility' and 'righteousness'; and in general, in cases where the <terms> on either side of the symmetry are asymmetrical they are opposed to both one another and to the due proportion.

"But air as well as earth conflicts with fire, each in virtue of something else, and falsehood and ignorance <conflict> with truth, but the former as contrary, the latter as privation. In the same way," he says here,[129] "upward movement conflicts with downward <movement> in virtue of the contrariety of places, but circular <movement conflicts> with each of the straight <movements> – not in virtue of the contrariety of places but in virtue of the form of movement itself.[130] For in the one case the movement <takes

126. The passage is ambiguous. It is not entirely clear whether Alexander spoke of lines or movements.

127. Philoponus only changed the definite article from the feminine to the masculine, reading *tôi kuklôi* for Alexander's *têi kuklôi* in lines 2 and 4.

128. Simplicius is referring to the next sentence: 'then, if it is not contrary to the circular', cf. 171,11f.

129. Move comma to after *ka'ntautha*.

130. For 171,25–27 cf. also 172,1–4.

place> from one point to the other and is unbent in every part, but in the other case <the movement> takes place from the same point to the same <point>, no part whatever remaining unbent. Further, the former cannot occur twice along the same <line> without having come to a halt whereas circular <movement> revolves infinite times in the same manner without pause. In consequence, if they are characterised by contraries they clearly ought to be contrary <movements>."

89 Simpl. *in de Caelo* 172,23–173,15: But if it is necessary that contraries of this kind, <i.e.> things that change into one another, are understood in terms of the contrariety of places,[131] <then the Grammarian> has, in the following, spent many words in vain striving to show that although the movements in a circle and in a straight <line> are not contrary in virtue of <contrary> places, they are still opposed <to one another> in other ways, and <to show> that it would be more sensible <if> circular movement were said to be contrary to straight <movement> because it is opposed <to it> in many ways, rather than <to say> that upward movement <is contrary to the movement> downwards, <the latter> only possessing the contrary in terms of place. For even though the things which are generated and destroyed are similar to each other but opposed to the ungenerated and indestructible things in many ways, their relation towards one another is said to be one of contrariety, in virtue of which they change into one another, but in relation to the things which are ungenerated and indestructible they are not <said to be contrary>. But since he said earlier that even two things in conflict with a single thing are contraries, just as earth and air <are contrary> to fire, the former as cold to hot, the latter as fluid to dry, the excess of thoughtlessness seems to me remarkable. For he has maintained frequently that they are not contraries *qua* earth and *qua* air and fire and in general *qua* substances. How then does he not understand that, if the hot is contrary to the cold and the dry to the fluid, there are not two things but a

131. Simplicius has just objected that contrariety in the Aristotelian sense involves both opposition of place and the capability to change into one another, cf. 172,5–7. Philoponus' concept of the contrariety of circle and straight line (cf. previous fragment) is not contrariety in this sense. In support of his refutation Simplicius cites a passage from the fourth book of the *contra Aristotelem* where Philoponus argues that the heavens are the most important and essential part of the world, cf. 172,20–22 with fr. IV/75: 138,32–34 and fr. IV/80: 142,17–20. The implication is that Philoponus did not realise that an interchange of the substances of heaven and earth is impossible.

single thing contrary to another in virtue of which the elements also change into one another? Speaking generally, if two things are contrary to a single thing, not in virtue of the same but each in virtue of something different, as <the Grammarian> says, and if in the case of 'excess' and 'deficiency' as well as in his numerous examples of this kind both <things> conflict in virtue of something different – in equality in virtue of their common inequality and in symmetry in virtue of the common asymmetry, but <conflict> with each other in virtue of something different – again, in what sense are there two things contrary to one and not one thing <contrary> to one? For asymmetry[132] is one thing and inequality is one thing.

"But if the place above towards which the ascending <bodies> are carried is the concave circumference (*hê koilê periphereia*) of the lunary sphere, and if the place above is contrary to the <place> below, <then> the heavens partake of one of the two contrary places, and in virtue of this they will be contrary to something, just as fire is <contrary> to water. Although they are not contraries *qua* bodies or substances, they are still contrary in virtue of contrary qualities."

Fragments 90–91

Philoponus picks up Aristotle's own suggestion (*de Caelo* 1.4, 270b35) that concave (*koilos*) and convex (*kurtos*) are contraries. He then suggests that they are properties of the celestial body. If participation in any kind of contrariety entails that a thing will suffer generation and destruction, the heavens too are generated and destructible.

90 Simpl. *in de Caelo* 173,25–174,13: Next <the Grammarian> says "convex and concave (*to kurton kai koilon*) are opposed as contraries; for they are not <in opposition> as relative terms because they do not always coexist. For first 'convex' applies to the spherical surface which is not concave, given that the sphere is solid, and 'concave' applies to roofs which are vaulted on the inside but flat on the outside. Secondly they are not <opposed> like 'state' and 'privation'. For each of them <sc. the convex and concave> is a quality."

As it seems, this rash man is ignorant of the fact that privation too is one form of quality. So how did he mean that 'convex' and 'concave' are not opposed as state and privation because they are
174, 1 qualities? But he says that "neither are they <opposed> as affirm-

132. Read *asummetria* with MS D.

ation and negation." It remains therefore that 'concave' and 'convex' are opposed as contraries.

"If they are some kind of qualities or properties of the celestial body, then the celestial <body> is a recipient of contraries, and consequently of destruction and generation as well."

Here, is he not obviously twisting completely the aim of what has been said <by Aristotle>? First, while Aristotle assumed 'concave' and 'convex' in the case of a line along which circular movement takes place (for every movement takes place along a line), he understood <'concave' and 'convex'> as belonging to a solid, saying that a line cannot exist by itself without body; rather, all natural lines have existence in body. In fact, the 'concave' and 'convex' exist in different boundaries of the spherical body. And he therefore finds fault with Alexander as well who said that if the 'concave' is considered to be contrary to the 'convex' in the case of a single line, then the line would be contrary to itself.

91 Simpl. *in de Caelo* 175,13–22: Moreover, he does not draw a profound conclusion at all when he says:

"If they hold that participating in whatever kind of contraries, either in both or in one of them, is universally a proof of the fact that the thing which partakes <of these contraries> is generated and destructible, then, seeing that the celestial body is a recipient of contrariety in terms of 'concave' and 'convex', and that the 'concave' of the lunary sphere is one of the contrary places, they ought to say that the heavens are generated and destructible as well. But if not every kind of contrariety is the cause of generation and destruction of bodies, just as moving in space in contrary directions upwards and downwards is in fact neither generation nor destruction, then the things that are deprived of contrary movements in space are not deprived of generation and destruction simply because of this."

Fragments 92–93

Against Aristotle's second argument, *de Caelo* 1.4, 271a5–10: curved movements from point A to point B are not contrary to curved movements from B to A because there is an infinite number of curves (connecting the points).

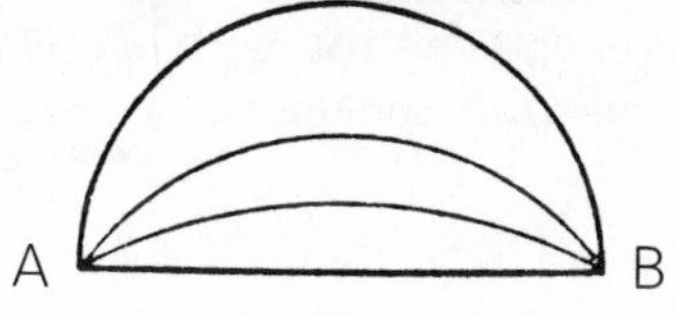

Simplicius outlines the rationale behind Aristotle's arguments for the absence of contrary places on a circumference and the impossibility of contrary movements along a curve. Philoponus objects that, since the number of circumferences drawn through two points A and B is infinite, there will be an infinite number of contrary movements. Or, since the movements in each direction are similar, all curved movements from A to B will be contrary to the movements from B to A. The same is true in the case of straight movements because the singular centre is opposed to an infinite number of termini at the periphery of the world (fr. 92). Philoponus objects against Alexander's interpretation of Aristotle's argument that it is impossible to prove physical things on the basis of geometrical principles. Instead, Philoponus assumes the largest possible circumference, the perimeter of the universe, in order to show that there are contrary places on the circumference of the universe, and that the movements between them can be contrary movements (fr. 93).

92 Simpl. *in de Caelo* 176,13–177,22: In this way, then, this worthy man wrote down in vain many sentences which object to the first of <Aristotle's> arguments. Let us see how he replies to the second proposition.[133] Now on the grounds of what has been laid down before Aristotle held that (i) the <movements> from contrary places are contrary movements of place, and that (ii) the <places> at the greatest distance (*hoi pleiston diestêkotes*) are contrary places, and that (iii) the greatest distance (*diastasis*) is determinate, just as the smallest <distance>, and that (iv) every distance possessing a determinate length is measured by the straight <line> between the distances; for the <distance> is one and determinate, which is why it is the shortest of the <paths> having the same termini, whereas the curves which are linked at those same points are infinitely many. And therefore they are indeterminate and hence do not determine the distance between <points> A and B. And because of this the greatest distance is not the one along the <circumference>, and the places of <points> A and B are not contrary <places>, and therefore the movements from A and B are not contrary <movements>, given that <the movements> take place along the circumference and not along the straight <line>. Although Aristotle has proved these <propositions> in this way by entirely indisputable lemmata, this man <sc. the Grammarian>, who does not comprehend the things laid down, says:

"I have been wondering considerably whether the Philosopher <sc. Aristotle>has not used this sort of argument in jest rather than in earnest."

133. Cf. *de Caelo* 1.4, 271a5–10.

And it is clear that he, who considers this stringent sequence of propositions as a jest but <his> own arguments – of which we shall hear – as serious business, would evidently be a very important person. For having cited first Themistius' paraphrase of the Aristotelian passage and subsequently the exegesis of Alexander of Aphrodisias in order that here too he may appear clever, he sets out to repudiate Aristotle's position according to either of them. And so, when Themistius says that those who hold that there *are* contraries on the circumference are driven to the absurdity that infinites are put in opposition to one, because the <number of> circumferences to be drawn through points A <and> B is infinite, this man imitates the argument childishly, saying that an infinite <number of> movements has an infinite <number of> contraries. For he says that along each of the infinite <number of> circumferences there are two movements contrary to each other. Even to this point he does understand that, given that the <movements> from contrary places are contrary movements, each of the infinite <number of movements> from B will be contrary to one movement from A. So that the <contraries> are infinite and Themistius' argument is correct.

Secondly, <the Grammarian> objects to the argument <in question> that even if the circumferences through A <and> B were infinite <in number>, they would still be similar to one another, and because of this all <movements> from A, <taken> as one, are opposed to the <movements> from B, <taken> as one. Then, giving superfluous examples, he says:

"I wonder, how he[134] did not realise that the same follows in the case of straight movements. For while the centre of the universe towards which all heavy <bodies> move is one, the light <bodies> moving away from the centre towards the periphery do not terminate at *one* point, but at an infinite <number of points>."

And here he is inelegant enough not to refrain from drawing diagrams depicting the centre of the universe, the peripheral circle, and the movements away from the centre, he who, again, is not able to understand the same which also gave rise to his ignorance earlier, <i.e.> that the <movements> from contrary places are contrary movements, that the <places> furthest away from one another are contrary places, <and> that these <places> are determinate and possess a determinate distance between <them>.

134. It is not immediately clear whether Philoponus is arguing against Themistius or Aristotle.

93 Simpl. *in de Caelo* 178,7–26: Alexander more appropriately brings the argument down to this: the <movements> along the circumference are not at all contrary because <points> A and B are not furthest away from each other on the circumference, as shown <by the fact> that an infinite <number of> circumferences with different lengths can be drawn through points A and B. But this man again speaks arrant nonsense (*makra phluarei*) as he finds fault with the attempt to demonstrate things of nature from geometrical principles.

"For the possibility of drawing circumferences *ad infinitum* through the same points until no larger <circumference> can be assumed is spoken of correctly in the case of mathematical <entities> arrived at by abstraction, but in the case of natural <entities> which are assumed <to have> a quality and matter, <this> is impossible. It is therefore <possible> to take the largest natural circumference in the universe. Certainly then, the things moving along the largest circumference of the universe in opposite directions away from the limits of the diameter of the universe are moving with contrary movements because the points from which they have been moving are furthest away from each other on the circumference. For the existence of a circumference larger than the one of the extremity of the universe is impossible. Now, if the two circumferences move in contrary directions to each other away from those points on the diameter in which the boundaries of the outer spheres are in contact with each other, <i.e.> the concave <boundary> of the fixed and the convex <boundary> of the planetary <sphere>, <then> the inner <circumference> and the outer <circumference> move with contrary movements, and in consequence of this their bodies are contrary as well."

Fragments 94–100

Against Aristotle's third argument, *de Caelo* 1.4, 271a10–13: a movement from C to D along a determinate semicircle is not contrary to a movement from D to C because the semicircle does not determine the distance between C and D. Philoponus objects that it is not true that every distance is

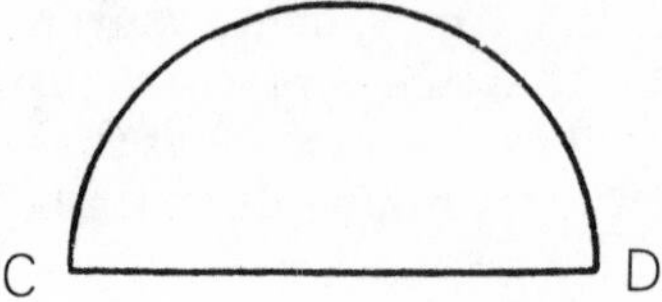

measured and determined by the straight line. Measures must be applicable to the measured object, but the straight line is not applicable to the curve (fr. 94). But even if it were true that any distance is measured along the straight line, it would still be true, according to Philoponus, that the movements along a semicircle in opposite directions are contrary movements. The greatest distance between places can be determined both by the distance in a straight line and by the distance along the circumference (fr. 95).

Along these lines there follows a discussion of Alexander's interpretation of Aristotle's third argument (fr. 96–100).

94 Simpl. *in de Caelo* 179,24–180,23: But when this man <sc. the Grammarian> attempts to disprove Aristotle's third argument[135] which says that even if the countermovement is assumed not along an indeterminate circumference, because it is possible to draw an infinite <number of> circumferences through the same points, but along one determinate <circumference>, for instance the semicircle, then the distance between <points> C and D will also in this way be measured by the straight <line>, he <sc. the Grammarian>, who neither understands Aristotle's arguments nor those of the commentators, spins out a mass of words in order to show that the straight <line> is not necessarily the measure of every magnitude or of every line. It is <the measure> only of things which are of the same kind, with which it conforms, and it does not conform with the circumference. And in this way he constructs all the arguments as if Aristotle and the commentators said that the length of the circumference is measured by the straight <line>. And for those in doubt it is perhaps necessary to cite some of the things said by him:

"If the straight <line> is indeed the shortest line drawn through the same points, it does not at all <follow> immediately that it is necessarily the measure of every line as well as every magnitude, but evidently <only> of things which are of the same kind and with which it conforms. However, <the straight line> does not conform with the circumference nor is it of the same kind. In consequence, it cannot be the measure of <the circumference>." Is he not manifestly believing that they <sc. Aristotle and the commentators> held that the circumference is measured by the straight <line>? But if this does not suffice to reveal his stupidity, listen also to the following:

"For even if some curved artifacts are often measured by craftsmen with a straight <line>, for instance the cubit, they still do not

135. Cf. *de Caelo* 1.4, 271a10–13.

measure the curved line as such with the cubit, as <they do> in the case of rectilinear artifacts where the cubit is directly applicable to the straight line of the artifact. But in the case of a circumference they do not apply the cubit to the circumference in this way. For that is impossible. Rather, in taking straight intervals of the circumference they measure these <intervals>, so that the measured <distance> is again similar to the measure. But if, since in knowing the length of the diameter of a circle the <length of> the perimeter is known as well, one will regard the straight <line> as the measure of the circumference, then, since by the circumference being known it is also possible to know the diameter, one ought to say too that the circumference is the measure of the straight <line>. And that the three sides of an equilateral triangle are equal to one another we do not find out in any way other than by means of circles drawn over one of the sides of the triangle as diameter.[136] Why then, is the circumference calculated by the straight <line> rather than the straight <line> by the circumference?"

95 Simpl. *in de Caelo* 181,16–33: But this man is ignorant of the aim of the present <arguments>, because in order to refute them – as he thinks – he put forward that those measuring the curves of artifacts measure the straight intervals of the curve taken beforehand by means of the straight <line>, not realising that this is what Aristotle said: 'For we always measure how far away each thing is <along the straight line>.'[137] But as usual, after conceding in turn that it is true that the straight <line> is the measure of any distance, he says that even in this way the argument will not bring them any nearer towards proving that the movements from the limits of the semicircle in opposite directions are not contrary <movements>.

"For since the circle is a magnitude," he says, "some of its parts are further away from each other and <others> are nearer. For <the zodiac sign> Gemini is further away from the beginning of Aries than Taurus, and Cancer is even further <away> than these. Accordingly, in this <circle> there are also <signs> which are at the greatest distance, for example Aries and Libra. For their distance along each semicircle is the same. Let us take Aries and

136. This does not seem to be right. In order to find out by means of a compass whether all sides of a triangle are equal, one has to draw two circles with one side as the radius.

137. Cf. *de Caelo* 1.4, 271a13 and MS D.

Scorpius: even though their distance is greater along one part of the circle because they are seven zodiac signs apart from each other, they are still rather close to each other along the remaining <part of the circle>, for <here> they are five zodiac signs apart. Therefore only Aries and Libra and, in general, the <signs> that divide the circle into two equal parts are at the greatest distance on both sides."

96 Simpl. *in de Caelo* 182,14–25: <The Grammarian> agrees that along the diameter the greatest distance is that between <points> C and D, yet he claims that along the circumference this is the greatest distance too because C and D are equally apart whichever way round you go. But what does this contribute to the greatest distance which exists between contrary places, <places> from which contrary movements <commence>? Pursuing his lack of knowledge and rashness again in the following, he says:

"For Alexander <of Aphrodisias> this was the basis of a trick. For he assumed that the straight <line> is a measure, and that it belongs to the measure to find the <points> that are furthest away from each other and contraries, the consequence <of which> is to draw the conclusion saying: 'Therefore it belongs to the straight <line> to find in distances the <points> furthest away from each other and contraries.' But mischieviously <Alexander> added 'on it' <sc. the straight line> when he says: 'For in distances the contrary is <found> by the straight <line> and on the <straight line>,' an assumption he did not have in the premises."[138]

97 Simpl. *in de Caelo* 183,21–184,7: But <the Grammarian>, who understands nothing of what has been laid down, spends many arguments showing repeatedly that the points which are furthest away from each other – given that we are measuring with a cubit – neither exist in the measuring cubit nor are they at the greatest distance in it. And he was not able to understand that if the distance were a single cubit, the <points> at the distance would be at the limits of the cubit, not <, of course, at the limits> of the wooden or copper <cubit> but of the <cubit> along the straight <line> between <the points>, and that the greatest distance between them exists along this <straight line>, which measures *qua* determinate <line> because it is shortest, but which is measured as indeterminate distance. For the wooden cubit does not *add* the measure[139]

138. Cf. 182,31–183,2, where Simplicius cites Alexander's argument in detail.
139. 'Measure' here in the sense of 'actual length'.

but makes the inherent <length> visible. But he is so out of tune with the meaning of the things said that he literally writes this:

"In general, to say that the <points> found in the measured <distance> by means of the measure are also *in* the measure is very silly and absurd."

He does not understand in what sense the distance along the straight <line> is both <the> measure of the greatest distance and that which is measured. Instead, he witlessly collected a number of criteria, showing that the contrariety and distance of the things examined are not *in* the criteria.

"For the 'distance' between truth and falsehood is not *in* the proof," he says; "neither is the <'distance'> between good and evil. And 'white' and 'black' or 'running' and 'resting' are not *in* the visual faculty, and the high and low pitch are not *in* the acoustic <faculty>, and the warp is not *in* the ruler. The ruler does not possess that straightness which we have found out by means of the <ruler> to exist in, say, this piece of wood."

98 Simpl. *in de Caelo* 185,3–186,15: Now, it is necessary to listen also to the following <arguments>: is it not a case of complete contempt for the arguments to say that the opposition of movements along the semicircle is the same as the <opposition of movements> along the diameter because both the semicircle and the diameter are limited by the same points? You notice how he does not pay any attention <to the fact> that Aristotle does not say without qualification that the movements along the semicircle are the same as the ones along the diameter, but <they are only the same> when they are understood as contraries, which means as <movements> from contrary places,[140] which <i.e. 'contrary places'> is to say the same as <places> at the greatest distance, which is to say the same as possessing a determinate distance between <them>. For the greatest <distance> is determinate. But <'determinate distance'> is to say the same as <a distance> measured by the shortest <line>. For this is the determinate <distance>. But, in case he does not know, <the Grammarian> should learn that the shortest of all lines possessing the same limits is the straight.

But Alexander says that the things moving along the semicircle as from contrary places, even though they do not move along the straight <line>, nevertheless move in this way with a contrary

140. Cf. *de Caelo* 1.4, 271a12f.

<movement> – that is a movement between places furthest apart – because they move the same distance between the <two places> as extends along the straight <line>. <And the Grammarian> replies that in this way <Alexander> will not escape from conceding that the <movements> occurring along the semicircle in opposite ways are contrary <movements>, even though the <movements> have <the property> of being contraries not because of the circle but because of the diameter of <the circle>. Yet, if <they are contrary> because of the diameter, they are not contrary as things moving along the semicircle. For <points> C <and> D are not furthest away from each other as limits of the semicircle but as <limits> on the straight <line/diameter>.

Further, Alexander says that if all distance were measured not by the straight <line> but by the circumference, <then> nothing could possibly be assumed to be at the greatest distance,[141] because it is possible both to make a large circumference through <points> which are close together by drawing an exceedingly convex circumference and <to make> a smaller <circumference> through <points> at a great distance. This man <sc. the Grammarian>, again, spins out lengthy arguments striving to show that even in the case of a circumference the greatest distance is the one which is equally far whichever way round you go, as <for instance> the <distance> between Aries and Libra. He does not realise that 'equally far whichever way round' is different from 'greatest', and that the distance traversed from Aries to Sagittarius via Libra along the circumference is taken to be greater than the <distance from Aries> to Libra. However, if distances are taken along the straight <lines> between the limits, the greatest <distance> will be the one between Aries and Libra because the diameter is greater than all straight <lines> drawn across the circle. But if the distance is taken along the circumference, it will be possible to draw <even> greater circumferences through the same points, as Alexander said: the greatest <distance> would not at all be determinate because at different times the distance between the points is taken along a different circumference. But this man <sc. the Grammarian>, who again does not understand what has been said, replies:

"To say that it is possible to draw a smaller circumference through <points> far apart, and a greater <circumference> through points closely together, I cannot decide whether this is an

141. Read *diestos* with MS B.

intentional fallacy or a case of not knowing that it is unsurprising (*ou thaumaston*) that if in the case of different circles the points on one of these circles are close together – let the perimeter measure one foot and let <the points> be half a foot apart – <then> they are said to be furthest apart, but points on a <circle> measuring 100 feet in perimeter which are 25 feet away from each other are not furthest away from each other."

99 Simpl. *in de Caelo* 186,24–187,6: But since Alexander wanted to show that it is possible to draw both greater and smaller circumferences through the same points he unnecessarily brought in the argument, saying that in the case of different limits it is possible to draw both the greatest circumference through limits which are close together and a smaller <circumference through limits> which are very far apart. But if <this> is possible in the case of different <limits> it is evidently much more so in the case of the same <limits>. This is something <the Grammarian> does not understand, <and> he covers reams[142] in order to show that nothing is remarkable <about the fact> that in some magnitudes closer <points> are at the greatest distance whereas in other <magnitudes points> further apart are not.

187, 1 "Although we may draw both the largest and the smallest circumference through the same points," he says, "for instance <points> A <and> B, it will not follow that points A <and> B are at the greatest distance because of a greater circumference and at a smaller <distance> because of a smaller <circumference>. For if the remaining <sections of> the circumferences of the two circles were drawn as well, points A <and> B would potentially not be two but four <points>. For in each <circumference> of the circles they possess a different relation towards each other."

100 Simpl. *in de Caelo* 187,16–25: But <the Grammarian> does not realise[143] in what way the distance (*diastêma*) is said to be measured by the straight <line>, <i.e.> that it possesses its location along a straight <line> in such a way that the intermediate <points> run in line with the extremities. As opposed to this he thinks that it is said <to be> in a straight <line> because the straight <line> applied to the distance from outside makes <the distance> straight.

142. Literally: 'he stretches many arguments'.
143. Read *ennoêsas*.

"On what grounds does Alexander say that there are no points furthest away from each other in a circle, if <it is true that> not all distances are measured by the straight <line>? Any measure provides only knowledge of what is measured, not the being such as the measure reveals it to have by nature. For it is clear that the straight measure is applicable to the distance because <the distance> is straight."

Fragment 101

On Aristotle's fourth argument, *de Caelo* 1.4, 271a13–19: assume two semicircles H and I which, if joined together, constitute a full circle bisected by the diameter at points E and F. A movement from E to F along semicircle

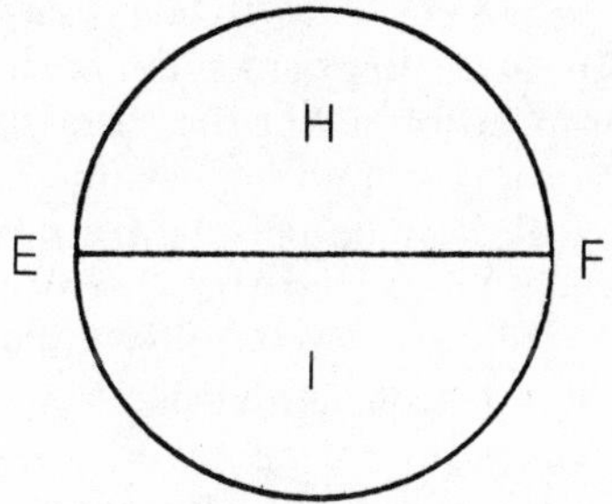

H is evidently not contrary to a movement from F to E along semicircle I. Philoponus agrees that the movements are not contrary movements.

101 Simpl. *in de Caelo* 187,28–188,25: <The Grammarian> also outlines the fourth argument[144] which shows that even if one assumed two movements in one circle – the one <movement> from E to F along semicircle H, the other from F to E along semicircle I – these movements would not be contrary because they do not 188, 1
<commence> from contrary places. For the <places> do not possess a determinate distance. This worthy man had such confidence in his vacuous assertions that he says:

"If the present <proposition> too is proved on the basis of the same arguments as the previous one, <then> there will be no need for us to argue against it because we have already met the previous <argument> to the best of our ability."

Then he finds fault with Themistius, who said that <here> the

144. Cf. *de Caelo* 1.4, 271a13–19.

same must be said as in the case of the <arguments> concerning the previous proposition about things moving along one semicircle, and <the Grammarian> says that the present proposition does not rely on the same hypotheses as the previous one. For the former hypothetically assumed that the movements take place in opposite directions along one and the same semicircle, but this <proposition> does not <take them to occur> in the same <semicircle> but assumes one movement along a circle, <the movement> being divided according to the division of the semicircles.

"It is reasonable," he says, "that these <movements> are not contrary. For if one assumed unification <of the two semicircles>, the two <movements> along the circle are one. For the movement from east to west along one of the hemispheres, for instance the one above the earth, is not contrary to the <movement> from west to east along the other <hemisphere> beneath the earth. For this reason the present proposition is not the same as the previous one."

And he was able to comprehend on the one hand that the movements which take place along one circle are not contraries, <but> he adduced on the other hand that there are two propositions, one assuming hypothetically two semicircles joined together, saying that the movements along <the semicircles>, just as in the previous theorem, are only then contraries when they are theoretically considered as occurring along the diameter, which is also the distance between points E <and> F, the other argument allowing by agreement <in the premise> that even the <movements> along the semicircles are hypothetically taken to be contraries. But the locomotions along the whole circle, at any rate, are still not contrary to one another because of this. This man thought this to be the only argument establishing[145] that the movements in a circle are not contrary.

Fragments 102–104

Against Aristotle's fifth argument, *de Caelo* 1.4, 271a19–22: two movements around the same circle in opposite directions are not contrary movements because they always return to the same point; contrary movements must occur from one contrary to another contrary. Philoponus does not accept the point that movements in one circle in contrary directions are not contrary movements. He objects that the definition of contrary motions, i.e. motions between contrary places, does not apply to the case of contrary

145. *legonta* here means more than just 'stating'.

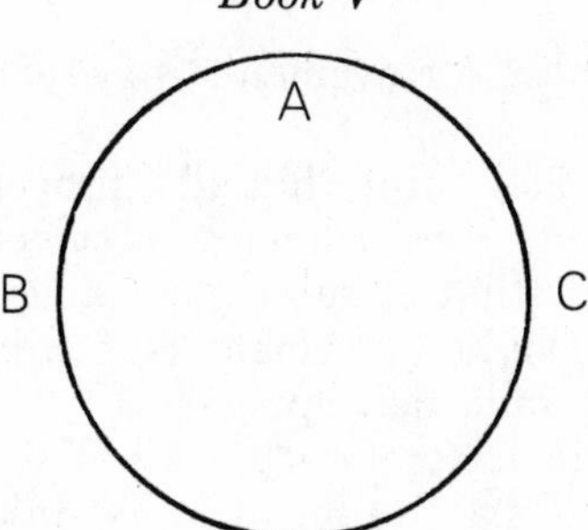

circular motion. A different kind of contrariety is involved, for circular motions are different in kind from rectilinear motions (fr. 102). Thus, Philoponus would say that the movements of the planets are in fact contrary to the movement of the fixed sphere (fr. 103). Simplicius attempts to show that Philoponus' criticism is inconsistent and self-contradictory. In fr. 104 Philoponus explains contrariety in circular motion with reference to planetary motion and the movement of the fixed sphere.

102 Simpl. *in de Caelo* 189,22–190,31: But he has armed himself against the fifth argument[146] as well, the <argument> about two movements occurring in the same circle from the same <point> and to the same point, but in contrary directions – one moving from A to A via semicircle B, the other from A again to the same <point> A via the other semicircle C. And <this argument> shows that these <movements> are not contraries because they take place between the same <points>, whereas contrary <movements occur> from a contrary to the contrary. <But> since he has exhausted, as it seems, his objections and is in in a corner, he now objects to the <proposition> that these contrary movements are universally <movements> between contrary places, despite <the fact> that Aristotle used <precisely> this axiom in the other arguments as well and in consequence of this <axiom> rejected <the proposition> that there is a movement contrary to circular movement, the reason being that in the circle no places are furthest 190, 1
apart from each other unless they are determined in terms of the diameter. So this man says that the contrarieties of things differing in species are different as well. Therefore, if contrary straight movements occur between contrary places, it is not immediately

146. Cf. *de Caelo* 1.4, 271a19–22.

necessary that circular <movements> are contrary in the same way as well.

"For if", he says, "they think that all <properties> which belong to straight movements also belong to <movements> in a circle, <then> it will follow that circular <movement> is no movement at all. For every straight movement is a transition from this to that. Natural and simple movements <occur> from one contrary <place> to the other contrary <place>. For the ascending locomotion of light <bodies>, fire for instance, takes place from below to above – 'above' being contrary to 'below' – and the <movement> of heavy <bodies>, earth for example, <takes place> in the opposite direction. And in the case of quantitative and qualitative change the changing object always changes from something to something else. Therefore, if all <kinds of> motion <take place> from one contrary to the other contrary or simply from something to something else, and if no circular <movement takes place> from something to something else but <always> from the same to the same,[147] then circular <motion> will not be any movement at all."

But why do I <sc. Simplicius> need to cite so many of this man's words and burden myself with the nonsense these <sentences> contain? But as regards these <sentences> as well as what is said by him in the following it is necessary to understand first that he evidently agrees that there is no movement contrary to circular movement – <contrary> in the sense of '<occurring> between contrary places' – <and that> the <places> at the greatest distance are evidently contrary places, and yet he employs so large a number of arguments, showing that in the circle the parts on the diameter are furthest away from each other, and in the 25th chapter of the fifth book he writes this in these very words:

"Since the limits of the semicircle are at the greatest distance the movements which take place between them in opposite directions[148] are, in consequence of the definition of contraries, necessarily contrary as well." Notice, how what is said here accords with these <sentences>: "Therefore, if all <kinds of> motion <take place> from one contrary" and so forth.[149] Secondly, we should understand that <even> more superfluously <the Grammarian> attempted to show what is stated by Aristotle, <viz.> that there is

147. For 190,13f. cf. also below fr. V/103: 192,9f.

148. Read *ap' autôn ep' enantias*.

149. Cf. above 190,12ff. Simplicius is being ironical.

no movement contrary to circular movement, <the proposition> against which he set forth his whole repudiation when he said:

"Let this be our task that we will prove that none of the arguments proving <the proposition> that no movement is contrary to circular movement is sound."

103 Simpl. *in de Caelo* 192,5–14: In consequence,[150] the movements opposed in such a way that they do not take place from contrary places but only in contrary directions, as <for instance> the <movement> of the planetary and <the movement> of the fixed <sphere> – for this man <sc. the Grammarian> would consider calling them contrary – are not relevant to the argument because they do not occur between contrary places, which <the Grammarian> even concedes when he says:

"None of the circular <movements> occur from something to something else but from the same to the same."[151]

<Movements> of this kind Aristotle would emphatically not consider calling contrary; he even distinguishes them from contrary <movements>, for he says in the fifth argument:[152] 'But it is not even the case that circular locomotion from A to B is contrary to the <movement> from A to C. For the movement <occurs> from the same to the same <point> whereas contrary locomotion is defined <as occurring> from one contrary to the other contrary.'

104 Simpl. *in de Caelo* 192,15–193,19: But <the Grammarian> said that the contrarieties in circular and rectilinear motion are different in species – he said so both in the words which I have already mentioned[153] and at the beginning of the so-called refutation of the sixth argument[154] where he writes:

"It has been pointed out that because straight and circular movement are admittedly different, the contrarieties must be different as well," he says. In general, if you want to see the absurdity of what is said by <the Grammarian> and <to see> that he only set out to contradict every single phrase, no matter what it is, <then> listen to the things said here where he states that a different species

150. Simplicius has just pointed out that in Aristotle contrary locomotion is defined as movement between contrary places, cf. 191,28–192,5.

151. Cf. above fr. V/102: 190,12–15; also 191,15–17.

152. Cf. *de Caelo* 1.4, 271a19–22.

153. Cf. above fr. V/102: 190,2–15.

154. Aristotle's sixth argument, see *de Caelo* 1.4, 271a22–33.

of contrariety belongs to straight and to circular motion, and to what is stated in the <sentences> against <Aristotle's> first argument, where he considers circular movement to be in opposition to straight <movement> more than straight <movements are> to each other.[155] However, if the contrarieties were different in species, <then> circular <motion> would not be opposed to straight <movement> at all. But in the former <passage> he wrote this:

"Perhaps one could with better reasons allow circular movement to be contrary to straight <motion> more than ascending and descending <movements are> to one another."[156]

However, in this <passage> he wrote this:

"Therefore it is not the case that whatever belongs to contrary straight movements also belongs to contrary circular <movements>. For since the species of motion are different it is necessary that the contrarieties of each species, whatever they may be, are different as well, just as both colour and flavour are doubtless qualities, but since they are different in species the contrarieties in these species are different as well."

Yet, if circular <movement> is contrary to straight <movement>, as he said earlier, both must necessarily share one and the same contrariety.[157] And again, having forgotten what has been said here he affirms in the following:

"What prevents straight movement from being contrary to circular movement in genus?"

But in this vein he would say that 'white' is contrary to 'sweet', seeing that he says in a similar way that circular movement is different from straight <movement> as taste <is different> from colour. He also adds the following nonsense of the same kind:

"For just as in the case of contrary straight movements," <the Grammarian> says, "the conflict of the contraries takes place because the <movements> use the termini interchangeably (*tois perasin enêllagmenôs kekhrêsthai*). For what is the starting point for light <bodies> becomes the terminus for the heavy ones. The case is similar in circular motions: although they are alike <in occurring> from the same to the same, the conflict between the contraries takes place because wherever one <movement> begins, the other <movement> terminates. For if two movements begin, say, at Aries, the outer moves, say, to the <signs> in front (*epi ta*

155. Cf. above fr. V/88.

156. Cf. above fr.V/88. Apparently, this citation belongs to the context of that fragment.

157. i.e. 'one and the same pair of contraries'.

hêgoumena) of Aries to Pisces, Aquarius and so forth.[158] But the inner <moves>, say, to the <signs> behind (*epi ta hepomena*), I mean Taurus and Gemini.[159] And what the outer <movement> has, so to speak, assumed[160] as the beginning of the movement after Aries, <namely> Pisces, this <configuration> the planetary <movement> assumes as the terminus. And the <configuration> which the planetary <movement> possesses as beginning after Aries, I mean Taurus, is the terminus for the <movement> of the fixed <sphere>."[161]

Fragments 105–107

Against Aristotle's sixth argument, *de Caelo* 1.4, 271a22–33, which is an appendix to the fifth argument: if movements in a circle could be contrary one to the other, one of them at least would be cancelled out and therefore be useless (*matên*). But God and nature do not produce anything useless. Philoponus asks why Aristotle discussed motions in opposite directions only along a single circle, and not along different circles, as is the case in the movements of the celestial bodies (see introduction to fr. 6–8). Alexander is cited in support (fr. 105). After all, the theory of aether is a physical theory, and Aristotle seems to have argued beside the point (fr. 106). On the other hand, if one conceded that movements in opposite directions in a circle do not occur in nature because they would cancel each other out and be useless, precisely the same difficulty would be entailed by Aristotle's conception of rectilinear movements (fr. 107).

105 Simpl. *in de Caelo* 194,6–30: However, if it seems proper we will also obliterate what has been said by <the Grammarian> against what he calls the sixth argument.[162] And first, at any rate, <it must be said> that he did not even realise about it that it is part of the fifth argument,[163] despite <the fact that> Alexander said that it is an unnecessary additional argument. Although I <sc. Simplicius> have already elucidated Aristotle's whole intention to the best of my ability by an interpretation of his text, it is still necessary to recall now some of the things said there. <For instance,> after having shown that the movements which occur in

158. i.e. contrary to the order of the signs. Strictly speaking, Aries, Pisces, Aquarius etc. are not references to the constellations of the zodiac, but rather the names of well defined 30° segments of longitude sub-dividing the circle of the ecliptic (the circle described by the apparent annual movement of the sun).
159. i.e. following the order of the signs.
160. Literally: 'has made for itself.'
161. For 193,8–19 cf. also 196,34–197,3.
162. i.e. *de Caelo* 1.4, 271a22–33.
163. According to Simplicius *de Caelo* 1.4, 271a19–33 is one argument.

opposite directions (i) along a circumference, (ii) along one semicircle, and (iii) along two semicircles, are not contrary <movements>, <Aristotle> proceeded to the remaining <section and> set out to demonstrate the present <proposition> that not even the <movements> occurring in opposite directions along a whole circle are contrary <movements>. And although he has shown this before on the basis of the definition of contrary movements, he shows the same now through a *reductio per impossibile*. And it is not necessary to repeat these things because they have been pointed out a short while ago, but it is necessary for one who encounters these things to realise that <the Grammarian> failed to understand the course of the argument, and because of this he thought it to be a sixth argument for the fifth hypothesis, which examines the <movements> occurring in opposite directions along one circle, <and thought it to be> a different mode of proving this <hypothesis>.

This man asks for the reason why <Aristotle> assumed the movement in opposite directions along one circle and not along two, as in the case of the fixed and the planetary <movements>, despite the fact that he inquired into the heavens.[164] And <the Grammarian> says that Alexander realised that the present argument is rotten <and> did not hesitate to attempt to assist the proposition. He <sc. the Grammarian> says:

"Contrary straight movements take place from contrary <places> and to contrary places, and even if they do not occur along one and the same straight <line> they are none the less contrary <movements>; but <movements> that take place along a circle and in opposite directions occur, if they are to be contrary, along *one* circle. For <Alexander> points out, but does not add or devise an explanation why, that it is most absurd that the movement which takes place along one circle should be contrary to the <movement> along another <circle>."

106 Simpl. *in de Caelo* 195,9–17: But if the contrariety comes out more clearly when <the movements> are assumed on the same straight <line>, <then> it is necessary rather to approve of Aristotle assuming things moving in opposite directions along one circle. For if they have a contrariety, it will be more apparent when they are moving along one circle; in consequence, had he attempted to

164. Move colon to after *zêtôn*.

show this for the case of two <circles>, this would have been more suspicious.

"But because", <the Grammarian> says, "the present theory on e heavens is a physical <theory> it was necessary to show for the spheres of the fixed stars and the planets that they do not possess contrary movements, so that Aristotle has focused upon something else beside the point and foreign to the subject-matter without proving the issue in question."

107 Simpl. *in de Caelo* 196,34–197,15: But in his superficial manner <the Grammarian> also said the following:

"Just as in the case of <bodies moving> in a straight <line> the point above is the terminus for the light <bodies> but the beginning for the heavy <bodies>, and vice versa for the <point> below, precisely the same <is true> in the case of <bodies moving> in a circle as well, even though the same point is used both as a beginning and as a terminus, only in different relations. For it is the beginning[165] of the one <body moving> westwards, and of the other moving eastwards."

How does he explain this? The same point, for instance the east, is the beginning for both the body of the sphere of the fixed stars and of the sphere of the planets. For both <move> *from* the <east> and *towards* the west, only in the case of the sphere of the fixed stars it is the hemisphere above the earth, and in the case of the planetary <sphere> the <hemisphere> beneath the earth. But since Aristotle says[166] 'if one circular movement were contrary to another circular movement, the second one would be purposeless' because <bodies> coming from contrary places and being in conflicting dispositions have the effect that the prevailing <body> cancels the movement of the subordinate one,[167] this man <sc. the Grammarian> objects to this passage, asking why does the same absurdity not follow in the case of <bodies> moving in opposite directions along the straight line as well, i.e. <that the one movement> is purposeless because the other one prevails? Or if they are equal in force they would halt each other and both would be purposeless, given that we take 'purposeless' to mean 'not actualising its own active force'. But this is absurd because neither God nor nature act without purpose.

165. Read *hê arkhê* with MSS A and B.
166. Cf. *de Caelo* 1.4, 271a22f. and 29–33.
167. Literally: 'the overpowered (or conquered) <body>'.

BOOK VI

In the sixth book Philoponus criticises Aristotle's arguments for the eternity of motion and time, *Physics* 8.1. Beginning with a critique of Aristotle's definition of motion and the consequences drawn from it, Philoponus continues with an attempt to establish the possibility of creation *ex nihilo*. He then shows that neither time nor motion are eternal; they must have had a beginning and will have to come to an end.

Prologue Simpl. *in Phys.* 1117,15–1118,11: One of our contemporaries who has become a Telkhin[168] regards slandering mere men as nothing bold and consequently extends his slander to heaven itself and the whole world. He regards the eternity of these things as terrible and entertains certain philosophical misconceptions in an unfortunate and unreasonable manner. He has written five long books against what has been shown <by Aristotle> in *On the Heavens* concerning their[169] eternity. In my exegesis of the first book of the treatise *On the Heavens*, I <sc. Simplicius> have tried to point out that these <writings> are rotten and have stood up only against stupid pupils. His sixth book takes up arms (*anezôsato*) against the eternal motion and eternal time established in this treatise,[170] because if these things remained undisputed it would be wholly necessary that that which is moved eternally with an eternal motion should be itself eternal. For these reasons I thought it right in going through this book to point out to people who are fonder of learning what the objections <he> raises against it are like and from what state of mind they have issued. And I will try to put to the test <his> objections <against Aristotle> by juxtaposing them right here after the exegesis of Aristotle's words.

Fragments 108–113

In *Phys.* 8.1, 251a9f. Aristotle defines motion as the actualisation (*energeia*) of the movable *qua* movable and infers from this definition that the potentially moved object pre-exists the motion in time, 251a10–23. Philoponus objects that this definition does not apply to every kind of movement, for in the case of eternal motion no potentially moved object pre-exists the motion in time. He confronts the Neoplatonists with three unacceptable

168. On the meaning of this term cf. above, n. 28.
169. i.e. the heavens; read *autou* in line 1.
170. i.e. *Physics* 8.

alternatives: (i) either the definition does not apply to all movements; (ii) or if it does, eternal motion will not be eternal because one must conclude that some potentially moved object pre-exists that motion as well; (iii) or, if eternal motion exists, the prior existence of the potentially moved object does not follow from the definition of motion, as Aristotle supposed (fr. 108).

Philoponus then attempts to demonstrate that the third alternative is correct, thereby undermining Aristotle's argument for the eternity of motion. He first re-interprets Aristotle's notion of 'capacity/potentiality' (*dunamis*) as something like 'internal force'. The point is that motion can only take place in the presence of a *dunamis*, and that *dunamis* immediately results in motion (fr. 108), unless some external force (*bia*) prevents it, (see fr. 111). He then shows that this concept of *dunamis* applies to cases of simultaneous generation and motion of elementary bodies. In consequence, it is not universally true that the potentially moved pre-exists the motion in time (fr. 109). If this were true, any motion would be natural for any body, which is absurd (fr. 110). Therefore Aristotle's definition of motion does not warrant the conclusion that motion must be eternal (fr. 112–113).

108 Simpl. *in Phys.* 1129,28–1131,7: Now since this Grammarian has heaped a lot of dirt not so much on the <Aristotelian proofs> 1130, 1
but on thoughtless men, let us invoke the <river> Alphëus together with Herakles, so that we may clean the dirt out, to the best of our ability, from the minds of those who have accepted it. Having set forth Aristotle's argument and the complete exegesis of Alexander <of Aphrodisias>, and having added Themistius' paraphrase as well in order that his work, having become more voluminous, may terrify any ignoramus by sheer volume, he adduces in the following his own objections to the proposition,[171] the first <of which> runs as follows. He says:

"When Aristotle defined motion as the actuality[172] of the movable *qua* movable, he covered by this definition (*horismos*) all motion in general, yet he assumes that some motions are eternal whereas others possess a beginning and an end. Now, what are his grounds for assuming as a consequence of the definition of motion that the things that are going to be moved necessarily pre-exist in time the non-eternal motion, which possesses a beginning of existence, as things that possess only the capacity (*dunamis*) of motion without the actualisation (*energeia*)?"

171. The proposition referred to is the definition of motion as the actuality of the movable *qua* movable in *Phys.* 8.1, 251a9f.

172. Philoponus here follows the MS tradition according to which *Phys.* 8.1, 251a9f. defines motion as *entelekheia tou kinêtou hêi kinêtou* (in agreement with *Phys.* 3.1, 201a27–29), instead of *energeia* . . . etc.

That this is not true <the Grammarian> attempts to prove in the following way:

"Every definition", he says, "is predicated of all things defined with equal validity (*isotimôs*),"[173] and he lengthens <his> argument at this point with examples. "In consequence," he says, "the definition of motion applies equally (*homoiôs epharmottei*) to beginningless motion – if there is such a thing – and to <motion> which possesses a beginning. Then, if it follows from the definition that in the case of non-eternal <motion> the moved object must pre-exist the motion in time, the same will follow in the case of eternal <motion> too. If this is true the definition is necessarily either (i) not valid (*mê alêtheuein*) in the case of eternal motion, despite the fact that it was presented as a general <definition>, which is paradoxical. Or (ii) if it were true also in the case of <eternal motion> that the moved object pre-exists the motion in time – so that too the substance of the heavens pre-exists the circular motion in time – <and if> none of the things that possess something pre-existing in time before them is eternal, then eternal motion in this sense will not be eternal, and the argument has turned the tables on itself (*autôi peritetraptai*). Or (iii), in case they[174] want motion to be eternal, <then> it is not true that it necessarily follows from the definition of motion that the movable pre-exists the motion in time. For in the case of eternal motion it does not pre-exist."

Then he endeavours to show next that when Aristotle gave the definition of motion he did not have the same idea (*ennoia*) of the potential (*to dunamei*), <i.e.> as something that can be separated from the actualisation (*energeia*), that is to say, the motion; but <his idea was> that motion exists as long as the potential is present (*heôs enesti to dunamei*), and that the potential exists as long as
1131, 1 there is motion. For when the motion stops whenever the moved object has reached its completion (*telos*), then the potential stops as well. And in support <of this> he cites a passage from Aristotle which says:[175] 'But when there *is* a house, there is no longer something buildable, but the buildable is built.' In addition, he relies on

173. At 1133,7–9 Simplicius continues this quotation: '. . . just as the definition of substance is not understood (*noeitai*) in one way in the case of eternal substances, and in a different way in the case of <substances> that are subject to generation and destruction.'

174. Presumably Peripatetic philosophers of Philoponus' time, who, as he says, want to be misled by fallacious reasoning, cf. below 1131,6f.

175. See *Phys.* 3.1, 201b11f.

the commentators[176] on these lines as witnesses <for the claim> that in the present passage Aristotle understood 'capacity' (*dunamis*) as being together with motion and not as <anything> separate from the actualisation, as now all those who want "to be misled by fallacious reasoning (*paralogisasthai*)", he says, use <the term>.

109 Simpl. *in Phys.* 1133,16–1134,29: But <the Grammarian> introduces a second argument <against> what is said by Aristotle; it runs as follows:

"And in the case of motions", he says, "which indisputably possess a beginning and an end of being, if it were shown that some of the things moving in this way are brought into being and possess as an immediate accompaniment (*euthus sunepomenên*) the motion that belongs to them by nature, <then,> I think, it would become entirely evident that the definition will <not>[177] apply to their motion as well. For they are <both> moved and potentially moving, <and> they move in this way while the capacity (*dunamis*) still remains. It is not the case that things <moved> pre-exist the motion in a merely potential state."

So in this way he lays down the challenge and attempts to show that some generable things are no sooner generated than moved with <their> natural motion. And he says that fire, assuming that it is generated in the lower region, at the same time both becomes fire and, concurrently (*sundromon*) with its essence (*ousia*) – possesses upward locomotion. Similarly, the water which precipitates in the clouds: it moves downwards at the same time as it precipitates, given that nothing is going to prevent <it>. Next, as if he is rejecting an objection which says that wood – which is potentially fire – pre-exists the upward motion of fire whenever fire is generated out of wood, he says:

"It was not the wood which possessed the capacity of spatial movement upwards. For the change of wood into fire is generation, and not motion. But the aforementioned definition is not about generation but about motion (i.e. the actuality (*entelekheia*)", he says, "of the movable *qua* movable).[178] Therefore, if locomotion upwards is <in fact> motion and not generation, <and if> the change (*metabolê*) of wood into fire is generation and not motion –

176. Philoponus cited at least Themistius' paraphrase on *Phys.* 3.1, 201b11f., see Simpl. *in Phys.* 1132,26–1133,3.

177. Read *ou* before *epharmosei* in line 20.

178. For lines 1133,31–33 cf. also 1136,26–28.

even though there is no generation without motion – then the upward locomotion of fire was not the actuality of the wood's capacity. For things moving within each species of motion move in such a way that they remain the same substances and are not destroyed, but the wood does not remain wood when it moves upwards. Rather, since it has perished and changed into fire, it does not move <at all> (for how could it, since it has perished and no longer exists?); however, the fire generated out of it <moves>."

Not satisfied with these arguments, he adduces others as well in his attempt to show that it is not wood which possesses the capacity of moving upwards, but fire. From this he thinks to show that it is not true <to say> that what potentially moves pre-exists the motion <in time>, which was the basis for the proof of the eternity of motion.

"For wood", he says, "pre-exists the upward movement of fire because it also pre-exists the fire which is generated out of it. But fire is no sooner fire than <it is> on the move upwards."

By this means, then, he persists in showing that the pre-existing thing, for instance wood, is not the thing which possesses the capacity of moving, but the moving thing itself (for instance the fire which is co-existent with the movement) itself possesses the capacity of moving as well.

"For if someone said", he says, "that locomotion upwards is an actuality (*entelekheia*) of wood, then, first, the actualisation (*energeia*) and motion of contraries will be the same. For wood is heavy, but fire is light. So if the upward movement is the actualisation of fire as well as the <actualisation> of wood having changed into <fire>, then the actualisation and motion of contraries will be the same, and they will be the same not in some other respect[179] but in the respect in which they partake of contraries. And lightness and weight are contraries. But not only that: each of the contrary movements will be an actuality (*entelekheia*) and actualisation (*energeia*) of the same thing,[180] if indeed both downward and upward locomotion are the actuality of wood – the latter being the movement of the fire generated out of it. So if", he says, "wood, as long as it is wood, does in fact not move naturally with a spatial movement upwards, it will not possess the capacity of upward locomotion, and the upward motion of fire is not the actualisation and perfection of <wood>."

179. e.g. visibility.
180. For lines 1134,17–24 cf. also 1137,24–26.

110* Simpl. *in Phys.* 1134,29–33: Next, he adduces yet a third argument against the same <proposition>[181] as follows:

If all elements and the bodies composed of them are capable of changing into one another – either immediately or again by way of other intermediates (for water would change into fire by way of the intermediate air), <then> it will follow that any kind of motion is an entirely natural <motion> both for a light and for a heavy <body>.

111 Simpl. *in Phys.* 1134,33–1135,15: And the fourth <argument>:

"If indeed growth", <the Grammarian> says, "is the actuality of the increasable as such, for instance of flesh, and if bread and wine become flesh when they have undergone a change in the animal, <then> the growth would also be the actualisation and actuality of bread and wine. But this is impossible, for what is fed increases, <and> animals are fed; the food feeds – but it is not fed. Therefore, the growth of flesh is not the actuality of the food whose change produced the flesh. Hence, neither is the upward movement of fire the actualisation and motion of wood, but that whose immediate nature it is to move with such a motion while remaining[182] in its own nature and not being destroyed – that is what we call a potentially movable with that movement. For instance, a human being is capable of walking, not the elements.[183] Also, we say that motion is the actuality of the immediate capacity. So if fire", he says, "and not wood is the potentially movable, and if it is no sooner generated than on the move towards the upper <region>, unless some force prevents it – and similarly the water in the clouds, then it is not true <to say> that in the case of non-eternal motions[184] the potentially movable pre-exists the active motion in time."

112 Simpl. *in Phys.* 1135,28–32: And what do I <sc. Simplicius> reply to this?[185] That this man has clearly been blinded by the contentiousness of his objection.

"For at the moment", he says, "we do not ask whether the things generated are generated out of existing or non-existing things, nor <do we ask> whether there is some kind of primary motion or not;

181. i.e. against Aristotle's definition of motion.
182. Read *menon* with 1138,22.
183. For lines 1135,7–10 cf. 1138,21–24.
184. Read *epi tôn mê aidiôn kinêseôn*.
185. Simplicius is referring to the argument of the previous fragment.

rather <we state> that the proposition assumed on the grounds of the definition of motion[186] is in fact not true."

113 Simpl. *in Phys.* 1140,4–8: In consequence, <the Grammarian> boasts at the end of the argument in vain:[187]

"If it has been shown to be false," he says, "that what is potentially moved pre-exists the motion <in time>, then that which is proved on the basis of this <proposition>," as the Grammarian writes, "<namely> that motion is beginningless, has been disproved as well."

Fragments 114–116

The only way to show that motion is eternal, according to Philoponus, is to show that the principle 'nothing comes to be from nothing' is true (fr. 114). Philoponus therefore attempts to falsify this principle. He first concedes that it may be true in the case of nature, but it is by no means true in the case of God. God, as opposed to nature, is able to create out of nothing by creating both form and matter simultaneously without a process in time (fr. 115). Next he shows that the principle is not even true in the case of nature and art (fr. 116).

114 Simpl. *in Phys.* 1140,11–17: Yet, having spat upon the Aristotelian principles of demonstration (*arkhai tês apodeixeôs*) this man wants us to be introduced to his own method; he says:

"It could only in this way be shown that motion is beginningless, if indeed the well-known axiom, as they call it, of the Physicists is true, <namely> that 'nothing is generated out of what is completely non-existent', but that all things are subject to generation out of something which pre-exists."

And he censures Aristotle for not accepting this proposition in order to infer that motion is without a beginning.

115 Simpl. *in Phys.* 1141,5–30: Nevertheless, since <the Grammarian> – who thinks that the proposition saying that 'nothing is generated out of what is completely non-existent' is easily demonstrated <to be> false – maintains that motion would be eternal only if it were proved true that nothing is generated out of what

186. The definition of motion is 'the actuality of the potential *qua* potential'; the assumed proposition (*axiôma*) is that the movable must pre-exist the motion in time, cf. *Phys.* 8.1, 251a8–16.

187. Simplicius says this after having rejected Philoponus' criticism of Aristotle's definition of motion.

is completely non-existent, let us also examine these subtleties (*adoleskhias*) of his. He remarks that they have been thoroughly explicated by himself in the ninth and the eleventh <book> *Against Proclus*,[188] intimidating us with the numbers of books written against famous men. Even now he expounds <the arguments> at length:

"First," he says, "even if nature produces the things it creates out of what <already> exists because it has its own reality and actualisation (*energeia*) in a substrate, and because <nature> is not able to be or to act in separation from <a substrate>, it is not necessary that God, who has his reality and actualisation separate from all beings, create out of existing things as well. For otherwise he would not be superior to nature.[189] And yet God not only produces the forms (*eidê*) of the things directly generated by him, but is believed to originate and to create even matter itself. For only what is primary is ungenerated and without a cause. So if God gives existence (*huphistêsin*) even to matter, <and if> matter does not need any other matter for existence (for it is the primary substrate of all natural things), then <it is> not <true> that everything which is generated is generated out of what exists.[190] For regardless of whether matter is created by God always or at some time,[191] it will surely not need any other matter because it is itself the first substrate (*to prôton hupokeimenon*) of bodies. Therefore, if the things generated by nature are generated out of existing things, it does not necessarily follow that the things directly generated by God are generated out of existing things as well, given that nature on the one hand needs some time and <a process of> generation in order to create[192] each of the physical objects and that God on the other hand gives existence (*huphistêsin*) to the things directly generated by him without a time lapse and without <a process of> generation, that is to say <without> a gradual forming and shaping of the <objects>. For mere willing suffices for him to give substance to things (*eis tên tôn pragmatôn ousiôsin*)."

116 Simpl. *in Phys.* 1142,1–28: Next he reminds us of yet another proof which is stated in the eleventh <book> of the *contra Proclum*.

188. Cf. *contra Proclum* 9.8ff.; 11.3ff.
189. Cf. also 1145,15f.
190. For lines 1141,19–22 cf. also 1143,27f.
191. i.e. regardless of whether one assumes a continuous divine creation or a single act of creation in the beginning.
192. Read *dêmiourgêsêi* in line 26.

By means of this <proof> he has shown, supposedly, that even the things which are generated by nature as well as by art come into existence out of not-being and perish into not-being.

"For the things created in this way", he says, "are compounds (*sunthetôn ontôn*) of matter and form, and prime matter is not generated or destroyed by nature, nor surely the compound of matter and form taken as a whole (for otherwise it would follow that matter *is* generated and destroyed). It <therefore> remains that only the form is subject to generation and destruction. Now if the colours and the shapes, the irrational and natural capacities (*dunameis*) of the soul[193] and, in general, the corporeal forms (*ta enula eidê*) possess existence over a portion of time (I mean the individual forms (*ta atoma eidê*) in each natural thing, for these are the things subject to generation and destruction), <and> if upon the destruction of the bodies these <corporeal forms> change into complete non-existence, then it is clear that they have also attained existence out of not-being and did not exist in any way before."[194]

Then, in addition, he adduces: "But perhaps this will not be of any use for us against the present hypothesis. For even if the corporeal forms are brought into being from not-being, <it is> still <true that> no natural generation takes place without motion. For generation is always accompanied by motion, so that if there was always generation there was always motion as well. But why <should it be true> that there was always generation? For someone who says that there was always generation says nothing other than that there was always motion. Hence, he commits a *petitio principii* and begs the question."

Then, I <sc. Simplicius> suppose, he adds to this next in a strange way:

"For the things created by God immediately are neither generated out of something pre-existent nor by way of <a process of> generation or a stretch of time. For God brought into existence both matter itself and time simultaneously together with the universe, so that motion did not pre-exist the world <in time>. So from this it is evident that if no argument will show that the world is without a beginning and without an end, <then> it cannot possibly be demonstrated that motion is eternal.[195] Then, since all the propositions from which they concluded that the world is eternal are

193. Philoponus thought the rational soul to be immortal, cf. the proemium to his commentary *in de Anima*.

194. For lines 1142,8–14 cf. also 1146,1–4.

195. For lines 1142,24–26 cf. also 1146,21–23.

refuted, the consequent <proposition> is necessarily refuted as well."

Fragments 117–120

Any motion may be analysed in terms of two relatives, the mover and the moved object. Aristotle argues in *Physics* 8.1, 251b5–10 that if the two have not always been in motion, there must have been a *prior* motion which caused one or the other or both of them to enter into that relationship of mover and moved, thereby making the motion possible. But the same is true again of the *prior* motion, and so on. Hence it is impossible to assume a *first* movement. Philoponus objects that there are things which are related to something else as soon as they come into being. The things related do not necessarily pre-exist the relation (fr. 117–118). Then he raises an objection against his own argument: everything still comes to be by virtue of motion, and it is impossible to assume a first motion. Philoponus replies that God creates out of nothing, and therefore originates motion as well (fr. 119–120).

117 Simpl. *in Phys.* 1147,10–31: For again, in referring backwards <the Grammarian> claims that in his opinion it has been demonstrated that some of the things generated do not pre-exist their natural movement in time – which, as we have learned, he has not demonstrated – and he attempts to demonstrate the same once again, and to refute the Aristotelian proposition which says that in the case of relatives either both or one of them must be in motion in order that they may acquire their relationship.[196]

"For Aristotle took for granted", as this man says, "that the relatives must exist first and then acquire the relationship between them, so that it is not possible for something no sooner to be than to be in a relationship, and concluded in this way that in all cases either both or one of the things must be moved <in order to> acquire the relationship between them."

And again, in citing the Aristotelian passage as well as Alexander's exegesis he attempts to show the same, <i.e.> that the fire which has been generated in the lower region and the water which precipitated in the upper region possess <their> generation and their own movement from the same moment, and it is not the case that the movable nature of the substrate pre-exists <the motion> in time.

"If the natural capacity (*hê phusikê dunamis*) inside it is the motor (*kinêtikon*)," he says, "and if the body underlying this <capacity> is the moved (*kinêton*), and if the moved and the motor are

196. Cf. *Phys.* 8.1, 251b5–10.

relatives and it is necessary that they pre-exist the relation between them in time, as Aristotle says, then fire will not be moved towards the upper region from the moment it exists as fire – provided that it has been generated in the lower region; this seems to be contrary to the evidence. Also in the case of the parts of animals: at the same time as they are formed they acquire the relationship of left and right, and it is not the case that they become parts first and only then acquire the relationship."

118 Simpl. *in Phys.* 1148,19–1149,4: So what did you <sc. the Grammarian> gain by spending so many words in order to show that the relatives do not pre-exist the relationship <in time>, by denouncing (*sukophantein*) Aristotle, and[197] by writing:

"Therefore, it is not true that in all cases relatives, if they do not belong to <the class of> things that are eternal, pre-exist their relationship in time." [23 . . . 29] "For if", he says, "the natural capacity inside fire is the motor, and if the body which underlies the <capacity> is the moved, and if as soon as fire is generated the former moves and the latter is moved, <then it is> not <true to say> that what is capable to move and to be moved pre-exists the motion in time, nor <is it true that> the relatives <pre-exist> the relationship between them <in time>, if mover and moved are indeed relatives."

119 Simpl. *in Phys.* 1150,16–25: Finally he puts forward an objection to himself that even if, in the case of relatives, the things do not always pre-exist the relation <in time>, they still pass into existence by way of motion[198] (for the parts <of animals> came to be because the seed has been moved, and the seed <came to be> because something else had been moved before; similarly also in the case of fire and the other <elements>, so that it is impossible to assume a first motion). Having objected in this way he removes <the objection> again. He says:

"If nature creates out of things which exist, it is not necessary that God does so as well. For if the world did not exist always, it is evident that God created it out of not-being." And <he says> that if <God> produces in the same way as nature, he will not be different from nature, and that he has created the matter of bodies out of not-being; for he certainly did not <create it> out of a substrate.

197. Read *kai graphein* with Diels.
198. i.e. motion in the sense of any kind of change.

120 Simpl. *in Phys.* 1151,8–21: <The Grammarian> says: "Just as, say, this <particular> matter has become fire from some pre-existing fire, and the latter <became fire> from yet another <fire>, <and just as> it is possible to stop ascending at some point at some fire which did not come to be from some other fire when its matter was kindled, but <came to be> due to friction or due to some other cause, but not from fire at any rate, so it is equally not impossible to see the same happening also in the case of the generation of things from one another. Now," he says, "whatever is generated by nature is the result of successive generation, but it is nevertheless possible that they possess a beginning of existence, and that there is some first thing in each kind of case which did not attain generation from some pre-existing similar or dissimilar thing. And <this is true> *a fortiori* in the case of the first elements themselves, for <they> co-existed with the primary formation of the world by God. For the things <composed> of elements, even if they first <came to be> then, have none the less come to be out of the <elements> and <only> in that way. Therefore, as we have already said before, if the world is not shown to possess a beginningless existence in time, neither can motion be shown to be beginningless."

Fragments 121–122*

In *Physics* 8.1, 251b10–28 Aristotle argues that time must be eternal. There are three arguments which Philoponus attempts to refute successively.

First argument: There must always be time because there is always a 'before' and an 'after' to any event, 251b10f. Philoponus replies with two speculative arguments, showing that the locutions 'before' and 'after' do not necessarily indicate the presence of time. First, the intellects of angels and spirits think discursively, i.e. there is a 'before' and 'after' in their thoughts, but they are nevertheless unrelated to time, given that time is the number of motion of bodies. Secondly, God exists over and above time; nevertheless, he has knowledge of the 'before' and 'after' of events in time (fr. 121). Temporal reasoning is due to the limitations of the human intellect; just as God contemplates temporal things atemporally, the human intellect cannot think about atemporal things without reference to time (fr. 122*).

121 Simpl. *in Phys.* 1156,28–1158,29: Thus, what has been said by Aristotle here[199] in a rational and divine manner towards a proof that motion is eternal has received powerful clarity through the

199. i.e. *Phys.* 8.1, 251b19–28. Aristotle argues that time is eternal on the basis of the notion of the 'now'.

commentators. But since the Grammarian, again, attempts to object to these <commentators> too, we shall see how he appears once he is examined closely. Having conceded that motion is in the same position as time as regards eternity, generation and destruction, he fights against the eternity of time and strives contentiously to overturn the arguments which prove it. <These arguments> can be divided into three <kinds>. The first of them was straightforwardly designed as an argument from the 'before' and 'after'. For whoever says that motion is generated does not say anything else than that it did not exist before but does exist after. And whoever says that it is destroyed does not say anything else than that it did exist before but does not exist after. Therefore, if the 'before' and the 'after' are parts of time, there will be time both before and after the motion. But whenever there is time there always is motion as well. In consequence, even before the supposedly first motion there <will> always <be> motion, and after the supposedly last motion there will again be motion. Therefore motion is eternal. In order to challenge this argument this man has presupposed three quasi-axioms for his remarkable proof. First, that time possesses a third <kind of> reality after <physical> bodies – or fourth, as he says, correcting himself later. For body is the first, its kinetic capacity the second, and motion is the third; and thus, in connection with actual movement (*epi têi energêtikêi kinêsei*), time is the number of motion. Secondly, he says that the intellectual substances (*tas noeras ousias*)[200] transcend any <kind of> body both in reality (*têi ousiâi*) and in actualisation (*têi energeiâi*), and he praises Plato and Aristotle and the other philosophers who have proved this. And thirdly:

"As regards the intellect[201] let it be agreed that its conception[202] of intelligible objects (*ta noêta*) has in fact no parts (*amerês*) and no extension (*adiastatos*), and it is not in need of calculation (*sullogismos*)[203] for the apprehension (*katalêpsis*) of an intelligible object as if it proceeded by discursive thought (*dianoiâi*) from proposition to proposition, but <the intellect> either makes contact or does not make contact. Yet again, as regards the actualisation (*energeia*)

200. e.g. the human soul, in particular the intellect. Philoponus would have included in this category spiritual beings such as angels.

201. Read *tou nou* for *tou nun* in line 13.

202. Literally: 'its hitting upon' (*epibolê*). In Epicurus, *epibolê* means the application of the mind to an object of perception.

203. Cf. e.g. Aristotle *Metaph.* 9.10, 1051b27–1052a4. On the problem of non-discursive thought cf. Sorabji, *Time, Creation and the Continuum* (London 1983), 139ff.

of the intellect, let this at least be also agreed that it does not simultaneously possess complete understanding of all the things that exist. For <the intellect> cannot simultaneously think about God as well as an angel, the differences and associations of the souls (*tas tôn psukhôn diaphoras te kai koinônias*), bodies and time and eternity (*aiôn*) and the other things that exist. For this is the characteristic property of the divine thinking, if I may so call it, alone: the indivisible, simultaneous cognition (*gnôsis*) of all things that are, have been and will be. But", <the Grammarian> says, "our present argument is not concerned with the divine intellect, but with the one beneath it, be it either angelic or psychical, or of any other kind. The intellect, then," he says, "which proceeds progressively (*metabatikôs*) from thought to thought does not simultaneously admit of two thoughts together at the same <time>, but it understands one <thought> first, then the second, then the third."

Having presupposed these <propositions> as if they were axioms he adduced the following:

"If the intellect is separated from the relationship to bodies both in reality (*têi ousiâi*) and in actualisation (*têi energeiâi*), <then> it is clear that it is to a still further degree deprived of the movement of bodies as well as of time. So if the intellect *qua* intellect bears no relation to time, <and if> it does not simultaneously possess the understanding of all intelligible objects – but in thinking, say, this intelligible object first, it successively proceeds to another and so forth[204] – there exists therefore in the process of thought of the intellect a thought before and <a thought> after, even though <the intellect> is dissociated from any <kind of> temporal relation. So not everything that is thought or said to be before and after in any sense whatever immediately carries a reference to time. But if time, according to Plato," he says, "came to be together with the heavens: if one destroyed <all physical> bodies, one would also destroy time; yet one would not destroy the intellect. Therefore, if the actualisation of the intellect is progressive, and time did not exist, it is <still> necessary that <the intellect> thinks one <thought> first and the other second. For this," he says, "is its essential property. So not everything spoken of as before and after in any sense whatever immediately carries a reference to time.[205] But if", he says, "one 1158, 1
did not concede that the intellectual substances are independent of

204. For lines 1157,31–34 cf. also 1161,2f.
205. For lines 1157,35–1158,1 cf. also 1161,23–28.

<any> relationship to time, one would at least regard the creator of time as superior to and to be beyond all time. So if God created the heavens directly, he also caused them to move in the way they do.[206] Now, the movement of the celestial <bodies> is irregular. So if one imagined the planets to be in conjunction in the same division of the zodiac,[207] it is evident that each of them will return to the same point in a different time. Therefore, when in completing its circle the moon arrives at the same point in which all <planets> had been together before, God, who arranged this, indubitably knew that the <moon> has completed its circle, but that the other <planets> have not. In consequence, if he knew that one of the stars has completed its circle before, and the other after, there is – as far as the Aristotelian argument is concerned – a 'before' and an 'after' in the divine thoughts as well, and therefore also time. For they will not claim that <God> is ignorant of the things of which he is the immediate creator. And <the 'before and after' is> not only in his thoughts, but also in the <acts of> his will. For when the moon has reached the same point, God indubitably wanted it to do so, but the other <planets> he wanted not to. And when he wanted the sun to stand still, he did not <want>, say, Mercury to do so, or any other <planet>.[208] In consequence, even in the <acts of> God's will there is a first, a second, and a third will – and therefore time. In addition, God possesses knowledge of that which will be. But universals are not <the sort of> things that will be, rather particulars and individuals like Socrates, before he came to be, and Plato. Therefore, if God knows a future event, he knows that it is not yet present. On the other hand, when it is present, he knows that it has become present. And whenever it perishes, he knows that it is past and is no longer existent. In consequence, the cognition (*gnôsis*) in virtue of which he knew that it will be is before the one in virtue of which he knows that it no longer exists. Therefore, if time clearly arises (*emphainetai paruphistamenos*) in direct consequence of the phrase 'before' and 'after', <then> we will not place the creator of time outside the relationship of time."[209]

206. For lines 1158,1–4 cf. also 1162,13–16.

207. This actually happened in May 529 as recorded by Philoponus in *contra Proclum* 579,14–18; cf. Wildberg, 'Prolegomena to the study of Philoponus' *contra Aristotelem*', in Sorabji (ed.), *Philoponus and the Rejection of Aristotelian Science*, 201.

208. Cf. Joshua 10:12f.: ' "Sun, stand thou still upon Gibeon; and thou, Moon, in the Valley of Aijalon"; and the sun stood still, and the moon stayed.'

209. For lines 1158,23–29 cf. also 1162,22–26.

122* Simpl. *in Phys.* 1158,29–1159,7: Having said this[210] <the Grammarian> attempts to prove next by means of many <sentences> that we are using temporal words because we are incapable of either thinking or expressing things which are over and above time. For in the same way as God thinks temporal things atemporally, we <think> the things that are over and above time temporally. So if we say 'time did not exist always' or 'it did not exist before it was generated', or <if> we use some other phrase that expresses a temporal notion, it is not immediately necessary that time is also implied (*sunepinoeisthai*) by the phrases, but only that time did not exist always.[211] For <the fact> that temporal phrases do not always signify time however they are used he says to have demonstrated in the fifth <book> of the *contra Proclum.*[212] And he asks the readers to pick out the arguments on this from there, so that – as the Grammarian says – he may avoid repetition (in which he has excessively rejoiced). Most of these sentences[213] I <sc. Simplicius> have cited directly because I fear that many will disbelieve that someone has dared to think and write such things in order to refute the masters of the philosophers.

Fragments 123–124

In a second argument Aristotle supports his claim that time is eternal by a reference to the fact that almost all Physicists are of the same opinion, *Physics* 8.1, 251b14–19. Philoponus replies that the truth is not found by democratic means; if it were, Aristotle's notions of aether and the eternity of the present cosmos, for instance, would have to be rejected immediately. He regards Plato as more consistent and trustworthy a thinker than the Physicists whose mere assertions ought not to be followed.

123 Simpl. *in Phys.* 1164,7–30: Listen to how this man <sc. the Grammarian> chose to object again to the second of Aristotle's arguments which argues for time being eternal on the grounds that all Physicists except one – Plato – evidently agree unanimously on the eternity of time, and that <time> is ungenerated.[214] And so <the Grammarian> says first:

210. i.e. the arguments of the previous fragment.

211. For lines 1158,32–35 cf. also 1163,26–28: 'For many temporal phrases (*lexeis khronikai*)' <the Grammarian> says, 'do not indicate time in all cases, but the phrase only means that time does not exist always.'

212. Cf. *contra Proclum*, 5.2–4.

213. This again refers to the arguments of the previous fragment.

214. Cf. *Phys.* 8.1, 251b14–19.

"Although the <Physicists> except Plato – perhaps five or ten men – agree with each other in saying that time is ungenerated, it is inappropriate to prefer these <men> to Plato simply because of this. For the truth must not be judged by the number of <men> having made assertions; for in this way, at any rate, Aristotle, who alone introduces the fifth substance of body, will receive the inferior vote because all or at least most <Physicists> say that the four elements, either all or some of them, <are> the principles of the world. In general, if one ought to follow the number of Physicists, how <is it possible> that – as <Aristotle> says in the first <book> of the *de Caelo*[215] – they all say that the world is generated, but he himself proves it to be ungenerated? Thirdly, if one ought to trust those who are consistent with themselves rather than those who are inconsistent, <and if> Plato says more consistently:[216] 'Time, then, came into existence along with the heavens', whereas the others say on the one hand that the world is generated, but on the other hand that time is ungenerated, despite the fact that neither of them possesses a separate reality from the other, <then> one must rather believe Plato who says that time too came into existence together with the world. Further," he says, "if in all the other physical <treatises Aristotle> has shown that the other Physicists missed the truth by far, how will we recognise that their testimony on time being ungenerated is trustworthy?"

And in addition to these <arguments> he claims that he is able to show that a larger number and more ancient <Physicists>, who are for many reasons trustworthy as well, have opposed those who said that time is ungenerated.

124 Simpl. *in Phys.* 1164,39–1165,3: But this Grammarian does
1165, 1 not recognise this as the aim of the arguments[217] since he objects to the evidence as if it were demonstrative:

"There is no need", he says, "to follow their undemonstrated assertions in the manner of irrational <creatures>."

215. Cf. *de Caelo* 1.10, 279b12ff.

216. Cf. *Timaeus* 38B6.

217. i.e. Aristotle's arguments attacked by Philoponus in the previous fragment. The aim Simplicius sees in these arguments is (i) to show that the Presocratics held the same opinion, and (ii) to offer an argument of persuasion in addition to the proof, cf. 1164,31–36.

Fragments 125–126

Aristotle's third argument runs as follows: Time cannot be or be conceived without the ‘now’. The ‘now’ is a mean, i.e. mid-point, between the past and the future; since there always was and will be time on either side of the now, time must be eternal, *Physics* 8.1, 251b19–28. Philoponus accuses Aristotle of *petitio principii:* the assumption that the ‘now’ is a mean of time is equivalent to the conclusion that time is eternal.

125 Simpl. *in Phys.* 1166,32–1167,16: The third of the Aristotelian arguments says:[218] ‘If it is impossible for time to be and to be conceived without the ‘now’ because one cannot take anything except the ‘now’ in time, and if the ‘now’ is a mean possessing the beginning of the future and the end of the past, <then> it is necessary that time exist always; but if time <exists>, it is evident that motion necessarily exists as well, if indeed time is a certain attribute of motion.’ Against this <argument the Grammarian> starts by saying:

“Astonishment comes over me at the Philosopher's <sc. Aristotle's> not realising that he had proved nothing but had begged the question. For the question <was> whether time was one of the things which existed always; in order to prove this <proposition> he used the axiom that the ‘now’ is a mean of time. However, this is the same as to assume that time is eternal, just as if someone who asked whether a line stretched to the maximum distance so that its limits are not visible was limited or unlimited, were to assume that every point on the line in question was a mean of <that> line. For if this <is the case>, then there is a line before and after any given point, and if this <is the case>, the line in question is unlimited. So just as, in this example, someone assuming that there is a line on either <side> of every point on the line in question assumes nothing else than that the line is unlimited – and has <therefore> included the question itself in the premise of the syllogism – in the same way, someone who wants to show that time is eternal and then assumes as an axiom and premise that time exists on either <side> of the ‘now’, has assumed the question itself, <i.e.> that time is without a beginning and without an end.”

126 Simpl. *in Phys.* 1168,34–1169,5: But as it seems, this man demolishes in his mind even the usual meanings of words when he wants to infer his own hypothesis:

218. Cf. *Phys.* 8.1, 251b19–28; Simplicius gives an abridged version of the argument.

"And it is not <possible>," <the Grammarian> says, "to show that the 'now' is a mean of time without having demonstrated before that time is eternal."

However, if demonstrations must be <based> on what is more evident, (and if the 'now' being a mean is more evident than time being eternal – for who does not know, even if he is not a gram-
1169, 1 marian, that the present time is a mean between past and future?), <then> Aristotle has rightly demonstrated the eternity <of time> on the basis of the <assumption that> the 'now' is a mean.

"But since," <the Grammarian> says, "time co-exists together with the heavens and the world, and since none of the arguments to show that the world is eternal have remained unrefuted, the assumption of the eternity of time will <therefore> surely have been refuted as well."

Fragments 127–131

Aristotle states that it is equally impossible to assume a last motion, *Physics* 8.1, 251b28–252a5. A movable object does not cease to exist at the same time as its motion ceases, and a destructive agent will itself be subject to destruction after it has destroyed. Therefore motion never ceases.

Philoponus objects that Aristotle's assumption is incorrect. There are things which both cease to move and cease to exist at the same time (fr. 128). In addition, there is, just as in the case of sudden generation, sudden destruction as well, so that it is not true that everything destroyed is destroyed by motion (fr. 129). Philoponus finally objects that not all things are destroyed by a destructive agent from the outside; rather, their natural capacity (*dunamis*) gradually decays until they perish eventually (fr. 130). There follows an argument against Alexander of Aphrodisias (fr. 131).

127 Simpl. *in Phys.* 1171,30–33: Then the Grammarian arrogantly says in the following:

"If the Philosopher <sc. Aristotle> establishes that motion is imperishable on the same grounds as he used to try to prove that it was ungenerated, then we have called to account the present <propositions> by the same <arguments> by which we have dissolved the other propositions too."

128 Simpl. *in Phys.* 1172,2–13: But since <the Grammarian> does not hesitate to use hereafter even more trivial arguments in abundance – just as if he had won the first bout[219] – let us examine these <arguments> too after we have cited <them>:

219. Simplicius is alluding to the sport of wrestling.

"For in the case of things whose being resides in their moving," he says, "or generally all things whose natural motion preserves and completes <their> being, <when> these things cease to move they cease to exist as well. <The> heart, at any rate, <the> arteries and <the> lungs, together with the cessation of motion, stop having the capacity to move and, more than that, stop even being the very thing they are said to be, and this applies to each of the other parts of the animal. And fire," he says, "which is in motion so long as it exists, stops being fire when it stops moving. It is therefore not necessary that after any hypothetical cessation of the last motion there <always> remains a further motion after the last one."

129 Simpl. *in Phys.* 1172,39–1173,15: But let us consider the following argument, which seems to be even more contrived than the former.

"Yet, even if it is true", <the Grammarian> says, "that after the 1173, 1
cessation of motion there remains something which possesses the capacity of being moved, <then> the Philosopher <sc. Aristotle> does not argue what follows correctly. For if not all things generated are generated by motion, but <if> there exists – according to Aristotle – sudden generation without motion and temporal duration, <then> there will be destruction of this kind as well, such as the arrival and retreat of complete forms in substrates, and such as points being generated in uniting, and as contacts and lightning and the apprehension of visual perception.[220] Therefore, not everything destroyed is destroyed by motion."

In consequence <the Grammarian> would say (for I think he left the argument inconclusive) that although that which destroys is destroyed, <it is> not always destroyed by motion.

"And if God," he says, "the creator, creates the heavens and the world, which are directly created by him without any stretch of time, whenever he wants the world to perish, the destruction of the world will involve no time either."[221]

He said these things because he wants <to show> that not everything destroyed is destroyed by motion.

130 Simpl. *in Phys.* 1175,11–26: Following next he objects, confusedly as I <sc. Simplicius> believe, to Aristotle who said: 'And the

220. On the problem of instant generation in Aristotle cf. Sorabji, *Time, Creation and the Continuum*, 11 n. 5.

221. For lines 1173,11–13 cf. also 1174,35f.

destructive agent will have to be destroyed once it has destroyed.'[222] <He also objects> to Alexander who said: '<Aristotle> assumed the destructive agent of something to be itself destructible as well, perhaps because destruction takes place either through the contrary or through the same',[223] and <who also said> that the destructive agent will either be moved again if it is to remain eternal, or will be destroyed if it is to be destroyed by motion. Objecting, then, to this <the Grammarian> claims to have shown in the fourth section[224] that the things generated are neither always generated out of a contrary, nor do the things destroyed <always> change into what is contrary to them, and that they do not submit to destruction because of a contrary since there is no contrary to everything generated and destroyed. Rather, there are things which are destroyed and do not possess an external cause of destruction but come to ruin because that which has been measured out as their natural capacity gradually decays in time, even though there was nothing external which ruined them.[225]

"It was therefore not necessary", <the Grammarian> says, "to ask in all cases where things perish if the cause of destruction possessing the capacity to destroy remains after the destroying, and whether this <cause> is eternal or perishable, and in this way to carry the absurdity to infinity by a sorites."[226]

131 Simpl. *in Phys.* 1177,10–26: But Alexander said that the things destroyed are destroyed by other things in motion – evidently the destructive agents (for Aristotle said so as well) – and if these are imperishable they will be moved again, but if <they are> perishable <then> in this way too there will be a <motion> after the last motion, namely, the motion generated in connection with their destruction. This man <sc. the Grammarian> does not understand, thinking that not the destructive agents but the things destroyed are said here by Alexander to be moved.

"Take for example the elements", he <sc. the Grammarian> says: "Because they are perishable they are also destroyed again when other things move, say matter and form; but matter, which is not

222. See *Phys.* 8.1, 252a1f.

223. Cf. also above 1171,10f. where the examples given are decay (*maransis*) and extinction (*sbesis*).

224. i.e. *contra Aristotelem* IV; cf. fr. IV/67–69.

225. For lines 1175,20–23 cf. also 1176,14–16.

226. Aristotle's argument by infinite regress relies on several implicit premises; Philoponus therefore regards it as a sorites (or heap) argument.

destroyed together with the things, remains <and> possesses the capacity to be moved."

He thus misunderstood <the sentence> and did not listen to Aristotle who said: 'And the destructive agent will have to be destroyed once it has destroyed, and that which is the destructive agent of it <will have to be destroyed> in turn later.'[227] <The Grammarian> repeatedly claims to have solved this impasse (*aporia*):

"For even if nature", he says, "does not make prime matter (*tên prôtên hulên*),[227a] God makes it, <and> not out of matter. In consequence, whenever <God> wants, he destroys <matter> into not-being, from which it came to be, just as form does not change into another form but turns back into complete not-being from which it came to be as well."

Fragment 132

After having refuted Aristotle's arguments for the eternity of motion and time, Philoponus finally adduces a remarkable proof showing that motion, and therefore time, must have been generated. Philoponus assumes three propositions, first, that everything generated needs something out of which it is generated; secondly, that it is impossible either to traverse or to increase the infinite; and thirdly, that something would not be generated if an infinite number of things were needed before it could be generated. As things are evidently generated now, it follows that the past process of successive generation must be finite. By implication, it is impossible that the movement of the heavens – which is the cause of generation and destruction – is eternal, which Philoponus also shows by an independent argument: it is impossible that the revolutions of any one of the planets should be infinite because this would involve multiplication of the infinite.

132 Simpl. *in Phys.* 1177,38–1179,26: Having said this,[228] he claims that he will show that the world does not change into absolute nothingness but into something different, greater and more divine.[229] And it is remarkable that on the one hand he 1178, 1
believes that the destruction of the world is a change into something which is and is more divine, yet on the other hand says that the generation <of the world> did not take place from what existed. He declares that this world changes into another world which is more divine – a <proposition> he elaborates in the following

227. See *Phys.* 8.1, 252a1f.
227a. On prime matter see above, n. 95a.
228. The reference is to the argument of the previous fragment.
229. Cf. also below, fr. VIII/134.

books[230] – not realising that this is not a destruction of the world but a perfecting. In concluding the arguments against the propositions which show motion to be ungenerated and indestructible he says that he has refuted them sufficiently – by this rotten chatter of his. And as if he has refuted these <propositions>, he even dares to demonstrate – according to himself – that it is impossible that motion should be ungenerated. For this proof he assumes three axioms beforehand: one <axiom is> that if in order to be generated, each of the things generated necessarily needs something which pre-exists, as for instance a ship <needs> wood, <then> it will not be generated if those things have not been generated before. The second <axiom> is that it is impossible for an infinite number to exist in actuality (*energeiâi*), or for anyone to traverse (*diexelthein*) the infinite in counting, and that it is also impossible that <anything> should be greater than the infinite, or that the infinite should be increased. The third one is: If it were necessary for the generation of something that an infinite <set of things> should pre-exist, one generated out of another, <then> it would be impossible for that thing to be generated.[231]

"For Aristotle himself", he says, "showed from this in the *de Generatione <et Corruptione>*[232] that it is impossible that the elements of bodies should be infinite in number,[233] if indeed one is generated out of the other. For the infinite cannot be traversed (*to apeiron adiexitêton*), so that fire, for example, would not be generated if it were generated <only> after an infinite <number of things> had been generated before. Let these <axioms>", he says, "be granted beforehand; now if the particular motion of this fire possesses a beginning of existence and an end, and if in order that this <motion> might be generated, another motion had to be generated first as a prerequisite for the generation of the body of the fire, from, say, air that was undergoing change, and again, if there was another motion before the motion of the air which changed into fire, <say> the <motion> of water in virtue of which the <water> changed into air, and if before this <motion> there was another one and so on *ad infinitum* – provided that neither the world nor the change of things into one another possessed a beginning, it was, then, necessary that an infinite <number of> motions existed first, in order that this particular fire might be

230. The treatise *contra Aristotelem* consisted of more than six books.
231. For lines 1178,14f. cf. also 1180,33–36.
232. Cf. *GC* 2.5, 332b30ff.
233. Omit *kai* in line 17 with editio Aldina.

generated. For it would not have been generated unless an infinite <number of motions> existed first, because of the first axiom," so he says. "Now if it is impossible for an infinite <number of> motions to have come to be in actuality (*kat' energeian*) because of the second axiom, it will then not have been possible for the motion of the particular fire to exist, both because of this and because of the third axiom, which says that that thing will not be generated for the generation of which[234] an infinite <number of things> must pre-exist. If, then, the motion of the particular fire came to be, an infinite <number> of motions surely did not exist first – according to the necessity of the conversion with negation (*sun antithesei antistrophê*)."[235]

(So he says, though ignorant of what conversion with negation is, as I <sc. Simplicius> have shown, I think, when I examined what he said against the first <book> of the *de Caelo*.)[236]

"So if nature", he says, "went through a limited <number of> motions in order to create the motion of the particular fire, there exists therefore some first motion which was not preceded by <any> 1179, 1 other <motion>. And the same account <applies> in the case of the other individual motions, and this is in agreement with the physical account (*phusikos logos*). For complete things are <prior> to incomplete, and actual prior to potential. So if on the one hand the ascent (*anodos*) took place *ad infinitum*, complete things would not precede the incomplete, and the actual not the potential; but if on the other hand <the motions> are limited <in number>, then the first <motion>, which evidently exists together with the universe, has made a beginning which starts from something actual[237] and complete for the subsequent motions. But if there is some beginning", he says, "of the particular motions, and if it is not possible to conceive of one motion before the other *ad infinitum*, then it is necessary that the circular motion of the things in heaven, too, had a beginning <and> did not exist before. For it is impossible both that the heavens move always in this way and that the generable and destructible things inside do not have their being in being generated and destroyed."[238]

As a fourth point he also adds this: "If the <motions> that will

234. Read *hou* in line 32.
235. i.e. transposition, cf. above, n. 4.
236. Cf. above fr. I/4 and Simplicius' criticism at *in de Caelo* 28,12–30,26.
237. Read *tou energeiâi* in line 6.
238. i.e. it belongs to the essence of sublunary things to be generated and destroyed.

be generated increase the number of the motions that have been generated when they are added to the latter, and if it is impossible to increase the infinite, <then> the motions that have been generated before will surely not be infinite <in number>."

And fifthly: "If the spheres", he says, "do not move with equal periods of revolution[239] but the one <revolves once> in thirty years,[240] another in twelve <years>[241] and another in turn in an even smaller length of time, so that the <sphere> of the moon <revolves once> within a month and the sphere of the fixed stars within a day, and if the motion of the heavens is without a beginning, <then> it is necessary that the sphere of Saturn has rotated with an infinite <number of> revolutions, but the <sphere> of Jupiter with nearly three times more <revolutions> than that. The <revolutions> of the sun will be thirty times greater <in number> than the ones of Saturn, the <revolutions> of the moon 360 times, and the <revolutions> of the sphere of the fixed stars more than ten thousand times greater. But how, if it is not <even> possible to traverse the infinite once, is it not beyond all absurdity to assume ten thousand times the infinite, or rather the infinite an infinite number of times? In consequence, it is necessary", he says, "that the circular motion of the heavens did not exist before <but> had a beginning of existence, <i.e.> at the same time as the heavens themselves" (as this man says, for this is not my argument) "began to exist."

133* Simpl. *in Phys.* 1182,28–36: Let this, then, be said against the sixth book of the Grammarian which attempted to deny the eternity of motion in order that the world might not be proved to be eternal on the grounds of <motion>. The single aim he proposed <is that> people who unfortunately listen to him should think that God is not unchangeable nor the world eternal. But having proceeded as far as what has been discussed he thought that the objection to the eternity of motion was, for him, complete. Even in this, he was unable to realise that the most important <arguments> for the proof are provided in the following, where Aristotle shows that of the things that exist some are immovable, others are always in motion, and <a third group> is sometimes in motion and sometimes at rest.

239. Literally: 'do not move regularly (*isokhronôs*)'.
240. i.e. Saturn.
241. i.e. Jupiter.

* * *

No fragments of the seventh book of the *contra Aristotelem* are known to be extant.

* * *

BOOK VIII

134 Brit. Mus. MS Add. 17 214, fol. 72vb,36–73ra,19: The title of the second chapter[242] of the eighth book[243] of John the Grammarian's *contra Aristotelem*:

"Our argument affirms that that which is subject to resolution into not-being is not wicked on its own and by itself, and that that into which the world will be resolved is not not-being."

From the second chapter: "However, the world will not be resolved into not-being, because the words of God are not resolved[244] into not-being either, and we clearly speak of new heavens and a new earth."[245]

242. *qpl'wn* is the Greek word *kephalaion*.

243. *m'mr':* 'discourse, sermon, homily; treatise, division of a book', is a greater unit than *qpl'wn*. In agreement with the translation of the Greek *biblios*, cf. Simpl. *in de Caelo* 75,16f. (fr. II/47), it is best translated 'book'.

244. Lacuna, read *ms<tryn>*.

245. Cf. Isaiah 65:17; 66:22; Revelation 21:1.

Indexes

There are four indexes to this volume: an English-Greek Glossary, a Greek-English Index, a Subject Index and an Index Locorum.

The Glossary lists key terms used in the English Translation and supplies the Greek words which they represent. This will incidentally help the reader to locate entries in the Greek-English Index.

The Greek-English Index is the most comprehensive. It lists key Greek terms and their uses, giving nearly all occurrences, and includes proper names. Each Greek word is followed by an explanation in English, which is not always a translation.

The Subject Index lists topics of particular interest, and cites only the most informative of the passages which refer to those topics. Further messages will normally be found in the Greek-English Index, under the corresponding Greek expression, which is listed in the Subject Index immediately after the Subject. In a few cases, however, the standard Greek expression is not used in the main text, and in those cases it will not be found in the Greek-English Index. The Subject Index includes references to the Arabic and Syriac fragments.

The Index Locorum lists all passages of all ancient authors referred to in the Introductions and in the Translation.

English-Greek Glossary

abstraction: *aphairesis*
absurd: *atopos*
actualisation: *energeia*
actuality: *entelekheia*
affirmation: *kataphasis*
air: *aêr*
alteration: *alloiôsis*
apprehension: *katalêpsis*
argument: *epikheirêma, logos*
attribute: *sumbebêkos*
axiom: *axiôma*

beginning (see also principle): *arkhê*
being (see also substance): *on, ousia*
body: *sôma*
boundary (see also end, limit, terminus): *peras*

capacity (see also force, potentiality): *dunamis*
cause: *aitia, aition*
celestial body: *to ouranion sôma*
centre: *kentron, meson*
change: *kinêsis, metabolê*
circle: *kuklos*
circular motion: *kuklophoria*

circumference: *periphereia*
commentator: *exêgêtês*
common ideas: *koinai ennoiai*
completion (see also perfection): *teleiôsis, telos*
concave: *koilos*
conception: *ennoia*
condensation: *puknôsis*
contiguous: *plêsiazos*
continuous: *sunekhês*
contrary: *enantion*
conversion: *antistrophê*
convex: *kurtos*
counternatural: *para phusin*
creation: *dêmiourgêma*
creator (see also god): *dêmiourgos*

deficiency: *elleipsis*
definition: *horismos, logos*
demonstration (see also distance, remoteness): *apodeixis*
destruction (see also perish): *phthora*
determinate: *hôrismenos*
diameter: *diametros*
difference: *diaphora*
dimension (see also distance, remoteness): *diastasis*
diminution: *meiôsis*
discursive thought: *dianoia*
distance (see also dimension, remoteness): *diastasis, diastêma*
down: *katô*

element: *stoicheion*
  first/fifth element: *prôton/pempton sôma*
end (see also boundary, limit, terminus): *peras*
essence (see also reality, substance): *ousia*
eternal: *aidios*
eternity: *aidiotês, to aiôn*
example: *paradeigma*
excess: *huperbolê*
exegesis: *exêgêsis*

fire: *pur*
firesphere: *hupekkauma*
fitness (see also suitability): *epitêdeiotês*
flame: *phlox*
force (see also capacity, potentiality): *bia, dunamis*
form (see also shape): *eidos, skhêma*

genus: *genos*
god (see also creator): *theos*

heaven, the heavens: *ouranos, ta ourania*
heavy: *barus*
hemisphere: *hêmisphairion*
hypothesis: *hupothesis*

ignorance: *agnoia*
immediate: *amesos*
immobility: *akinêsia*
impasse: *aporia*
impossible: *adunatos*
inclination (see also momentum): *rhopê*
incomplete: *atelês*
incorporeal: *asômatos*
increase: *auxêsis, auxanein*
indefinite: *aöristos*
indestructible: *aphthartos*
individual: *atomos*
infinite: *apeiros*
instantaneous: *exaiphnês*
intellect: *nous*
intelligible object: *noêton*

judgment: *gnôsis*

length: *mêkos*
light (as opposed to heavy): *kouphos*
light (i.e. illumination): *phôs*
limit (see also boundary, end, terminus): *peras*
line: *grammê*
locomotion: *phora*
lower region: *to katô*

magnitude: *megethos*
matter: *hulê*
  prime matter: *prôtê hulê*
mind: *nous*
momentum (see also inclination): *rhopê*
moon: *selênê*
motion, movement: *kinêsis*

natural: *kata phusin, phusei*
nature: *phusis*
necessary: *anankê, anankaios*
negation: *apophasis*
not-being: *mê on*

objection: *antilogia, enstasis*
opposite: *antikeimenon*

Greek-English Index

References are to the marginal numbers in this volume; unless otherwise stated, page numbers 25–199 refer to Simplicius *in de Caelo* (CAG VII), page numbers 1117–1182 to Simplicius *in Physica* (CAG X). Fragment numbers are given in parentheses after the page and line numbers.

178,16.21 (93); 180,13 (94); 194,16 (105); 1135,3 (111); 1142,26 (116); 1151,12 (120); 1166,32f.(125); 1178,8.12.14.16.29 (132)
see also 58,15 (35)

aêr, air
generates living beings by putrefaction, 124,5 (67)
is light, 74,19 (46)
its qualities, 123,34–124,7 passim (67)
its relation to the firesphere, 83,25–28 (54)
moves downwards, 158,14 (82)
moves in a circle, 34,8 (9); 37,28 (17*); 89,11f.(59); 163,28 (84); 164,24 (85)
moves upwards, 26,37 (1*); S.Seth 41,13 (2*); 158,14 (82)
moves with a composite motion, 36,12 (14)
moves with a simple motion, 37,3 (16); 37,22 (17*)
transparent, 89,1 (59)
yields, 75,32 (47)
see also 83,32.34; 84,1 (55); 124,4 (67); 126,14 (68); 171,22 (88); 172,35.36 (89); 1134,32 (110*); 1178,22–25 (132)

agenêsia, uncreatedness, of the world, 139,24 (77*)
agenêtos: meaning of, 119,13–120,12 passim (63)
of the heavens, 119,10.14.17.28; 120,8 (63); 142,10 (80); 156,29 (81)
of matter, 1141,19 (115)
of motion, 1178,5.9 (132)
of souls, 123,18 (67)
of time, 1164,9f.23–30 (123)
of the world, 119,17.28 (63); 136,13 (73)
ta agenêta, 172,31.33 (89)

agnoia, ignorance, of Philoponus, 126, 6.12 (68); 165,13 (86); 177,19 (92)
see also 171,23 (88)
agnoein, of Philoponus, 166,13 (86); 170,28 (87); 173,30 (90); 181,16 (95); 185,13 (98); 194,18 (105)

aïdios (see also *anarkhos*), eternal, of circular motion, 43,8 (20); 1156,29 (121)
of motion and time, 1118,5–7 (Prologue VI); 1130,9 (108); 1141,7 (115); 1167,4.13 (125); 1168,37.39; 1169,2 (126)
of the world, 1169,4 (126)
see also 1175,15.25 (130)
aidiotês: of the heavens, 80,24f.(52); of motion and time, 1134,12 (109); 1135,13f.(111); 1156,32.33 (121); 1164,9 (123); 1169,5 (126); 1182,29.33 (133*); of the world, 59,7 (36*); 1117,18; 1118,1 (Prologue VI)

aiôn, eternity, 1157,19 (121)

aisthêsis, sense-perception, 139,26 (77*)
aisthanesthai, 194,24 (105)
aisthêtos (see also under *haptein* and *horatos*), of the heavens, 113,29 (70)

Aithiops, Ethiopian, 157,30 (82)

aitia, aition, cause, reason, 35,31 (13*); 37,7 (16); 46,17 (26); 75,33 (47); 77,23 (48); 79,5 (49); 199,32 (50*); 158,19 (82); 175,19 (91); 177,19 (92); 182,19 (96); 1175,21.24 (130)

akinêsia (see also *kinêsis*), immobility, 122,7 (65)
akinêtos, 1183,36 (133*)

akribês, stringent, of an argument, 176,30 (92)

aktis, sunray, 83,7f.(54)

Alexandros, of Aphrodisias, 32,2 (7); 36,10 (14); 37,12.21 (17*); 42,30 (19); 46,6 (25); 46,31 (27*); 79,13f. (49); 121,12 (64*); 158,30 (82); 170,24.25.27; 171,1.6 (87); 174,11 (90); 176,33 (92); 178,7 (93); 182,19 (96); 185,14.23; 186,6 (98); 186,24 (99); 187,20 (100); 194,8.23 (105); 1130,4 (108); 1147,20 (117); 1175,13 (130); 1177,11.16 (131)

Alkaios, the poet, 156,26 (81)

alloiôsis, alteration, qualitative change, 37,5 (16); 88,1 (57*); 139,5 (75); 158,5.9 (82)
alloiousthai, 79,2 (49)

alogos, irrational, of beings/souls, 123,18.20 (67)

Alpheios, the river, 1130,1 (108)

anaitios, without cause, 1141,19 (115)

anaklasis, reflection, of sunrays, 83,8 (54)

analogia, proportion, 81,23f.(52)

anankê, necessary, necessity
logical, 30,31 (5); 42,28 (19); 56,32

(33); 58,21 (35); 71,5 (39); 75,30 (47); 79,5 (49); 134,13 (71); 158,33 (82); 172,23 (89); 179,31; 180,3 (94); 190,4.24 (102); 192,32; 193,3 (104); 1118,6 (Prologue VI); 1130,12.27 (108); 1141,14.25 (115); 1142,28 (116); 1147,13.25 (117); 1150,22 (119); 1158,34 (122*); 1166, 35.36 (125); 1172,12 (128); 1178,35; 1179,18.24 (132)
necessary condition, 142,16 (80); 170,17 (87); 1178,10.32 (132)
physical, 37,13 (17*); 84,2 (55)
see also 30.28 (5); 156,26 (81); 179,35 (94); 185,3 (98); 194,11 (105)
anankaios, 158,21 (82)
anapaula, rest, 78,24 (49)
anapherestai (see also *anôphoros, phora*), to be moved upwards, 158,20 (82)
anapodeiktos, 163,25 (84)
anarkhos (see also *aidios*), without a beginning, 141,17 (78)
of motion, 1130,17 (108); 1140,7f.(113); 1140,13.17 (114); denied, 1151,21 (120)
of time, 1167,15 (125)
of the world, 1142,25f.(116); 1151,20 (120)
anatolê, ascendent, east, of motion (*ap' anatolôn* = westward), 31,11 (6); 188,13 (101)
see also 82,29 (54); 89,15 (59); 197,4 (107)
aneidos, formless, of matter, 135,29 (72)
anepistasia, thoughtlessness, of Philoponus, 172,36 (81)
anepistatos, 183,34 (97)
anisotakhus, unequal in velocity, of the motion of the celestial bodies, 37,9f.(16); 1158,5 (121)
anô (see also *katô*), up, 26,37 (1*); 32,10 (7); 36,15 (14); 37,14.16.20 (17*); 71,1.5 (39); 71,32 (43); 158,14.17.19 (82); 172,29; 173,10 (89); 175,20 (91); 190,9.10 (101); 192,29 (104); 196,35 (107); 1147,21.27 (117)
ta anô pheromena, 66,18–23 passim (38)
anoêtos (see also *apaideusia*), foolish 25,30.35 (Prologue I); 122,2 (65); 162,33 (83*)
anoia, foolishness, of Philoponus, 46,18 (26); 156,27 (81); 182,18 (96)
see also 164,24 (85)
anôphoros, moving upwards, 66,23 (38)
antereisis (see also *antitupos, hupeikein, sterrotês*), resistance, 78,24 (49)
antikeimenos, opposite
of motion, 57,2 (33); 122,5 (65); 172,29 (89)
of privation, 122,5.8 (65); 131,23; 132,6; 133,23 (69); 134,14 (70)
of qualities, 165,23; 166,1 (86)
see also 123,5 (66); 139,3 (75); 172,31 (89)
antikeisthai, 170,31–34; 171,5.7 (87); 171,21 (88); 173,26.33; 174,11 (90); 177,12 (92); 192,24.27 (104)
antikinêsis (see also *kinêsis, phora*), movement in opposite directions, 179,25 (94)
antikineisthai, 197,11 (107)
antilêpsis, apprehension, of perception, 1173,8 (129)
antiperistasis, reciprocal replacement 76,19 (47)
antiperiistanai, 75,33; 76,11 (47)
antistrophê, conversion, 30,32 (5), 166,13 (86)
antistrephein, 58,6 (34); 163,22 (84); 164,23 (85)
sun antithesei antistrophê, 28,7 (4); 163,18 (84); 1178,34.35 (132)
antithesis, antithesis, 126,8 (68); 131,19 (69); 185,4 (98)
antitithenai, 165,22 (86)
antithetos, 166,3.7.9 (86); 192,5 (103)
antitupos, solid, 76,13 (47); 77,26.27 (48)
aoristos, indefinite, of a straight line, 46,35 (27*); 176,22 (92); 179,25 (94); 183,28 (97)
apaideusia, ignorance, of Philoponus 26.31 (Prologue I)
apaideutos, 26,3 (Prologue I)
apathês (see also *duspathês*), 73,13 (45*)
apeirodunamos, having infinite power, 79,5 (49)
apeiros, unlimited, impossible to increase, 1178, 12–14; 1179,13f.22–24 (132)
of celestial motion, 44,17 (22)

(80); 156,29; 157,22; 158,33 (82); 164,22 (85); 170,17–31 passim; 171,17 (87); 172,25 (89); 179,30 (94); 180,7 (94); 181,23 (95); 183,22 (97); 184,1 (97); 185,27 (98); 186,25.30 (99); 187,28 (101); 189,26; 190,20.27 (102); 194,12.15.17; 195,15 (105); 1118,1.4 (Prologue VI); 1130,29 (108); 1133,18.24; 1134,8.10.11.15 (109); 1142,2.25 (116); 1147,21 (117); 1151,20f.(120); 1168,36; 1169,4 (126); 1175,17 (130); 1177,38; 1178,6.16 (132)

deinos, clever, shrewd, (of Aristotle) 26,25.27 (Prologue I); 170,11 (87)
  deinotês, 170,12 (87)

deixis (see also *apodeixis*), proof, 45,3 (23); 136,17 (73); 1167,3 (125)

dektikos, fit for receiving (e.g. qualities)
  of substance, 158,1.28 (82)
  of the heavens, 174,3 (90); 175,16 (91)

dêlon (and *dêlonoti*), clear, evident, 66,13 (37); 72,15 (44*); 75,28 (47); 199,32 (50*); 83,25 (54); 83,34 (55); 88,13 (58*); 89,25 (59); 119,18 (63); 123,27.30.35; 124,16 (67) 142,23 (80); 178,9 (93); 183,29 (97); 1133,20 (109); 1142,25 (116); 1150,23 (119); 1151,19 (120); 1157,28; 1158,7 (121); 1179,5 (132)
  prodêlon, 67,16 (40*)

dêlôtikon, carrying reference to, 1157,35; 1158,1 (121)

dêmiourgos (see also *theos*), creator, 25,26f. (Prologue I); 1173,11 (129)
  creates immediately, 1173,11f.(129)
  of time, 1158,3.29 (121)
  outside any relation to time, 1158,29 (121)
  dêmiourgein, of God, 1141,16.18.26 (115); 1150,22.23 (119); 1158,4 (121)
  dêmiourgêma, 90,21 (60*); 1141,17 (115); 1142,22 (116)

diairêsis, distinction, division, 119,15 (63); 165,15 (86)
  diairein, 47,30 (29*); 188,11.12 (101)

diallêlos, circular (of a proof); 45,2.7 (23)

dialuein (see also *apelenkhein, dielenkhein, elenkhein, lusis*), to refute, 26,15 (Prologue I); 136,18 (73); 1171,33 (127)

diametros (sc. *grammê*), diameter
  of a circle, 180,16.18.21 (94); 182,14 (96); 185,5.6.20; 186,4 (98); 188,20 (101); 190,1.21 (102)
  of the universe, 46,31 (27*); 178,18.21 (93)

dianoia, (discursive) thought, 1157,15 (121)
  dianoeisthai, to think, 78,27 (49)

diaphora, difference
  of place, 70,34 (39); 73,6 (45*)
  of souls, 1157,18f.(121)
  of temperatures in different seasons, 82,5.10 (54)
  differentia, 135,23.24 (72); 166,7 (86)
  diapherein, 31,12.14 (6); 49,1 (32); 89,24 (59); 134,18 (71); 135,21.25 (72); 190,2 (102); 193,6 (104); of God and nature, 1150,24 (119)
  diaphoros, 26,33 (1*); S.Seth 41,4.9f.(2*); 28,1–11 passim (4); 31,9.10 (6); 49,6 (32); 89,3 (59); 178,11 (93); 186,11 (98); 186,29 (99); 190,2 (102); 192,17.18.25 (104); 193,1 (103)

didaskalia, education, teaching, 59,9f. (36*)
  didaskein, of Aristotle, 157,34.35 (82); 165,34 (86)

dielenkhein (see also *apelenkhein, dialuein, elenkhein, lusis*), to refute, 136,16 (73)

dogma, doctrine
  of men, 141,13 (78)
  of the philosophers, 26,11 (Prologue I)

doxa
  belief (in God) 26,8 (Prologue I)
  glory, of God, 90,16 (60*)
  opinion, 139,16 (77*); 177,1 (92)
  reputation, 25,33 (Prologue I)
  dokein, 25,36 (Prologue I); 79,8 (49)

dunamis
  capacity: of the elements, 74,22 (46); 75,19.20 (47); 83,31; 84,2.4 (55); 142,23 (80); immediate, 1135,10 (111); natural capacity decaying in time, 1175,21f.(130); of motion, 1130,13 (108); 1133,22.30; 1134,9.27 (109); 1147,24 (117); 1149,1 (118); 1157,8 (121); 1172,8f.(128); 1173,2 (129);

1175,24f.(130); 1177,19 (131); of the soul, 1142,9f.(116)
Aristotle's conception of according to Philoponus, 1130,20–1131,7 (108)
force, 199,29 (50*)
limited in a limited body, 79,4 (49); 142,23 (80)
dunamei, 46,10 (25); 1130,31 (108); 1133,23.29 (109); 1135,8.11.14f.(111); 1179,3.5 (132)
dunamenon, 1133,21; 34,11.15.17 (119); 1140,6 (113); 1149,1 (118)
dunasthai, 37,17 (17*); 46,30 (27*); 67,10 (40*); 75,20; 76,3 (47); 119,20; 120,11 (63); 163,2 (83*); 177,18 (92); 178,14 (93); 180,4.5 (94); 185,25 (98); 186,27; 187,4 (99); 1134,31 (110*); 1135,1 (111); 1141,14 (115); 1151,21 (120); 1157,20 (121)
dunaton, 164,23 (85); 178,10 (93); 179,26; 180,18 (94); 185,24 (98); 186,5.9 (98); 186,25.29 (99); 194,10 (105); 1178,31 (132)
kata tên dunamin, 26,15 (Prologue I); 188,5 (101)
kata to dunaton, 26,1 (Prologue I); 1130,3f.(108)
dusdiairetos (see also *adiairetos*, difficult to divide, 76,9.13 (47); 77,26 (48)
dusmê, setting, west, of motion (*apo dusmôn* = eastward), 31,11 (6); 188,15 (101)
see also 82,30 (54); 89,15 (59); 197,5 (107)
duspathês, hardly affected, 73,10 (45*)

eidopoiesthai, characterise, 75,19 (47)
eidos, form, shape, species
generated together with the substrate, 137,19 (73)
of contrariety, 192,22.31.32; 193,1 (104)
of created things, 1141,17 (115); 1142,5.6 (116); 1151,16 (120); 1173,5 (129); 1177,18.25 (130)
of an element, 26,36; 27,3 (1*); 67,5 (40*); see also 84,19 (56)
of the heavens, 76,23 (47); 132,5.7.11 (69); 133,22.23.25 (70)
of motion, 1134,4 (109)
of quality, 173,31 (90)
of the soul, 123,18.22 (67)
subject to generation and destruction, 1142,8.11f.(116)
eidos and *sterêsis* as contraries, 121,14 (64*); 122,9 (65); 123,6 (66); 131,19–132,11 passim (69)
eidos kai hulê, 157,35 (82); 165,35–166,9 passim (86)
kat' eidos, 31,9–14 passim (6); 135,23 (72)
atomon eidos, 1142,11 (116)
enulon eidos, 1142,10.16 (116)
ekkentros (see also *homokentros*), eccentric
of spheres, 32,8 (7)
elenkhein, (see also *apelenkhein, dialuein, dielenkhein, lusis*) 136,14 (75); 157,1 (81); 163,26 (84); 170,20 (87); 176,34 (92)
elenkhos, 135,28 (72); 181,17 (95)
eleutheros, free, of bodies from lightness and weight, 76,29 (47)
empsukhos, alive, having a soul
of a body, 91,5 (61*)
of the heavens, 91,6.17 (61*); 1135,4 (111)
enantios, contrary, general, 46,5 (25)
involved in generation and destruction, 119,23 (63); 121,6.12.13 (64*); 123,12–124,17 passim (67); 126,8,15 (68); 131,19–30 passim (69); 156,30 (81); 1175,14–20 passim (130)
no contrary to the heavens, 121, 26.28 (65); 156,31.33; 157.5 (81); cf. 173,13 (89)
no contrary to substance, 123,14 (67); 157,1 (81); 158,27 (82); 165,11–166,11 passim (86); cf. 165,12–27.33 (86); 170,15–34 (87); 171,1; 173,14 (89);
of body, 157,26–159,1 passim (82); 170,15 (87); 173,14 (89); 178,26 (93)
of concave and convex, 174,12 (90)
of form and privation, 122,9 (65); 123,5 (66); 131,32 (69)
of motion, 34,33; 35,5.7f.(11*); 56,31; 57.2.7 (33); 58,10 (34); 58,16f.(35); 121,7; 122,3 (64*); 157,3.6 (81); 157,23–159,1 passim (82); 162,20–163,3 passim (83*); 163,12–20 (84); 164,26 (85); 165,12–33 passim (86); 171,17–32 passim (88); 175,21 (91); 176,16.17.24; 177,6–8.19

(92); 178,8–25 passim (93); 181,23.24 (95); 182,17 (96); 185,8.15–21 (98); 188,1.12–25 (101); 192,5–14 (103); 192,28–193,12 (104); 194,11–30 passim (105); 195,16 (106); 197,8 (107); 1134,21 (109)
of natural and counternatural, 58,21 (35)
of place, 172,26–30; 173,12 (89); 175,17 (91); 176,17.24; 177,7.20 (92); 182,17 (96); 185,9.14 (98); 188,1 (101); 189,30; 190,9 (102); 194,25f.(105); 197,8 (107)
of qualities, 157,28 (82); 163,15–27 passim (84); 164,24 (85); 166,5 (86); 173,1–14 passim (89); 192,6 (104)
of straight and curved, 170,26; 171,2–5 (87)
hen heni enantion, 35,5 (11*); 56,31 (33)

enantiôsis, contradiction, contrariety 56,28 (33); 70,34 (39); 131,20.27 (69); 171,25.26 (88); 172,27 (89); 175,16.19 (91); 184,1 (97); 190,3 (102); 192,15–193, 3 passim (104); 195,10.12 (106)

enargês, clear, evident, 32,11 (7); 195,9 (106); 1147,28 (117)

endeiknunai (see also *deiknunai*), to declare, disclose 81,1f.(52); 156,28 (81); 1178,2 (132)

endekhesthai (see also *kôluein*), to be possible 28,7 (4); 36,15 (14); 57,4 (33); 58,2 (34); 158,20 (82); 174,8 (90); 1151,9.15 (120); 1179,10 (132)

energeia, actualisation; 197,14 (107)
of the intellect, 1157,17 (121)
of motion and change, 1130,13.31; 1131,6 (108); 1134,19–29 passim (109); 1135,2.6.14 (111)
of nature, 1141,13.15 (115)
see also 1157,11.28 (121); 1178,29; 1179,6 (132)
energeiai, 46,7.9.10 (25); 46,18.22.24 (26)
to energeiai, 46,10 (25); 1178,12 (132); prior to the potential, 1179,3.5 (132)
energein, 197,14 (107); 1141,14 (115)

ennoia, conception 26,13 (Prologue I); 48,21 (31); 49,3.5 (32); 183,30 (97); 194,10 (105); 1130,30 (108); 1158,34 (122)
koinai ennoiai, 141,13 (78); 1168,36 (126)
ennoiein, 67,7.14 (40*); 199,32 (50*); 135,25 (72); 183,24.33 (97); 185,29 (98); 187,16 (100)

enstasis, objection, 25,24; 26,2.8.15.16 (Prologue I); 26,31 (1*); 42,19f.(18); 73,4.10 (45*); 126,9 (68); 1118,10 (Prologue VI); 1130,6 (108); 1133,28 (109); 1150,16.21 (119)
enistanai, 34,22 (10*); 46,30 (27*); 68,8 (41*); 189,29 (102)

entelekheia (see also *energeia*), actuality, of motion, 1130,8 (108); 1133,33–1134,24 passim (109); 1134,34–1135,10 passim (111)

ephienai, to desire, of elementary bodies, 67,7–12 passim (40*)

epibolê, conception, of the intellect, 1157,14 (121)

epideiknunai (see also *deiknunai*), show, prove, 46,5f.(25); 170,12 (87); 1118,3.9 (Prologue VI)

epikheirêma (see also *apodeixis, logos, tekmêrion)*, argument, proof, 56,28 (33); 59,8 (36*); 66,13 (37); 170,24 (87); 176,14.29 (92); 187,28 (101); 189,22.30 (102); 192,12 (103); 192,17.24 (104); 194,6.8.19 (105); 1133,16; 1134,8 (109); 1134,29 (110*); 1164,7 (123); 1166,32 (125); 1172,3f.(128); 1172,39 (129); 1178,6 (132)
epikheirein, 136,18 (73); 170,19 (87); 179,24 (93); 188,4 (101)
epikheirêsis, 176,31 (92); 194,24 (105)

epikratein, to prevail, of motion, 71,31 (43); 197,12 (107)

epikuklos, epicycle, 32,7 (7). 36,23 (15)

epinoia (see also *nous*), notion, thought, 46,33 (27*)
epinoein, 79,10f.(49); 1179,8 (132)

epipedos, plane, flat, 46,6 (25); 173,29 (90)

epiphaneia, surface, 48,8 (35*); 173,27 (90)

epipherein, to move about, 37,13 (17*)

epistanai, to understand, 66,20 (38); 91,17 (61*); 190,17.26 (102); 1182,33 (133*)

epokhê (astronomical) position, 83,2 (54)

48,18 (31); 170,26; 171,4 (87); 174,6–13 passim (90); 179,31 (94); 180,1–11 passim (94); 185,13 (98); 1167,5–16 passim (125)
requires body for existence, 174,8–9 (90)
grammikos, of a circle, 46,22 (26); 48,15 (31)

haplos (see also *sunthetos*), simple
of bodies, 31,15 (6)
of motion, see under *kinêsis* and *phora*
haptein, to touch
of celestial spheres 37,18 (17*)
of the intellect, 1157,16 (121)
haptos (see also under *aisthêsis, horatos*), of the heavens, 89,16.19.20 (59)
hedra (see also *topos*), abode, of the stars 72,13 (44*)
hêlios, sun, 82,17.27; 83,1.5.7.19 (54); 84,22 (56); 88,9 (58*); 1158,18 (121); 1179,20 (132)
hêmikuklos, semicircle, 179,27 (94); 181,23.28 (95); 185,4–21 passim (98); 187,30; 188,7–22 passim (101); 189,24.25; 190,23 (102); 194,12.13 (105)
hêmisphaira, hemisphere, 188,14 (101); 197,6 (107)
hen, the One
procession from, 135,25 (72)
Hêraklês, 119,12 (63); 1130,2 (108)
Herôdianos, 26,22 (Prologue I)
heterophulos (see also *homoeidês, homophuês*), different in kind, S.Seth 41,7f.(2*)
holos, whole
of an element, 34,11 (9); 37,5 (16); 37,16.19 (17*); moves in a circle, 36,14f.(14); 80,21f.(51*); moves in a straight line, 36,17f.(14)
of the heavens, 32,18 (8); 142,21 (80)
see also 1142,6 (116)
holotês, totality, of an element, 35,16 (12*); 35,29 (13*); 45,29 (24); 67,6.11.16 (40*); 71,23 (43)
homoeidês (see also *heterophulos, homophuês*), of the same kind, 177,10 (92); 179,31; 180,3.4 (94)
homokentros (see also *ekkentros*), homocentric, 32,7 (7)
homophuês (see also *heterophulos, homoeidês*), of the same nature
of the celestial and sublunary regions, 28,8f.10 (4); 34,6 (9); 35,32 (13*); 71,24 (43); 73,5 (45*); 77,25 (48); 81,10 (52); 82,9; 83,25 (54); 89,25f.(59)
of God and man, 90,20 (60*)
see also 27,2 (1*)
horatos (see also under *aisthêsis, haptein*), visible, of the heavens, 89,16 (59)
horismos (see also *aphorizesthai, logos*), definition, 46,20 (26); 48,21 (31)
of motion, 1130,9–27 passim (108); 1133,21.32 (109); 1135,31 (112)
horizein, horizesthai, 48,21 (31); 49,5 (32); 66,18 (38); 176,23 (92); 185,11 (98); 190,2 (102); 1130,7 (108)
horismenos, 176,18–20; 177,21 (92); 179,27 (94); 183,28 (97); 185,19.12; 186,7 (98); 188,2 (101)
horos, 43,25 (21); 47,28 (29*); 164,23 (85)
hormê, impulse, of the soul, 79,12f.(49)
hudôr, water
becomes hail, 76,24 (47)
moves downwards, 26,35–27,4 passim (1*); S.Seth 41,12 (2*); 28,2.6 (4); 31,13 (6); 34,23 (10*); 36,16 (14); 37,10 (16); 74,18 (46)
its qualities, 89,1 (59); 124,1.3 (67); 157,29 (82); 173,13 (89)
yields, 75,32 (47)
see also 158,15 (82); 1178,24 (132)
hudatinos, 88,14 (58*)
hugros, wet, 27,4 (1*); 28,3 (4); 123,33 (67); 172,35; 173,2 (89)
hugrotês, 87,30 (57*)
hulê, matter
created by God, 1141,18–22 passim (115); 1143,23f. (116); 1150,24 (119)
distinction celestial-terrestrial matter, 135,21–23 (72)
first substrate, 1141,23f. (115)
incorporeal and formless, 135,27.29 (72)
Philoponus' conception of, 134,9f.(71); 135,26–30 (72); 166,3 (86)
prime, 1142,5 (116); 1177,23 (131)
recipient of all forms, 134,20–24 (71)
see also 123,6.7 (66); 132,5.14 (69); 134,9–24 passim (71); 157,35 (82); 165,27.35; 166,1.6.7.9 (86); 42,4.6.7

kaustikos, capable of burning
of fire, 82,26 (54)
denied of the heavens, 81,7 (52); 82,9 (54)
kenodoxos, vainglorious, of Philoponus, 26,31 (Prologue I); 90,13 (60*); 131,32 (69)
kenon, empty, vacuum, 76,5.7 (47)
as motive force, 158,17.19 (82)
of Philoponus' arguments, 46,33 (27*); 188,3 (101)
see also 74,20 (46)
kentron (see also *meson*), centre
of a circle, 46,7 (25); 46,19–25 passim (26)
of the spheres, 32,6 (7)
of the universe, 32,3.4 (7); 79,11 (49); 177,14–18 (92); earth and water move towards it, 26,36
kephalaion, chapter (of a book). 190,21 (102)
khitôn, *keratoeidos khitôn*, cornea of the eye, 47,12f.(28)
khôra, space, 72,14 (44*); 158,16.20 (82)
khrôma, colour, of the stars, 88,10.12 (58*); 89,3.4 (59)
see also 123,35–124,8 passim (67); 157,31 (82); 192,33; 193,7 (104); 1142,9 (116)
khronos, time
eternal, 1118,5 (Prologue VI); 1156,33–1157, 2 passim (121); 1164,8–30 passim (123); 1166,35–1167,16 passim (125); 1168,37.39 (126)
generated together with the heavens, 1157,36 (121); 1164,22 (123); 1169,3 (126)
its relation to body and motion, 1157,6–9 (121)
its relation to the intellect, 1157,27–35; 58,1f.(121)
its relation to the now, 1166,32–35 (125); 1168,36–1169,5 passim (126)
measure of motion, 44,15f.(22); 1157,9 (121)
necessary for natural generation, 1141,26 (115)
see also 1130,12–28 passim (108); 1135,14 (111); 1142,10.24 (116); 1147,11 (117); 1151,20 (120); 1157,19–58,29 passim (121); 1158,31–59,2 passim (122*); 1167,2 (125); 1175,22 (130); 1179,16 (132)
akhronos: of generation by God, 1141,27 (115); of God's thought, 1158,31f.(122*)
huperkhronos, 1158,30.32 (122*)
kinêsis (see also *phora*), motion, movement, change
cessation of, 1172,12.13 (128); 1173,1–15 passim (129); 1175,11–26 passim (130); 1177,10–21 passim (131)
circular (see also *kuklophoria, phora*), complete, 42,29 (19); 45,4–6 (23); 48,19f.(31); definition of, 32,3 (7); has no contrary, 58,18f.(35); 121,7 (64*); 157,3 (81); 157,24 (82); 163,28–30 (84); 170,29f.; 171,1–8 (87); 171,17–32 passim (88); 172,26–30 (89); 197,1.7–10 (107); incomplete, 43,9 (20); 48,17f.(31); unlimited, 43,10 (20); see also 80,15f.21f.(51*); 78,19 (49); 164,25 (85); 170,18.20 (87); 199,28 (50*); 174,7 (90); 187,29; 188,10–25 (101); 189,22–190,31 passim (102)
contrariety of motions, 34,33–35,8 passim (11*); 58,16f.21f.(35); 159,1 (82); 162,20–34 (83*); 163,12–30 (84); 164,26 (85); 170,15–33; 171,1 (87); 171,17.21.28 (88); 172,26.28 (89); 175,21 (91); 176,16.25; 177,4–7.20 (92); 178,19.25 (93); 181,24 (95); 182,17 (96); 188,1.14–25 (101); 189,23–190,30 passim (102); 192,5.14 (103); 194,13–29 passim (105); 197,10 (107)
definition of, 1130,7–1131, 7 passim (108); 1133,32f. (109); 1135,10 (111); 1135,31 (112)
eternal (see also *aïdios, anarchos*), 1118,4–6 (Prologue VI); 1130,9–29 passim (108); 1134,8–12 (109); 1141,6–8 (115); 1156,29.32 (121); 1166,36 (125); 1182,29.33 (133*)
arguments for its eternity, 1134,8–12 (109); 1141,6–8 (115); 1156,36.57,4 (121); 1164,7–10 (123); 1166,32–37 (125); 1175,11–16 (130); 1177,10–15 (131)
not eternal, 1142,20.26 (116); 1151,21 (120); 1178,5–1179,26 passim (132)
first, 1135,30 (112); 1150,20f.(119)

generated, 1156,36 (121); 1171,31 (127); 1178,8f.(132)
of the heavens, S.Seth 41,6 (2*); 32,5 (7); 42,21 (18); 44,15 (22); 58,5–10 passim (34); 138,34 (75); 142,19 (80); 157,6 (81); 188,14 (101); 192,5–7 (103); 1179,9.18 (132); is not circular, 32,8f.(7); has no contrary, 121,7 (65); irregular, 37,9f. (16); 1158,5f. (121); is not rectilinear, 58,6 (34); 58,20 (35) see also 1142,24f.(116)
of relatives, 1147,14.25 (117); 1148,29–1149,4 (118); 1150,18 (119)
of the sublunary elements: caused by nature, 26,33; 27,1 (1*); S.Seth 41,4–14 passim (2*); 35,15.18 (12*); 157,6 (81); 1133,19f.(109); 1134,32f.(110*); circular, 34,8 (9); 35,7.8 (11*); 35,29f.32 (13*); 36,14 (14); 37,19.21 (17*); 42,22 (18); 56,29–57,6 passim (33); 58,2–4 (34); 89,11f.(59); composite, 36,10f.(14); 37,15.22 (17*); downwards, upwards, 34,24.32 (10*); 35,6 (11*); 76,5f.(47); 158,14.18 (82); 171,25 (88); 1135,6f.12 (111); forced, 34,22 (10*); local, 37,6.10 (16); 37,25.26 (17*); 78,29f.(49); 80,19 (51*); rectilinear, 31,8 (6); 37,22 (17*); 67,7 (40*); 76,28f.(47); simple, 31,7 (6); 32,5.9 (7); 35,30.32 (13*); 36,17 (14); 36,25 (15); 37,4f.7f.(16); 37,26 (17*); 56,35 (33); 58,8 (34); 58,19 (35); 162,34 (83*); 190,8 (102)
privation of motion, 122,3–8 (65)
quantitative and qualitative, 190,11 (102)
rectilinear, 42,30f.; 177,13 (92); 196,35 (107): complete, 43,10 (20); 43,23f.(21); contrary to circular motion, 170,29–171,7 passim (87); 171,17–32 (88); 172,26–30 (89); 190,3–7 (102); 192,15–193,8 passim (104); 194,25–27 (105); denied of the heavens, 75,21–23 (47); eternal, 43,8f.(20); of a star, 72,15 (44*)
relation of *kinêsis* to: *genesis*, 1134,2f.(109); 1135,11–15 (111); 1142,16–18 (116); 1147,21–28 (117); 1148,29–49,4 (118); *dunamis* and *energeia*, 1130,29–1131,7 (108); 1133,16–1134,29 passim (109); 1140,5f.(113); *nous*, 1157,29 (121); *sôma* and *khronos*, 1157,6–9.30 (121)
kinêtikos, 1147,23.25 (117); 1148,29 (118)
kinêtos, 1130,8 (108); 1133,33 (109); 1135,9.11.15 (111); 1147,24.25 (117); 1149,1 (118)
kinoumenon, S.Seth 41,6f. (2*); 31,12 (6); 33,19 (8); 35,17 (12*); 36,23 (15); 157,29–159,1 (82); 162,21–163,1 (83*); 163,13 (84); 165,18–20 (86); 170,21 (87); 173,10 (89); 177,15 (92); 178,19 (93); 185,14.21 (98); 188,7 (101); 190,12 (102); 195,11.12 (106); 1118,7 (Prologue VI); 1130,19.23 (108); 1133,18; 1134,4.16 (109); 1149,4 (118); 1182,36 (133*)
koilos (and *kurtos*), concave (and convex), 173,11 (89); 173,25–174,12 passim (90); 175,16.17 (91); 178,23 (93); 185,26 (98)
koloios, jackdaw, of Philoponus, 42,17 (18)
kôluein, to prevent, 158,18 (82)
ouden kôluei, 28,8.10 (4); 30,28 (5); 46,32 (27*); 58,5f.(34); 71,30 (43); 72,13 (44*); 80,29 (52); 83,35 (55); 133,27 (70); 1135,12 (111)
komêtês, comet, 89,14 (59)
korax, crow, of Philoponus, 42,17 (18)
koruphê, *to kata koruphên sêmeion*, zenith, 83,9 (54)
kosmos (see also *ouranos, pan*) world
changes into a new world, 1177,38–78,5 (132); (see also fragment 134)
eternal, 59,7f.(36*); 139,24 (77*); 1142,25f. (116)
generated and not eternal, 1151,20 (120); 1164.19.23 (123); 1169,3–5 (126); 1178,26 (132); 1182,29f.31 (133*)
not heavy or light, 71,27–30 (43)
perishable according to Philoponus, 25,26 (Prologue I); 119,17.21 (63); 132,7–15 (69); 136,13.16 (73)
see also 72,12 (44*); 73,12 (45*); 76,15 (47); 80,19 (51*); 83,13 (54); 138,33 (75); 142,16.20 (80); 1117,17 (Prologue VI); 1142,27 (116);

1150,23 (119); 1151,18 (120); 1169,3 (126)
kouphos (see also *barus kai kouphos* under *barus*), light, 30,27.29.31 (5); 37,9 (16); 37,14 (17*); 66,12.14 (37); 66,18.21 (38); 68,9.10 (41*); 74,17–24 passim (46); 1134,19 (109)
kuklophoria (see also under *kinêsis, phora*), circular motion, 34,34 (11*); 37,27 (17*); 79,4f.(49); 1130,23 (108); 1179,25 (132)
kuklophoreisthai, 199,34 (50*)
kuklophorêtikos, 157,22 (82)
kuklos, circle, 45,3.4 (23); 46,35 (27*); 47,13 (28); 164,25f.(84); 171,8 (87); 177,17 (92); 180,15–22 (94); 181,25.30.33 (95); 185,19; 186,3.11.12 (98); 187,4.6 (99); 187,20 (100); 187,29; 188,11–16.24 (101); 189,23–190,27 passim (102); 192,9.13 (103); 192,15–193,11 passim (104); 194,14.20–29 (105); 195,11.12 (106); 197,1.8 (107)
mathematical, 46,6 (25); 48,15.21 (31)
more complete than straight line, 46,5 (25)
of the moon, 1158, 9.11 (121)
physical, 47,1 (27*)
kuklikos, 47,11 (28); 48,17f.(31)
kurios, principal, proper, 32.2.4 (7)
kurtos, see *koilos*

lêmma, lemma, statement, 176,27 (92)
lexis (see also *logos*), sentence, 34,33 (11*); 131,18 (69); 194,11 (105); 1131,2 (108); 1159,5 (122)
temporal, 1158,33.35; 1159,1 (122)
logos, account, 1179,2 (132)
argument (see also *apodeixis, epikheirêma, tekmêrion*), 45,7 (23); 56,27 (33); 67,6 (40*); 75,19 (47); 78,18 (49); 81,10 (52); 81,23 (53*); 83,20.26 (54); 90,22 (60*); 91,3 (61*); 123,22 (67); 126,12 (68); 131,17.26; 132,12 (69); 134,11.16 (71); 136, 14 (72); 139,24.27 (77*); 156,27 (81); 162,34 (83*); 166,12 (86); 170,18.28 (87); 177,4.9 (92); 185,27 (98); 186,27.30 (99); 188,21.24 (101); 190,19.29 (102); 192,8 (103); 194,18.30 (105); 1130,15.26 (108); 1140,5 (113); 1142,25 (116); 1156,34; 1157,4.22 (121); 1165,1 (124); 1169,4 (126); 1171,33 (127); 1173,10 (129); 1175,17 (130); 1178,6; 1179,26 (132)
assertion, 188,3 (101)
definition (see also *horismos*), 48,6 (30*)
proposition (see also *lexis*), 31,7 (6); 34,22 (10*); 58,6 (34); 89,25 (59); 124,14 (67); 131,18 (69); 157,3 (81); 158,26 (82); 162,32 (83*); 176,15.30 (92); 188,6.8.16.18 (101); 194,24 (105); 1130,6 (108); 1141,5 (115); 1142,27 (116); 1147,13 (117)
ratio, 83,1 (54)
term, 142,24 (80)
word, 26,18 (Prologue I); 71,19 (43); 170,11 (87); 172,25 (89); 176,13 (92); 179,30 (94); 185,3 (98); 1148,20 (118)
lusis (see also *apelenkhein, dialuein, dielenkhein*), refutation, 26,17 (Prologue I)
luein, 66,13 (37); 73,9 (45*)
lutta, madness, of Philoponus, 58,15 (35)

manôsis, rarefaction, of sublunary elements, 36,13 (14); 37,4.5.8f.(16); 37,25 (17*)
mathêmatikos, mathematical, 46,9 (25); 46,23 (26)
megethos, (geometrical) magnitude, of a circle, 181,24 (95); see also 186,31 (99)
meiôsis, diminution, 142,14 (80)
meiousthai, 79,2 (49); 158,3 (82)
mêkos (see also *bathos*), length (first dimension), 48,7.10 (30*)
Menandros, 26,22 (Prologue I)
meros (see also *morion*) part
of an element, 34,11 (9); 35,15 (12*); 36,14 (14); 37,19 (17*); 67,12.18 (40*); 73,6 (45*)
of the heavens, 138,32 (75); 142,9.18.22 (80)
of time, 1142,10 (116); 1157,1 (121)
of the world, 142,17.19 (80)
see also 49,6 (32); 142,15 (80); 194,8 (105); 1141,28 (115)
meson, middle, centre, intermediate
of elemental change, 1134,32 (110*)
of time, 1169,1 (126)
of the universe, 27,1 (1*); 31,9.10 (6);

34.24.31 (10*); 36,18 (14); 37,6 (16); 66,22 (38); 76,5.6 (47)
see also *arkhê*, *meson*, *telos* under *arkhê*
mesotês: of a line, 1166,34; 1167,3 (125); 1168,36.38; 1169,2 (126); of the now, 1167,7 (125)
metabolê, change
of food into flesh 1135,1–5 (111)
of place, 158,10 (82); 190,7 (102)
of the world, 1177,39 (132)
substantial, 158,9 (82)
see also 139,2.5 (75)
metaballein, to change, 73,9 (45*); 124,4 (67); 134,25.28 (71); 136,20.22 (73); 142.9 (80); 172,24.32; 173,3 (89); 1178,4 (132)
metabolê eis allêla, of elements, 82,9f. (54); 134,22 (71); 1133,23; 1134,2 (109); 1134,30–32 (110*); 1178,26 (132)
methekhein, to partake of, 71,6 (39); 71,21.24 (43); 75,21.25.26 (47); 78,28 (49); 88,10 (58*)
methodos, method, 1140,12 (114)
metron, measure, 179,30; 180,2.5.19 (94); 181,21 (95); 182,19.20 (96); 183,29–33 (97); 187,22–24 (100)
metrein, 176,19 (92); 179,28.34; 180,6–15 (94); 181,17.19 (95); 183,23–33 passim (97); 185,11.23 (98); 187,17.22 (100)
mixis, mixture, of elements, 84,17 (56)
miktos, of motion, 36,10 (14); 37,15 (17*)
moira, portion
of an element, 84,21 (56)
of the zodiac, 1158,6 (121)
monas, monad, 78,27 (49)
morion (see also *meros*), part
of a circle, 181,25.30 (95); 190,21 (102)
of an element 33,19 (8); 36,16 (14); 37,3.10 (16); 73,9–14 passim (45); 75,32; 76,11–19 passim (47); 77,27 (48); 142,11 (80)
of the heavens, 76,8 (47); 77,24 (48)
see also 47,30 (29*); 1147,28.30 (117); 1150,19 (119)

nous (see also *epinoia*), intellect, mind, 199,35 (50*); 1157,13–38 passim (121)
its relation to body and time, 1157,27–37 (121)
noein, 72,14 (44*); 173,28 (90); 1157,20–39 passim (121); 1158,30.32 (122); 1166,33 (125); 1177,15.20 (131)
noêma, 1157,24f.32–34 (121)
noêsis (see also *dianoia*), 1157,18.21.31.33; of God, 1158,13f.16 (121)
noêtos, 89,26 (59); 133,29 (70); 1157,14.15.31 (121)
nöoumenon, 1157,34 (121)
nun, the now, its relation to time, 1166,33–1167,16 passim (125); 1168,36.38; 1169,2 (126)

on, being, something that exists, (and *onta*), 1135,29 (112); 1141,12.16.24.25 (115); 1148,22 (118); 1150,22 (119); 1157,20.21; 1158,25.27 (121); 1178,1.2 (132); 1182,35 (133*)
aei onta, 1167,2 (125)
mê on, *mê onta*, 1135,30 (112); 1142,13.14 (116); 1150,23.25 (119); 1177,24.25 (131)
nothing comes to be from not-being, 1140.14f. (114); 1141,6.7 (115)
onkos, bulk, mass, 81,24 (53*)
onoma, name, word, 49,2 (32)
ouranos (see also *kosmos*, *pan*), heaven, 26,5 (Prologue I); 28,9.10 (4); S.Seth 41,2 (2*); 33,18 (8); 34,9 (9); 36,24 (15); 45,7 (23); 57,4 (33); 66,19 (38); 67,13.17.18 (40*); 75,20–76,29 passim (47); 83,32 (55); 88,29; 89,13 (59); 156,29.31.33; 157,4 (81); 175,18 (91); 194,23 (105); 1117,17 (Prologue VI); 1130,24 (108); 1157,36 (121); 1164,22 (123); 1169,3 (126); 1179,10.18.26; 1179,9.25 (132)
does not affect the sublunary bodies, 83,13–15.23 (54)
generated by God, 1157,36; 1158,4 (121)
generated and perishable, 34,6 (9); 132,7–15 passim (69); 134,14 (71); ungenerated and imperishable, 119,10.16.17; 120,8 (63); 132,2 (69); 141,16 (78); 156,29 (81)
hard and solid, 75,31 (47); 77,23f.(48); 83,28f. (54)

phthora (see also *genesis*), destruction, 126,8 (68); 139,1.3 (75); 158,8 (82); 174,4 (90); 175,19.20.22 (91); 1156,33 (121)
instant, 1173,5–15 (129)
of the world, 1178,1.4f. (132)
phthartos, perishable: of individual forms, 1142,8.12 (116); of the heavens, 26.6 (Prologue I); 28,11 (4); 34,5 (9); 81,11 (52); 132,2 (69); 134,14.15 (71); 142,24f. (80); 175,15.18 (91); of motion (see also *pauein*), 1172,8.12 (128); 1175,19.21.24 (130); of the world, 25,26f. (Prologue I); 119,8 (63)
phtherein, *phtheiresthai*, 37.29f. (17*); 76,13 (47); 79,7 (49); 83,31 (55); 121,6 (64*); 123,21 (67); 131,34; 132,6.8 (69); 1134,6.7 (109); 1142,4.6 (116); of motion, 1173,8–15 passim (129); 1175,11–26 passim (130); 1177,10–21 passim (131)
phtheiromenon, 172,30 (89); 1134,5 (109); 1135,8 (111); 1158,25 (121); 1173,8.14 (129)
phtheiron, 1173,10 (129); 1175,15 (130)
phusis, nature
does not act without purpose, 197,15 (107)
does not create prime matter, 1177,22 (131)
of elements, 34,8 (9); 76,24 (47); 79,5.8 (49); 1135,8 (111); 1141,16 (115)
of things, 26,23 (Prologue I); 46,32 (27*); 79,5 (49); 142,15 (80); 159,1 (82)
of the world and the heavens, 119,18 (63); 132,11 (69); 134,19 (71); 142,21 (80)
principle of generation, 1142,2 (116); 1151,14 (120); creates out of existing things, 1141,12–14.24 (115); 1150,21f.24 (119); 1178,38 (132); needs time for its generation, 1141,26 (115)
principle of motion, 26,34–27,4 passim (1*); S.Seth 41,5–14 passim (2*); 28,1–11 passim (4); 79,10 (49); 157,6; 158,6 (82); 1133,19 (109); 1147,23 (117)
huper phusin, 35,13.19 (12*); 80,23 (51*)
kata phusin, 31,13 (6); 34,9 (9); 34,23.31.32 (10*); 34,33–35,8 passim (11*); 35,12–20 passim (12*); 37.18.27 (17*); 56,30–35 passim (33); 58,9 (34); 58,20.21 (35); 76,5 (47); 80,18–21 passim (51*); 157,4.5 (81); 1133,24f. (109); 1134,33 (110*); 1172,6 (128)
koinê phusis, 135,22f. (72)
para phusin, 33,20 (8); 34,9–11 (9); 34,33–35,8 passim (11*); 35,17 (12*); 37,28.29 (17*); 56,30–57,5 passim (33). 58,2–10 passim (34); 58,20.21 (35); 71,22 (43); 78,23 (49); 80,17–23 passim (51*)
phusikos: of the celestial form, 133,22–25 (70); of change, 158,8 (82); of a circle, 46,23 (26); of the circumference, 178,17 (93); of a line, 46,9 (25); 174,9 (90); of motion, 56,34 (33); 58,19 (35); 122,4–5 (65); 138,34 (75); 142,19 (80); 157,5 (81); 158,13.18 (82); 162,34 (83*); 190,8 (102); natural things, 157,5 (81); 165,28; 166,1.4 (86); 178,12.15 (93); Physicist, 1140,14 (114); 1164.17.26.27 (123)
Pindar, 42,18 (18)
planômenê (sc. *sphaira*)
planetary sphere, 36,24 (15); 178,24 (93); 192,6 (103)
planetary movement, 31,12 (6); 193,17.18 (104); 194,23 (105); 197,5.6 (197)
planômenos astêr, 1158,6 (121)
The Planets: (see also *hêlios*, *selênê*): *Aphrodisiakê* (sc. *sphaira*), sphere of Venus, 71,4 (39); *Ermaikê* (sc. *sphaira*), sphere of Mercury, 71,5 (39); *Heôspheros*, morning star, (Venus), 36,22 (15); *Zeus*, Jupiter, 1179,19 (132); *Kronos*, Saturn, 88,12 (58*); 1179,18.21 (132); *Stilbôn*, Mercury, 1158,19 (121)
Platôn, 66,33; 67,2.4f. (40*); 68,6.8.10 (41*); 78,17.23 (49); 80,14.15.17 (51*); 81,1.2 (52); 84,15.22 (56); 1157,11.36; 58,23 (121); 1164,9.12.13.21f.24 (123)
pneuma, wind, 36,17 (14)
poiotês, quality
of the elements (see also under

dunamis), 81,23 (53*); 82,19; 83,24 (54); 83,35 (56); 123,32 (67); 157,30 (82); 163,15–27 (84); 164,25.26 (85); 165,19.22 (86)
of the heavens, 87,29–88,1 (57*); 88,9 (58*); 173,14 (89); 174,2 (90)
general, 157,28; 157,7 (82); 165,23; 166,2.4.5.9 (86); 173,29.31.32 (90); 192,33 (104)
posotês, quantity, 158,7 (82); 190,11 (102)
pragmateia, treatise, 26,1.12.16 (Prologue I); 74,17 (46); 78,22 (49); 1118,3 (Prologue VI)
praxis, activity, of the stars, 78,28 (49)
Proklos, see under *Philoponos*
proödos, procession, from the One, 135,26 (72)
propeteia, rashness, of Philoponus, 182,18 (96)
see also 173,30 (90); 158,33 (82)
prosauxêsis (see also *auxêsis*), increase, 43,12 (20)
prosauxein, 47,12 (28)
pros ti, relative, 123,29 (67); 1147,14–25 passim (117); 1148,20.22; 49.3 (118); 1150,17 (119)
protasis (see also *hupolêpsis*, *hupothesis*, *sunêmennon*), premiss, 121,5 (64*); 133,21 (70); 182,25 (96); 1157,15 (121); 1167,12.14 (125)
prothumia, desire, eagerness, of Philoponus, 25,28 (Prologue I)
prôtos, first, primary, of the celestial body, 42,20 (18)
proüparkhein, to pre-exist, 136,15; 137,18 (73)
of movable and moved, 1130,7–29 passim (108); 1133,22–1134,17 passim (109); 1140,5f.(113); 1140,15 (114); 1142,24 (116); 1147,11.21.25f. (117); 1149,4 (118)
of relatives, 1147,16 (117); 1148,20.23 (118); 1150,17 (119)
of things necessary for generation, 1178,10–79,1 passim (132)
see also 1151,16 (120)
psukhê (see also *sôma*), soul, celestial motion due to it, 78,19–79,8 passim (49)
forms of the soul, 123,18.22 (67)
as a principle of motion, 79,10.12 (49); 163,1 (83*)
see also 141,14 (78); 1142,9 (116); 1157,18 (121)
psuxis, coldness, 30,28.31 (5); 81,25 (53*); 89,19 (59)
psukhein, *psukhesthai*, 37,7 (16); 83,34 (55); 88,12 (58*); 158,3 (82)
psukhros, 30,30 (5); 81,26 (56*); 88,13 (58*); 123,33 (67); 157,29 (82); 163,17 (84); 165,21.25; 166,10 (86); 172,35; 173,2 (89)
psukhrotês, 47,28 (29*); 87,29 (57*)
puknôsis, condensation, of sublunary elements, 36,13 (14). 37,4.5.9 (16); 37,25 (17*)
pur (see also *phlox*), fire
downward motion counternatural to it, 35,6 (11*)
absolutely light (*kouphos*) according to Aristotle, 74,17 (46); not light in its proper place, 71,23f. (43)
distinction celestial-terrestrial fire, 81,7–9 (52); 83,11–28 (54)
light (*phôs*) according to Plato, 67,4f. (40*); 124.8f. (67)
moves in a circle, 35,2 (11*); 35,19f. (12*); 89,11f. (59)
moves with a complex motion, 37,22 (17*)
moves upwards, 26,37 (1*); S.Seth 41,13 (2*); 31,9 (6); 36,15 (14); 67,2–4 (40*); 190,9 (102); 1133,25–1134,29 passim (109); 1135,6.11.12 (111); 1147,21f.27 (117)
possesses two natural movements, 35,14f. (12*)
see also 47,29 (29*); 80,23–81,11 passim (52); 88,10 (58*); 124,4.15 (67); 126,14 (68); 157,29 (82); 163,16 (84); 165,20.24 (86); 171,22 (88); 172,34; 173,1.13 (89); 1134,32 (110*); 1149,1 (118); 1150,20 (119); 1151,9–11 (120); 1172,10f. (128); 1178,19–38 passim (132)
purios, 88,14 (58*)
to ouranion pur: not capable of burning, 81,2.8 (52); 81,7f. (52); 82,9 (54); see also 82,15 (54); 84,15–22 (56)

rhêma, word, verb, 66,10 (37); 1158,31 (122*)
rhêsis, passage, 37,13 (17*); 1147,20 (117)

rhopê, inclination, momentum
downwards, 31,13 (6)
of elements, 67,9.12.17 (40*); 70,7 (42*)
natural, 79,12 (49)
proper, 37,13f. (17*)
rhepein, 67,8 (40*)

selênê, moon
its periods of revolution, 1158,9.17 (121); 1179,17.21 (132)
its sphere, 37,18 (17*); 71,4 (39); 173,11 (89); 175,17 (91)
ta hupo selênên (see also *stoikheion*), the sublunary bodies, 26,6 (Prologue I); 28,9f. (4); 35,32f. (13*); 73,5 (45*); 77,25 (48); 81,11 (52); 83,12.18.23 (54); 90,15 (60*); 134,17–28 passim (71); 135,22 (72); 139,1 (75)
sêmainein, to mean, signify, 66,20.21 (38)
sêmeion, point, 83,1.9 (54); 171,27 (88); 176,21; 177,15 (92); 178,10–22 (93); 179,29, 180,1 (94); 183,22 (97); 185,6; 186,5.14 (98); 186,25; 187,1–4 (99); 187,21 (100); 188,21 (101); 189,23 (102); 196,35; 197,1.4 (107); 1167,7.10f.(125); 1173,6 (129)
of the zodiac, 1158,8.9.17 (121)
Simplikios, referring to himself, 25,31.34.36; 26,14.18f.29 (Prologue I); 82,13 (54); 89,20 (59); 134,27 (71); 135,31 (72); 194,10 (105); 1118,7 (Prologue VI); 1173,9 (129); 1179,26 (132)
skhêma (see also *eidos*), form, logical, 166,12 (86)
phusikon, 76,18f. (47)
sphairikon, 76,1.8f.14f. (47); 89,9 (59)
see also 76,14 (47); 123,26–28 (67)
skhesis, relation, state, 74,23 (46); 187,5 (99); 197,2 (107); 1147,15–31 passim (117); 1150,17f. (119)
of body and intellect, 1157,28.36f. (121)
of God and time, 1158,28f. (121)
of time and intellect, 1157,29–34; 58,1f. (121)
skopos, aim, purpose, 67,15 (40*); 72,11 (44*); 78,14 (49); 80,24 (52); 181,16 (95); 195,16 (106); 1165,1 (124); 1182,30 (133*)
skotos (see also *phôs*), darkness, 124,11.13 (67)
Sôkratês, 1158,22f. (121)
sôma (see also *ousia*, *psukhê*), body
always in a place, 71,1 (39)
contrariety of, 157,26–159,1 passim (82); 162,22–30 (83*); 163,13.20 (84); 165,32; 166,6.7 (86); 170,15.16.21 (87); 173,14 (89); 178,26 (91)
generation and destruction of, 175,19 (90)
its relation to the intellect, 1157,27–29 (121)
its relation to motion and time, 1157,6–9 (121)
limited body has limited capacity, 79,4 (49); 142,22f. (80)
three-dimensional, 48,5 (30*); 89,23–25 (59); 135,30 (72)
see also 47,1.2 (27*); 47,11 (28); 83,13 (54); 88,33 (59); 89,6 (59); 134,10 (71); 138,34 (75); 142,20.23 (80); 166,1.4 (86); 174,9 (90); 1142,12 (116); 1147,24 (117); 1150,25 (119); 1157,10 (121); 1178,17.23 (132)
empsukhos, 91,5 (61*)
euthuphoroumenon, 75,24 (47)
haplon, 31,15 (6)
kuklophoroumenon, 58,7f. (34); 157,22 (82)
ouranion, see under *ouranos*
pempton, (see also *ouranos*), S.Seth 41,2 (2*); 76,25f.(47); 1164,15 (123)
suntheton, 1134,30 (110*)
sphairikon, 174,10 (90)
sophia, wisdom, 25,33 (Prologue I)
sophos, 26,28 (Prologue I); 48,14 (31); 175,13 (91); 176,34 (92)
sôritês, heap, of an argument, 1175,26 (130)
sperma, seed, 1150,19 (119)
sphaira, sphere, 31,15 (6); 32,5.8 (7); 36,22 (15); 47,2 (27*)
fixed sphere not in a place, 71,3 (39); is hot, 82,14–83,29 passim (54)
of the moon, 37,18 (17*); 71,4 (39); 173,11 (89); 175,17 (91)
of the sun much greater than the earth, 83,1 (54)
periods of revolution, 1179,15–22 (132)
spheres are contiguous, 67,9.10 (40*)
see also 173,28 (90); 178,22 (93)

sphairikos, 45,28.29 (24); 47,11 (28); 76,1 (47); 89,9 (59)
sterêsis (see also *eidos*), privation
generation from, 123,13; 124,7.11 (67); 126,13.15 (68)
belongs to sublunary matter, 134,15 (71)
of motion, 122,5–7 (65)
see also 171,24 (88); 173,29.30.32 (90)
sterêsis and *eidos* as contraries, 121,13 (64*); 121,28; 122,8 (65); 123,6 (66); 131,17–132,17 passim (69)
sterrotês (see also *antereisis, antitupos, hupeikein*), solidity
of the heavens, 75,31.33 (47); 77,24 (48)
stereos, 174,8 (90)
stoikheion (see also *ta hupo selênên* under *selênê*), element
not heavy or light in their natural places, 71,20–27 passim (43); 74,21f. (46); 75,17f. (47)
the four sublunary elements, S.Seth 41,3 (2*); 31,8.16 (6); 42.21 (18); 56.29–57,6 passim (33); 66,11 (37); 73,5–15 passim (45*); 76,24 (47); 77,25 (48); 83,31 (55); 90,25 (60*); 1134,30 (110*); 1164,16 (123)
their totalities, see *holotês*
see also 33,17 (8); 34,6 (9); 34,35 (11*); 45,28 (24); 70,7 (42*); 81,5 (52); 81,23 (53*); 84,17.18 (56); 88,30f.; 89,10f. (59); 90,23.25 (60*); 91,5f. (61*); 163,27 (84); 173,3 (89); 1151,17.18 (120); 1177,16f.(131); 1178,17 (132)
sullogismos, argument, calculation, syllogism, 26,38 (1*); 28,5 (4); 1157,14 (121); 1167,12 (125)
sullogizesthai, 1140,16f. (114); 1173,3 (129)
sumbebêkos, attribute, 123,15.25 (67)
sumphônos, being in agreement, of Plato and Philoponus, 78,18 (49); 81,2f. (52)
sumplokê, composition (of a treatise) 26,26f. (Prologue I)
sunagein, to infer, 35,31 (13*); 49,7 (32); 175,13 (91); 176,27 (92); 182,21 (96); 184,1 (97)
sunekhês, continuous
of a body, 75,32 (47); 76,11 (47)
definition of, 46,20 (26)
of a circle, 46,8 (25); 46,19 (26)
sunekheia, 46,22 (26); 76,16 (47)
sunêgoria, 72,11 (44*)
sunêmennon (see also *hupolêpsis, hupothesis, protasis*), conditional premiss, 170,31 (87); 188,18 (101)
sunkrima, composition, of the celestial bodies, 84,20 (56)
sunkrinein, 88,12 (58*); 171,6 (87)
sunthetos (see also under *ousia*), composite, 75,26 (47); 89,11 (59); 91,5 (61*); 135,22 (72); 157,35 (82); 165,35; 166,1.6.8 (86)
of matter and form, 1142,4.6 (116)
sustasis, composition, formation, 157,4.5 (81); 1151,18 (120)

takhus, fast, 31,12.14 (6); 37,19 (17*)
taxis, arrangement, order, 74,27 (49)
tekmêrion (see also *apodeixis, epikheirêma, logos*), proof, 141,15 (78)
tekmairesthai, 165,14 (86)
teleios, complete
of the circle, 42,27 (19); 45,3 (23); 46,5.10f. (25)
definition of, 42,28 (19)
of the four elements, 42,22 (18)
of heaven and world, 119,18.26 (63)
of motion, 42,29 (19); 43,24 (21); 44,18 (22); 45,4–6 (23)
prior to the incomplete, 1179,3.4 (132)
see also 43,25 (21); 47,28 (29*); 48,21 (31); 48,36f.; 49,8.11 (32); 1179,6 (132)
teleiôsis: of motion, 1134,28 (119); of the world, 1178,5 (132)
teleuton, 177,16 (92)
telos, end, 1131,1 (108); 1140,5 (113); 1150,16 (119); 1182,32 (133*)
thaumastos, remarkable, surprising, 48,36; 49.10 (32); 77,23 (48); 80,13 (51*); 172,35 (89); 186,11 (98); 186,31 (99)
thaumazein, 176,28; 177,12 (92)
thelein, to want, will, of God, 1141,29 (115)
Themistios, 68,6 (41*); 70.2f. (42*); 71,20 (43); 72,10 (44*); 131,21.22.24 (69); 176,32; 177,1.9 (92); 188,6 (101); 1130,4 (108)
theos (see also *dêmiourgos*), God, 26,8 (Prologue I); 88,30; 89,26 (59); 90.16,20.21 (60*); 197,15 (107);

Subject Index

References are to the marginal numbers in this volume; unless otherwise stated, page numbers 25–199 refer to Simplicius *in de Caelo* (CAG VII), page numbers 1117–1182 to Simplicius *in Physica* (CAG X). Fragment numbers are given in parentheses after the page and line numbers.

actualisation (see also potentiality), *energeia*
  of motion, 1130,13–1131,6 (108); 1134,17–29 passim (109)
  of the potential 1130,31 (108)
actuality (see also potentiality), *entelekheia*, of motion, 1130,8 (108); 1133,33–1134,29 passim (109); 1134,34–1135,10 passim (111)
aether (see also under element), *aithêr, pempton sôma* or *pemptê ousia*
  Aristotle's argument for, S.Seth, 41,1–8 (2*);
  Philoponus' arguments against, S.Seth, 41,8–14 (2*); Farabi, 9–15 (3); 56,28–57,8 (33); 58,5–10 (34); 58,19–22 (35); 59,6–10 (36*)
air, *aêr*
  moves in a circle as a whole, 34,5–11 (9); 164,24f.(85)
  moves up and down due to the force of vacuum, 158,14–24 (82)
apogee (and perigee), *apogê, perigê*, 32,11 (7); 36,23 (15)

capacity (see also actualisation, actuality, potentiality), *dunamis*
  in the motor, 1147,23f.(117); 1148,29–1149,4 (118)
  limited in bodies, 142,22–25 (80)
  not separate from actualisation, 1131,4–6 (108); 1133,17–23 (109); 1135,10 (111)
  of motion, 1130,13; 1130,30–1131,7 (108)
change (see also motion), *metabolê*
  of all elements into one another, 1134,29–33 (110*)
  of wood into fire, 1134,1f. (109)
circular motion (see under motion)
circumference, *periphereia*, of the universe, 178,16f. (93)
complete, completeness, *to teleion*
  Alexander's definition of, 42,27–31 (19)
  Aristotle's definition of, 48,35–49,1 (32)
  Philoponus' objection to both definitions, 47,27–30 (29*); 48,14–22 (31); 49,3–5 (32); cf. also 48,5–11 (30*)
  of the circle, 42,27–31 (19); 45,2–7 (23); 46,4–11 (25); 46,17–25 (26); 48,14–19 (31)
  of the heavens, 45,27–29 (24)
  of the movements of the heavens, 42,27–31 (19); 44,15–18 (22); 45,2–7 (23)
  of the straight line, 43,8–12 (20); 43,22–25 (21); 46,4–11 (25); 46,29–47,3 (27*)
completion, *to telos*, of the potential and of motion, 1130,30–1131,7 (108)
concave (and convex), *koilos*, (*kurtos*), as properties of the celestial body, 173,25–174,13 (90); 175,13–22 (91)
condensation (and rarefaction), *puknôsis, manôsis*, of parts of the spheres of fire and air, 36,9–18 (14); 37,3–12 (16); 37,12–29 (17*)
contrariety, *enantia*
  of form and privation, 121,4–14 (64*); 123,4–7 (66); pertaining to the heavens, 121,25–122,9 (65); relevant for generation and destruction, 131,17–132,17 (69)
  impossible of substance, 156,33–157,1 (81); 157,26–159,3 (82); 165,10–166,13 (86)
  in the heavens, 173,10–15 (89); 173,25–174,13 (90); 175,13–22 (91); 181,25–33 (95)
  in circular motion, 157,21–25 (82); 176,13–177,22 (92); 178,7–26 (93); 185,3–22 (98); 187,28–188,25 (101); 189,22–190,31 (102); 192,5–14 (103); 196,34–197,15 (107)
  in motion and change, 162,20–163,3 (83*)

Index Locorum

Numbers in **bold** type refer to the works cited; numbers in ordinary type refer to the pages of this book.

Meteorologica **1.3,339b16–340a3**, 69n56; **1.3,340a1–3**, 49, 70n57; **1.3,340b32–341a3**, 47; **1.4,341b22–24**, 47; **1.4,344a11–13**, 47
de Anima **2.1,412a15f.**, 76n71; **2.7,418b4–9**, 74n66; **2.7,419a2–6**, 74n67; **2.11,423a12–15**, 76n71; **3.13,435a11–14**, 76n71
de Motu Animalium **2,698b9–18**, 66n46
Metaphysica **8.4,1044b3–8**, 85n96; **9.10,1051b27–1052a4**, 134n203

ASCLEPIUS
in Metaphysica **69,17–21**, 8n22; **71,28**, 8n22; **433,9–436,6**, 8n21; **433,16**, 8n21; **450,22**, 8n21

AS-SIJISTĀNĪ
ap. Anonymum Muntakhab Ṣiwān al Ḥikmah (ed. Dunlop) **326 (fr. 79)**, 25, 25n43, 30, 89f.

BASIL
Hexaemeron **3.9**, 76n73

BIBLE
Isaiah **65:17**, 148n245; **66:22**, 148n245
Joshua **10:12f.**, 136n208
Psalms **19:1**, 75n69
Revelation **21:1**, 148n245

DAMASCIUS
ap. Philoponum in Meteorologica **97,20f.**, 47

ELIAS
in Categorias **107,24–26**, 9n35; **123,1–3**, 8n19

FARABI
Against Philoponus (ed. Mahdi) **§7 (fr. 62)**, 25, 25n42, 77, 88n101; **§7 (fr. 76)**, 25, 25n42, 88; **§9–15 (fr. 3)**, 25, 25n42, 43f.

GEMISTOS PLETHON
contra Scholarii defensionem Aristotelii **PG vol. 160: col. 909**, 21n14; **col. 1002**, 21n14

IAMBLICHUS
ap. Eliam in Categorias **123,1–3**, 8n19

MANUSCRIPTS
British Museum Add. **17 214**: **fol. 72vb,36–73ra,19 (fr. 134)**, 26n45, 148; **fol. 73ra,17**, 33, 148n244

MARINUS
Life of Proclus **13.157,41**, 7n15

OLYMPIODORUS
in Meteorologica **2,21–29**, 47

PHILOPONUS
in Analytica Posteriora **242,14–243,25**, 8n21
in de Anima **21,20–23**, 10n38; **37,18–31**, 8n21; **341,10–342,16**, 82n86
in Meteorologica **97,20f.**, 47
in Physica **55,24–26**, 23n31; **225,4–226,11**, 8n21; **703,16–17**, 24n35
contra Aristotelem ap. Simplicium in de Caelo **26,31–27,4 (fr. 1*)**, 42; **28,1–11 (fr. 4)**, 44f.; **28,8**, 33, 44n5; **28,16–18**, 44n6; **30,26–34 (fr. 5)**, 45; **31,6–16 (fr. 6)**, 45f.; **32,1**, 27n50, 33, 46n7; **32,1–11 (fr. 7)**, 46; **33,17–20 (fr. 8)**, 46; **34,5–11 (fr. 9)**, 47; **34,21–24 (fr. 10*)**, 47; **34,30–32 (fr. 10*)**, 48; **34,33–35,8 (fr. 11*)**, 48; **35,12–20 (fr. 12*)**, 47, 48f.; **35,28–33 (fr. 13*)**, 49; **36,9–18 (fr. 14)**, 49; **36,21–25 (fr. 15)**, 49; **37,3–12 (fr. 16)**, 49f.; **37,12–29 (fr. 17*)**, 50; **42,17–22 (fr. 18)**, 51f.; **42,27–31 (fr. 19)**, 52; **43,8–12 (fr. 20)**, 52; **43,22–25 (fr. 21)**, 52; **44,15–18 (fr. 22)**, 52; **45,2–7 (fr. 23)**, 52f.; **45,27–29 (fr. 24)**, 53; **46,4–11 (fr. 25)**, 53; **46,9**, 52n19; **46,17–25 (fr. 26)**, 53; **46,22f.**, 52n19, 53n20; **46,29–47, 3 (fr. 27*)**, 53f.; **47,10–13 (fr. 28)**, 54; **47,27–30 (fr. 29*)**, 54; **48,5–11**